REN

H

RENEGADE AT HEART

AN
AUTOBIOGRAPHY

Lorenzo Lamas
with Jeff Lenburg

BENBELLA BOOKS, INC.
DALLAS, TEXAS

The events, locations, and conversations in this book, while true, are re-created from the author's memory. However, the essence of the story and the feelings and emotions evoked are intended to be accurate representations. In certain instances, names, persons, organizations, and places have been changed to protect an individual's privacy.

BENBELLA
BenBella Books, Inc.
10300 N. Central Expressway
Suite #530
Dallas, TX 75231
www.benbellabooks.com
Send feedback to feedback@benbellabooks.com

Printed in the United States of America
10 9 8 7 6 5 4 3 2 1

Library of Congress Cataloging-in-Publication
Lamas, Lorenzo.
   Renegade at heart : an autobiography / by Lorenzo Lamas ; with Jeff Lenburg.
      pages cm
   ISBN 978-1-941631-25-6 (trade cloth)—ISBN 978-1-941631-26-3 (electronic) 1. Lamas,
Lorenzo. 2. Actor—United States—Biography. I. Lenburg, Jeff. II. Title.
   PN2287.L242A3 2014
   791.4502'8092—dc23
   [B]

                                                                                    2014034982

Editing by Brian Nicol
Copyediting by Stacia Seaman
Proofreading by Michael Fedison and Chris Gage
Text design and composition by John Reinhardt Book Design
Cover design by Sarah Dombrowsky
Cover photography by Peggy Seagren McIntaggart
Printed by Lake Book Manufacturing

Distributed by Perseus Distribution
www.perseusdistribution.com

To place orders through Perseus Distribution:
Tel: (800) 343-4499
Fax: (800) 351-5073
E-mail: orderentry@perseusbooks.com

Significant discounts for bulk sales are available.
Please contact Glenn Yeffeth at glenn@benbellabooks.com or (214) 750-3628.

To Mom, an amazing woman and survivor,
I dedicate this book to you.

—Lorenzo

To Lorenzo, for your brotherhood, your friendship,
and for forging down this path together.

—Jeff

Contents

PROLOGUE

Remember, You Have a History!

AS WHITE-CRESTED WAVES crash on the shore with a loud thundering roar, I feel his presence stronger than ever, standing at our favorite spot on Will Rogers Beach in beautiful Malibu. This powerful, graceful, confident, conspicuous but refined man swimming like the champion he was. Laughing and breaking into that wide, infectious grin as he playfully lifts me up on his broad shoulders to surf ashore as crashing waves lather us in white foam. The same man I admired so much, the man who built his career through blood, sweat, and tears and fought hard every step of the way to become accepted, respected, and successful. My hero, my confidant...my father, Fernando Lamas.

As I gaze out at the blue Pacific sparkling like diamonds as the layers of dense fog give way to brilliant rays of sunshine, I truly miss him. That rich baritone and overdramatic lilt in his voice—surprisingly sounding more like Count Dracula than the native Argentinean he was—as he would offer his wise counsel and timely words of encouragement. Every time I come here it is only natural I think of Dad. This beach was *our* place. It is here we spent so many times together. Although the quantity was not there, what we had, as he used to say, was "quality." Something I would never trade for anything.

One of my father's favorite things was cruising up Pacific Coast Highway in his luxurious, shiny, tan-and-gold Rolls-Royce Silver Shadow so we could spend the day together on the beaches of Malibu. My father loved that car. It was a hard-won prize, representing years of toiling and paying his dues to make something of himself as a foreigner with a foreign name in an alien land. I can still hear him saying as if he were performing onstage, "In a Rolls, Lorenzo, you've arrrrrrr-ived!"

Dad left a major imprint on my life with his many life lessons and his penetrating words, none of which have lost their significance for me. If anything, unlike small grains of sand swept away by receding waves into the abyss, they have taken on greater importance with age. He was always sharing, always instilling, always preparing, always planting seeds. His eyes were on the future—my future, my life—and what he thought was best for me.

As the majestic waves crest out in the distance, I remember one such example clearly, like yesterday. Dad picks me up from school. I run out to the parking lot to find him in his usual parking spot, doing his usual thing—reading the newspaper. Looking up, he smiles when he sees me and excitedly honks the car's distinctive horn. I climb inside his sparkling Rolls to the usual looks of envy from other kids waiting for their parents. Then we speed off.

The glow of pride on my father's face instantly fades. He sees I have been crying. He knows why: Other boys have been teasing me about my name. There are no Lorenzos or Fernandos in the neighborhood where I live or in the school I attend. Dad never says a word to me about it. Instead, he heads down Sunset Boulevard toward the Pacific Ocean. He is on a mission. He has a point he wants to make.

"Aren't we going to Bel Air?" I ask. It is where he and my stepmom, movie star Esther Williams, have lived since he and Mom divorced.

"No, amigo, not yet," he says. He reaches over and gives me a reassuring pat on the leg. "I want to show you something."

We drive for what seems like thirty or forty minutes. Finally, Dad comes to a stop at a quiet intersection on a hillside high above the blue Pacific as the sun's golden light cascades over eucalyptus trees lining both sides of the street.

"Come over here," Dad says, as he gets out of the car and walks across the street. "I've brought you here to show you something, something I never want you to forget. Look up there and tell me what you see."

I stare somewhat blankly. "A street sign?" I ask.

"Exactly!" Dad points to the sign above the lamppost. "What does the sign say?"

"It says Lorenzo Place."

"That's right, Lo-ren-zo Place," he says, pronouncing the name in syllables. "You, *mi hijo*"—meaning "my son" in Spanish—"have a very important name!"

Father gestures with both hands toward the houses below and the ocean in the distance as if he were encompassing all of California, a reverse conquistador who has found the Promised Land. He calls out to the residents as if they are an audience waiting to acknowledge and applaud the names of the streets on which they live: "Santa Monica, San Vicente, La Cienega, La Jolla."

Father lets the moment sink in before concluding. "Remember, amigo, that before there was a Harry and a Chuck, there was a Pedro and a Lorenzo. Wonderful names with a history! A courageous band of settlers who built missions up and down the Pacific coast hundreds of years ago—El Camino Real!"

My beacon of light, Father always knew what to say and when to say it. Even at times when I did not agree with him and wish I had.

Lesson over, we walk back down to the car. Smiling, Father gently wraps his arm around my shoulder. Then, as only he could, he puts it all in perspective for me: "People may forget what you say or do, but never forget your history."

Father's wise words wash over me as we surge down the Pacific Coast Highway in his fancy chariot. They echo in my mind as the road gives way to the spectacular, unobstructed view of gigantic waves cresting and crashing on the brown sandy coastline below...and now again years later as I stand here on the beach thinking of him. I understand better now what he was trying to tell me: Be proud of who you are. Never have an ounce of "quit" in you. Always do your best. Let the chips fall where they may. And...

"*Mi hijo*, as important as the rest, live and love, make wise choices where your heart is concerned," Father says, even as he swerves to avoid a deep crevice in the road, "and remember, the true measure of a man is how he handles the curves in his life."

It has taken half of my life—four divorces, two broken engagements, more busted romances than I remember, millions lost, and many therapy sessions—not to mention years of guilt and heartbreak— to understand how right my father was. Why did nothing satisfy me, even after enjoying tremendous fame and fortune, owning spectacular mansions, airplanes, boats, and racing cars? Why did nothing fulfill me? Why did nothing complete me? Then it became clear to me: because I am a renegade at heart.

Renegades never settle. They are never satisfied. They keep exploring, keep discovering, keep trying until they get things right. They live every day more anxious about what lies around the bend than about living in the moment. They enjoy the thrill of the ride for however long, no matter where it takes them, regardless of the consequences, regardless of the outcome. It is all part of the journey . . . my journey (and I have the scars to prove it). It is exactly how my father would see things if he were here today, on this sandy coastline, reliving cherished memories with me.

"They . . . the choices, *mi hijo*," he pauses. "They define who you are as a person and a man."

I have lived those words as best I can. Not a day goes by that I do not miss my father. His spirit, his grandeur, his unsettling smile, his wisdom, and, yes, even his favorite pungent cologne, they are with me always, every second of every day. I am sure he would have wished he had attained the success I ended up having. He did not live to see it, but he wanted me to embrace his advice and go beyond anything he imagined for himself. I thank him for that.

The other great measure of a man, my father would say, is to "learn from your mistakes." I am here to tell you: I have. For the first time, I am at peace in my life. I am now a clear-minded father of six, with a woman I am with for all the right reasons, more satisfied and healthier than I have ever been, thanks to diet and exercise, and—most important—having so much to live for.

Father always encouraged me to remember my history. I do. All of it vividly, as if it happened yesterday. Every detail, every key moment, every turning point. And all the baggage that goes with them. It may not be exactly the life my father imagined for me after first laying eyes on me the day I was born. It is, however, my life, my career, my marriages, my romances, even my foolish mistakes. And nobody else's. Lived as only I know how . . . a true renegade.

ONE

Caught Between
Two Worlds

PEOPLE ASSUME just because you are the son or daughter of a celebrity, you spend your whole life around other rich and famous people, living in the upper echelon of society. You have it easy. In my case, nothing could be further from the truth. As I would come to learn, fame and fortune never solve. My parents are examples of that.

Both are highly talented professionals so busy working and so preoccupied with their careers that they never achieve true, lasting happiness together. Surely they have the right intentions when they marry, buy a home together, plan a family, and, of course, have me. To the world, they are Hollywood's happiest couple. Yet, as I discover at a very tender age, just because you make plans doesn't mean they will always work out as you hope.

My father, known to the world as Fernando Lamas, is a rakishly handsome, flamboyant, and athletic man who loves life and beautiful women—not necessarily in that order. Born on January 9, 1915, in Buenos Aires, Argentina, he grows up in a country imperiled by political and economic unrest and yet rises above it all. At a young age, after developing a love for theater, he studies drama at school. Later, he abandons his studies for athletic pursuits—horse riding, fencing, boxing (winning the middleweight amateur title), and swimming (becoming the South American freestyle champion in the 1937 Pan-American Games). While still in his teens, he returns to his first love—acting, appearing onstage, then on radio, before making his first motion picture at the age of twenty-four. By 1942, he establishes himself as an Argentine cinema celebrity, proudly starring in over a dozen pictures, producing six and directing two, and living up to his on-screen reputation as a ladies' man.

With a natural eye for beauty, Dad holds true to a basic philosophy when it comes to women, based on his old-world values: "Women are the same all over the world, and I say God bless them," he good-naturedly explains to a reporter—although with some differences, he points out: "American women are slightly different from Latins because they have more freedom. I take my hat off to them; the women here have earned their position of equality with men. They can influence men by direct means, whereas Latin women cannot. The Latin women have to remain in the home, and the man is the master. Whatever influence they have must come by indirect means."

Brought up to believe that a woman's place is in the home, Father is attracted to women with like values. In 1940, he falls in love with and marries fellow Argentine actress Perla Mux, who costars with him in fourteen films from the late 1930s to the early 1950s. The union lasts four years, producing a daughter, Christina, before ending in divorce. Then, in 1946, he marries a second time to Lydia Barachi. Six years later, in September 1952, they split after having a second daughter, Alexandra ("Alex").

In 1950, Dad flees to Hollywood to appear in a supporting role in his first American feature for Republic Pictures, *The Avengers*, before signing a contract with Metro-Goldwyn-Mayer to star as a romantic lead in English-speaking movies. After his MGM film debut in *Rich, Young and Pretty* with Jane Powell in 1951, he quickly becomes one of the most promising Latin actors since Rudolph Valentino and Ramón Novarro, as he climbs his way to international stardom. My father's story—a foreigner with a foreign name and accent making something of himself in an alien land—becomes a great example to me. It teaches me an important lesson: If you work hard and pay your dues, almost anything is possible.

Despite his success, my father is realistic about how fleeting fame is—a lesson he later imparts to me when I become an actor. "Hollywood is a momentary place," he says, "and I feel this is my moment. I like it here, and I'd like to stay. But perhaps two years from now, some fellow in the balcony of a theater in Kansas City will get up and say, 'Aw, I'm getting tired of seeing that guy on the screen.' Six other people might join him and that would be the beginning of the end."

Long before I am a twinkle in my father's eye, Dad's romances with many of his female costars become well-publicized affairs. His torrid relationship with tempestuous platinum-blond legend Lana Turner—sparked during their making of MGM's *The Merry Widow* (1952)—makes national headlines as the thrice-married actress seeks to make my father husband number four. The press turns their affair into a carnival; the two lovers are unable to even go out of town in order to retain some semblance of privacy. Finally, in October 1952, they call off plans to marry, although three months later Lana goes ahead and divorces her then-husband, wealthy sportsman Bob Topping, when rumors resurface that my father and she still might wed.

While on loan to Paramount in 1953 to star in *Sangaree*, a 3-D Technicolor drama for Pine-Thomas Studios, Dad meets his match. He falls in love with his luscious, flaming redheaded costar: my mom, Árlene Dahl. He is immediately attracted to her "softness," the thing he looks for most in a woman. Mom possesses that quality and more, and the fact that her father has raised her with that same old-world philosophy about women makes them a perfect match.

Mom is a Minneapolis native of Norwegian descent who worked various jobs through high school and was active in local theater groups before embarking on a show-business career. After starring on Broadway and in two features for Warner Bros., she finds her greatest success at MGM, just like my father. She costars as the female love interest in many successful feature films for the studio, including *The Bride Goes Wild* (1948) with Van Johnson and *Three Little Words* (1950) with Fred Astaire.

Mom becomes Dad's steady the same year MGM loans them out to costar in their second Pine-Thomas Studios film together, the independent romantic adventure for Melson Pictures Corp., *The Diamond*

Queen. At the same time, my father is seeking his release from his MGM contract after more than four years in the studio's service. Dad and Arlene are the talk of the town and are treated like Hollywood royalty everywhere they go. Their union does create quite a stir with the media because Mom is not yet divorced from her first husband, actor Lex Barker (who, after divorcing Mom, dates Lana Turner, the woman Dad almost married), and because Father is eleven years her senior.

Their relationship is contentious and rocky during their two-year courtship and even after I am born, as evident in this exchange with a reporter during a November 1953 interview:

"How about some pictures kissing her?" the photographer says to the reporter.

In no mood to act lovey-dovey, Mom, exhausted from her stage performance the night before with José Ferrer in *Cyrano de Bergerac*, turns away from Dad, who smooches her on the cheek and announces, "The patient will live!"

After considerable coaxing, Mom eventually complies after the reporter asks her, "What plans have you after this show?"

"I guess to get a good rest."

"Might as well quit fooling around," the reporter adds. "Do you two have any plans to get married?"

"You'll be the first one to know it," Dad says with an unctuous grin.

"Aw, tell her first," the reporter jokes.

The reporter excuses himself and pulls Dad outside. He asks him the same marriage plans question privately.

Dad says, "We may. We're thinking it over carefully."

"Are you free to marry?" the reporter asks.

"Of course. Since October!"

The reporter cracks a smile. "Sorry, but I can't keep up with you guys."

"Wait a minute!" Dad says seriously. "One marriage and one divorce ain't bad! We'll let you know."

On June 25, 1954, after deciding they cannot live without each other, they quickly marry in a simple ceremony at the Last Frontier Hotel's Little Church of the West. Former tennis champion Gene

Mako and his wife, Laura ("Larry"), serve as best man and matron of honor.

My parents move into a palatial spread in Bel Air, the same place I briefly call home after coming into this world on January 20, 1958. When Mom goes into labor, Dad is doing what any good actor does: He is working to provide for his family. He is in the middle of rehearsing for NBC's *Jane Wyman Theater* (yes, the same Jane Wyman I would costar with years later on *Falcon Crest*), which is broadcasting live that night, when the hospital calls to tell him, "Mr. Lamas, your wife is about to give birth."

Like most fathers, Dad always wanted a son. After receiving the news, he sprints from the set despite Jane protesting, "It's almost show time and we have no second act."

Turning to her as he runs past her, my father famously hollers, "My son is about to be born. I'm not missing it for anything."

On April 10, 1958, my parents baptize me at the Church of Religious Science in Hollywood. Laura Mako is my godmother; architect William Pereira is my godfather. Dr. Ernest Holmes, the church's founder, also attends; Dr. William Hornaday conducts the baptismal ceremony.

My early years are not always easy and happy. I never enjoy the standard Hollywood childhood most second-generation kids of celebrity parents do. In mid-February 1959, a month after my first birthday, Father is suddenly out of the picture when Mom sues him for divorce, claiming she has "lost all contact" with him. After a brief separation, they try to make the marriage work again. On the surface, it appears it is.

But even though my parents share a zest for life, they are polar opposites. Mom is a reserved yet fastidious overachiever; Dad is a gregarious and proud macho man. Mom dresses me impeccably in ruffled shirts and velvet pants; Father talks to and treats me like a little adult.

I come to revere and idolize my father as he whisks me off with him in his sporty Alfa Romeo convertible with the top down, taking me almost everywhere, including to meetings he has in Hollywood. He props me up on a chair, and I listen quietly to him and all these grown-ups talk about the business in my presence as if I am one of the guys. In reality, I am just a two-year-old, wet-behind-the-ears, snot-nosed kid who still pisses in his pants and has no idea what in the hell they are talking about.

Occasionally I also accompany Dad to the sets and locations for productions he is filming. Going to the studio is so surreal and magical. It is like watching a group of adults play dress-up like it's a real-life Mickey Rooney–Judy Garland Andy Hardy movie unfolding before my eyes. The sets are built and the cast members are in their costumes and makeup, ready to put on the "big show" and help save Farmer Tom from losing his farm.

Even then, I never quite understand what my father *does* for a living. He rarely talks about acting or moviemaking to me when driving us to the studios. Instead, he is like some kind of wise man on the mountaintop. He readily dispenses his wisdom to me on just about anything and everything, even though I am far too young to understand most of what he is saying. With the bravado that made him famous as an actor, he starts the same way every time: "Lorenzo, you'll be happy someday; I'm telling you this," and thrusts his forefinger into the air as if he is acting in a serious melodrama. I become a fast learner in the art of nodding.

I never knew then as I would later that Dad is the kind of person who always puts a positive spin on things. It is his nature. In June 1960, an Associated Press reporter sits down to interview my father and asks him to comment on his marriage to my mom. He famously proclaims that although it has had its share of rough sailing, their marriage is "succeeding" because "too many people in Hollywood forget that they are men and women first, and actors second. They bring their roles home from the studio and try to live them at home. A man is a man and a woman is a woman. No matter if he wins an Academy Award, it means nothing if he does not have understanding at home."

Father adds, "Women especially are emotional. That is their nature. An actress deals in emotions in her work. If she continues playing the part at home, the result is chaos. Man was meant to be dominant. When an actress's career zooms higher than her actor husband's, it is an impossible situation. Soon she starts paying the bills. He cannot stand by and retain his self-respect."

Because they are in step with the societal norms of the time, including male superiority in the household, Father and Mom have a very traditional marriage. As head of the household, he sets ground rules from the first day. He pays all the bills and lets Mom do whatever she wants with her earnings. Even as a married man, however, he remains the free-spirited individual he has always been, doing whatever he wants when he wants. So twice a week, he goes to the fights—boxing is one of his true loves. Sometimes he tells Mom; other times not. I am sure most men reading this love the fact my father lived such a footloose and fancy-free existence. But even back in that day, not every woman was as patient and subservient as my mother. In fact, she wasn't either.

The AP interview runs nationally, and once again, to the world, my parents appear happy in their marriage. As that two-year-old, wet-behind-the-ears, snot-nosed kid who still pisses in his pants, I never suspect anything to the contrary. Of course, my parents are *actors*.

Five months later, Mom suddenly flies off to Mexico to get a quickie divorce. On October 10, 1960, she files. Five days later, she marries wealthy Texas oilman Christian R. Holmes III, after he has finalized property settlement details of his divorce with his ex-wife. Mom and Christian are wed at a private estate in Cuernavaca in front of invited guests that include his business associates and socialites from nearby Mexico City. It is the third marriage each for Mom and Christian, a Marine captain during the Korean War who has oil interests in Texas, Louisiana, and South America. The following February, Mother's desire to have a church wedding prompts her and Christian to exchange vows again in the Lutheran Church of the Good Shepherd in Reno, Nevada.

Just like that, a new man suddenly moves in to live with us, while the man I have come to love and admire as my father, the one who whisks me off in his fancy convertible to Hollywood meetings, vanishes. My world shatters into a million pieces. I feel a huge loss, a huge void. The whole thing is like a bad movie I cannot get out of my mind. I cry myself to sleep many nights. It is all so confusing. The father I have grown to love in such a very short time is no more. My life, as I know it, is not the same. Nor will it ever be. My parents' divorce traumatizes me in ways that will not become evident until much later.

I do not ever remember Mom really talking to me about Dad, the divorce, or her marriage to Christian. Perhaps she thought I was too young or would not understand. Whatever the reason, it is as though that part of her life and my life with Dad is simply swept under the rug and forgotten. With her new man and new husband in her life, Mom carries on. I am expected to do the same. It takes a long time for me to warm up to Christian. He is not my father, despite his best efforts to fill his shoes, and I long for the day when I can see Dad again and be in his company.

In August of 1961, Mom and Christian welcome a baby daughter into the world: Carole Christine. Mom and Christian arrive in style, in a limo from the hospital, carrying her in a beautiful bassinet.

That same year Father reunites with his former flame and MGM screen star Esther Williams. The two of them pack their bags and move to Italy, where they work and live together for almost three years. Devoting her life to my father, Esther leaves her children in the care of her alcoholic ex-husband, Ben Gage, a decision she later pays dearly for. Naturally, the news Dad is moving far, far away devastates me. It is yet another reminder of the loss in my life: that Dad is not only not part of my life anymore, but he is now in a place halfway around the world where I will never see him. My separation from him and longing for his return dominate my existence. I miss him so much.

Meanwhile, Mom does everything to make her third marriage work while providing me with a safe and stable environment in which to grow up. My childhood home for the next eight years is a stunning one-story, rambling five-bedroom California ranch-style house with a shake roof and white stucco siding in Pacific Palisades, nestled between the Santa Monica Mountains and Santa Monica Bay, with a backyard overlooking the Pacific Ocean.

After divorcing my father, Mom bought the house in 1960 for $64,000. The home was originally built in the late 1950s by a local developer as part of two neighborhoods, or tracts, he developed near Will Rogers State Park: Villa Grove and Villa Woods. We are the last house at the end of the cul-de-sac in Villa Grove. As the only housing developments in Pacific Palisades at the time, we are completely isolated and protected from the rest of the world. It is a magnificent place to live. There is no crime, and my friends and I play ball until nine o'clock at night during the summer because it is so safe.

Because my first name is hard for them to pronounce, my play-mates settle on calling me "Lucky." The nickname sticks. After I become an actor, a fan has a T-shirt made for me with "Lucky Lamas" emblazoned across the front. As my life plays out, I start to believe "Lucky" is my real name.

With so many oil interests to manage, my stepfather Christian is frequently on the road on business. Mom is always super-busy working, too. She is either headlining a stage show in Vegas or going to New York to talk about her cosmetics business. She is hardly home herself. And even when she is, she is always too busy doing something. Most days I feel lost and lonely. I become a deeply troubled fat little boy who eats a lot out of frustration. I long for what my friends have and what every kid wants: normalcy. My friends all have *normal* lives with *normal* parents not in show business. They function and do everything like normal families. I do not have that. I have a mother who leads a fashionable jet-set life. Then, when she is home, she invites society and famous people over for dinner and requires me to dress up and sit there smiling like a dummy. Not only that, I have a father who lives far away, a father I never see and hardly know.

After school, I spend my time at friends' houses just so I can have a normal family dinner rather than help Mom entertain her adult friends, people I do not even know. I'm frequently wishing for what I do not have: wishing my parents were David's parents, or Jeff's parents, or Sally's parents. Dealing with such tumult and confusion is hard, especially for a kid my age.

When Mom flits out of town, she usually leaves my sister, Carole, and me in the care of our nanny, Emily Gibbs. Housekeepers come and go, but Emmy, as I called her, becomes the one constant in my life. She fills the void. She nurtures me. She consoles me. She disciplines me—almost always for good reason. She fills the hole in my aching heart. I count on her for everything. Emmy is there for me, from about age two until I turn eight (when Mom moves us to New York for the first time).

Emmy is this sweet, soulful, God-fearing woman with a heart of gold, a devout Christian who teaches me more about karma than any

New Age book ever can. One thing I learn from Emmy is to never, ever lie. She has me grab a switch from a hickory tree out back if I do (and if it is not a big enough switch, go get one *bigger*). Then she swats my ass so hard that I never think of lying again.

Besides many other wonderful lessons, Emmy teaches me how to pray. Every night before tucking me tightly into bed, she kneels and prays with me at my bedside. With my hands clasped and pointed toward the heavens, I silently pray for the same thing. One night, I turn to Emmy after praying and ask with all the innocence of a six-year-old, "Emmy, why are you black? Are black people bad?"

"Child," Emmy says, wagging her finger forcefully at me, "I never want to hear you say that again for the rest of your life."

"I'm sorry, Emmy," I answer quietly.

Emmy quickly softens and lowers her voice as she explains, "Honey, God gave us all different colors. God made us the colors of the rainbow. Each of us is judged not by our color but what we do in this world."

Heavy words for a six-year-old, words I have never forgotten. As I was growing up around Santa Monica in the 1960s, the only black people I saw worked as nannies, gardeners, and other service providers. That innocent question of a six-year-old and the honest answer from a woman who lived in the faith of God really set the tone for my acceptance of everyone. I learned how to be a Christian because of one Emily Gibbs.

From the time I turn three, I suffer from chronic bronchitis, a condition doctors think is either psychosomatic (from the separation anxiety of missing my father) or smog-related. Whatever the cause, I have serious trouble breathing at night. Like any good mom, Emmy is right there. The minute I start coughing in bed, she rushes into my room and sits next to me.

"You poor child," she says softly. "Emmy will get you better."

She then rubs Vicks VapoRub on my chest, puts a hot terry-cloth towel over it, sits, and waits patiently until I fall asleep.

Waking around seven o'clock every day, I usually run straight to Emmy's room because I know she makes me a big breakfast every morning. Nobody makes better breakfasts than Emmy. On the morning of Monday, November 25, 1963, I find her door mysteriously locked. I knock softly. Emmy greets me with tears streaming down her eyes and moon-shaped face.

"Emmy," I immediately ask, "why are you crying?"

"Oh, honey," she says, dabbing her eyes with a handkerchief, "it's a terrible day."

"What? Why?"

Sobbing, Emmy sinks into her armchair in her bedroom. On the black-and-white television in her room, a television news anchor is describing the action as a horse-drawn flag-draped casket proceeds reverently down the streets of Washington, D.C. It is the memorial service honoring President John F. Kennedy, assassinated three days earlier.

"A great man was shot," Emmy says, misty-eyed, "and he's going to be laid to rest today."

I climb into Emmy's lap. We sit there mesmerized for hours watching the funeral procession on television, just the two of us. Throughout the sad day, she reflects on what a great man and humanitarian the president was. It was a day the two of us, Emmy and I, grew even closer.

Despite Emmy being there to tend to my daily needs, what I lack is my mom's love and attention. Her absence truly saddens me anytime she whisks out of town on business and I begin to feel angry and resentful about her constant absences. Much later, as a mature adult who works his entire career to put bread on the table and is absent, sometimes for long periods, to earn a living, I come to realize Mom was just doing the same. However, back then as a six-year-old child, I fail to fully understand the sacrifices she is making and why. One day, just after Mom returns from a trip and the suitcase rack in her bedroom cradles her still-unpacked suitcase and she still holds her purse in her hand, I walk into her room and announce, "I want a ball and want you to take me to the store."

"Honey, I can't. Mommy is really busy," Mom says, turning her back on me. "Mommy is always busy."

It is not what I want to hear. Dressed in black boots with red tips, I get so mad I haul off and kick her right in the shin. Mom stands there wailing in pain. Emmy, who sees the whole thing, comes running into her bedroom.

"Lorenzo Fernando Lamas," Emmy bellows, "what did I see you do?"

I think, "Uh-oh, Emmy caught me. The wrath of God is going to land on me." Breaking into tears, I immediately beg for forgiveness. "I'm sorry, Mommy, I'm sorry."

Mom, still crying in pain, manages between sobs to ask, "Lorenzo, why did you kick me?"

I look at her. "I don't know. I just got angry."

Emmy grabs me, takes me out of the room, and says sternly, "Lorenzo, you go outside and find the biggest switch you can and bring it back to me. Right now!"

Now I am really sobbing. "All right, Emmy." Sniff, sniff. "I'll go."

I walk out crying crocodile-sized tears, go straight to the hickory tree, peel off about a three- or four-foot-long switch, and bring it back in to Emmy. She swats my ass with four or five of the hardest lashings I have ever received, and I cry my heart out with each whipping. I can assure you, I never did anything like that to my mom—or anyone else—again.

Despite the geographical distance between us, my father is never far from my mind. I often wonder if I will ever see him again and if he ever thinks of me. In 1962, I get a big surprise: He flies me to Italy to see him. It marks the first time we see each other since my parents' divorce and his leaving the country with Esther.

Because I am underage, Lola Leighter, a close friend of my father's and someone who is like a grandmother to me, accompanies me on the TWA flight to visit him. I cannot express how much that trip and seeing him means to me. We pick up right where we left off: He drives me around in his Alfa Romeo convertible to the ancient city of Rome and the harbor and beaches of nearby Ostia and spends every minute of every day with me. I am this chubby-faced, scrawny kid but he makes me feel very special. Despite everything, he is still my hero. I know the love is there. I know for certain he loves me and I love him.

Father captures every moment with his Brownie camera. He shoots countless black-and-white photos of me that he then turns into little handmade storybooks, complete with handwritten captions with each photo describing in a charming, funny way where we are and what we're doing. Although their pages have yellowed and frayed over the years, those simple storybooks have not dimmed with age. They tell about the special bond between a father and son.

One of my favorites is one he titles *The International Sheriff*, featuring photos from our day trip to Rome, including outside of St. Peter's Cathedral. In it, I star as the macho, gun-slinging sheriff (as "a stand-in for Mr. Lamas...his father") who comes face-to-face with a vicious Indian (played by yours truly in a dual role).

"Where is he?" I ask in one caption, with a scowl on my face. "I got to find him."

"Looking for me, Sheriff?" It is him—I mean, me, the Indian.

"Draw, you dirty Indian! I got you. I'm tough...I'm Lorenzo Lamas!"

It's as if my father was already laying the seeds for my acting career without me even knowing it. Little do I realize that the renegade in me is starting to surface. I starting to come out of my shell—thanks to a little nudge from my father.

In the storybook titled *La Dolce Vita*, I play this swinging bachelor much too busy reading my *Pinocchio* comic book to talk. Finally, I instruct my chauffeur, "To my cabin on the beach, Perkins, and don't bother me, I'm reading!" In no time, I am spending the day at Ostia Beach (in a small storybook, it is amazing how fast time flies!), walking the sand and swimming nude as if I am some kind of ladies' man: "This is the life! No clothes, my beach house, my boat and a few girls. Hah!"—my father's words!

Father goes to great lengths to show his love for me on that trip, as evidenced in *The Two Guys*, the third and final storybook he does for me. Inside are panels of old two-by-three-inch photographs of us lovingly cobbled together—"two happy guys"—on Ostia Beach and "two not-so-happy guys" in front of his classic Alfa Romeo convertible at Fiumicino Airport moments before my flight back to the States. The final captions on the last page in Dad's handwriting say it all about the bond between us, as well as his deepest regrets over our separation:

"I'll see you soon, Daddy!"

"Be a good boy, eh?"

"NO ENDING!"

Our actual final minutes together are bittersweet. Tears well up in my eyes when I say goodbye to Dad as Lola and I board the plane. It is so hard, not knowing when I will ever see him again, that my heart aches just thinking about it.

"Daddy, Daddy," I say, running into his arms, sniffling, "please come with us, Daddy."

"Someday, Lorenzo, someday," he says. We lovingly embrace. "Promise."

One last embrace, then Lola pulls me away with "Lorenzo, we need to board."

For a moment, I see real emotion in my dad's eyes. He feels the same pain, the same turmoil, the same tug-of-war with his feelings I do, even though he does not outwardly show it like I do.

"Goodbye, Son!"

At that, Lola and I walk off. Lola tugs me along as I keep glancing over my shoulder. Father is still standing where we left him. He is watching my every step. I pause a second and wave. Dad smiles broadly and returns the favor as Lola and I make our way to the plane. Then I suddenly lose sight of him and he disappears into the mass of humanity moving about.

Every day I hold on to that promise that I will see my father again. In 1963, it comes true when Dad and Esther move back to Los Angeles. The news makes me the happiest boy on the face of the planet. It means my father and I can see each other any time we want. Earlier, when I said I prayed the same prayer every night, it was that my father and I would be together again. Finally, we are.

Dad and Esther rent a guesthouse on Lola's sprawling estate off Sunset Boulevard in Brentwood until they buy their own house in Bel Air four years later. That February, for my fifth birthday, Dad and Esther throw a lavish birthday costume party at Lola's in my honor. They dress me up as a pint-sized caballero. Actor Chad Everett (later of TV's *Medical Center* fame) is among the invited guests. He brings a pony for all us kids to ride. Dad even gives me my earliest tips on picking up women when he introduces me to a little señorita who catches my fancy. Of course, by now, I am a master at nodding and letting him do all the talking.

It is the most time my father and I ever spend together. From kindergarten through third grade, he picks me up every day from school and drops me off at Lola's main house while he hangs out with Esther at the guesthouse. For me, Dad becomes the image of what it is to be a man, and quite an image it is: this huge voice and grand presence always willing to share and teach me many important lessons on becoming a man. One of my favorites is his teaching me how to give a person a firm handshake.

"Look them right in the eye, Son," he says and then practices with me. I am only six years old. "Now shake my hand."

I extend my right hand, grip his loosely, and shake.

"That's not firm enough," Dad admonishes me. "Don't give me a fish. Give me a handshake."

I try again.

"In the eye, look me straight in the eye," he reminds me.

I stare so hard into his eyes, mine tear up from the strain.

"Good. Now again."

Anytime I come over to visit or stay for dinner, Esther is always accommodating. She is an honest-to-goodness home-loving wife and mother through and through. She is also a terrific cook, as I quickly discover, and is truly in her element whenever she entertains. Even when we all go together to the beach with my friends, she really puts out a feast. She cooks the kind of meals served for dinner on Saturday night—mouthwatering, home-cooked lamb shanks or pot roasts as the main course, with roasted corn, potatoes, and asparagus—all made in a hibachi right on the beach. Dad makes it my job to load Esther's Mustang convertible before we pick up my friends Bill and Dave, or Jay and Jeff, all of whom live up the street (they are so skinny Dad collectively nicknames them "The Bird"), and head to the beach.

My father makes a circle in the sand with the heel of his foot around him and Esther and the food every time we go to the beach. It means that area is off-limits. Dad says, "You boys stay out until you are called."

Of course, my father has an ulterior motive: The last thing he wants is a bunch of crazy kids kicking up sand on his lamb shanks!

As Esther cooks and Dad sits and reads the newspaper, we do what most kids do when they go to the beach: frolic and have fun. We have a blast together—body-surfing, digging holes in the sand, chasing each other, tackling each other. The water is so cold we come out freezing and shivering, and bury ourselves in the sand from head to toe to keep warm.

One of Dad and Esther's favorite pastimes is gardening. They love it as a stress reliever and enlist me, whether I want to or not, to assist them. It is again all a part of my father's effort to instill responsibility in me at an early age. He is of that old-fashioned mind-set that if I am old enough to hold a trash bag, I am old enough to stand there and hold it for him.

"Over here, amigo," Dad says before instructing me exactly on how to hold the bag as he stuffs in ivy clippings, overgrown brush, or whatever else he is cutting back for the fire season.

After we finish, my quirky father throws all this stuff—large bags of clippings and bundles of branches twined together—in the back of Esther's stylish Mustang convertible as if it is a dump truck and takes it all to the nearby dump. Incidentally, million-dollar homes in the very affluent neighborhood known as Summit Ridge now sit on that dump site. Today, every time somebody successful tells me they live in Summit Ridge, I laugh because those homes are built on top of crap and God knows what else.

Any spillage from the bag is also my responsibility. Dad points to some clippings that never quite make it inside. "Be a good amigo and pick those up, too," he says, "and when you are done, help Esther."

Esther never really needs my help. She seems to have things under control. My father, however, believes it is the responsibility of a man to do what women cannot do for themselves. The first time I walk over to help Esther, she smiles down at me. I never say a word to her and do exactly as told. After bagging the last of the garden clippings and mess, she pats me on the shoulder and says, "It's okay if you help, but your father is the one who really needs your help."

We look over. Dad is struggling to lift two large bags of clippings and deposit them in her Mustang. The bags are so overfilled and top-heavy they look as if they are ready to split at the seams. Just as my father starts to toss them, the top bag explodes like an overstuffed Mexican piñata, and everything rains down on him at once, covering him in dirt, leaves, branches, and debris. It is like a scene out of a slapstick comedy. Esther and I giggle under our breath. Suddenly Dad blinks his eyes open. After he wipes away the grit, he hollers comically, "Lor-en-zo!"

Esther and I start laughing, and Dad does, too. He realizes the silliness of the moment and embraces it.

Lola has never had any children herself, and so she always treats me like her little prince any time I visit. In fact, she gives me the book *The Little Prince* to read and is always encouraging my imagination. When I turn five, she takes me to Disneyland, introducing me to all of the great Disney fantasy characters. Her property is expansive, with clusters of big and small trees she calls her "Enchanted Forest." I find it all very enchanting indeed, spending hours there with her, taking long walks with her through the forest. I discover empty Coke bottles and leave messages in them in the trunks of those trees. Every time I go back to Lola's with Dad, I want to see if my bottled messages are still where I have left them. One message I write to Pinocchio asks, "Why does your nose grow?"

One time, to my astonishment, a message I left is missing. "Lola, where did the message go?" I ask.

"Pinocchio took them," she says, enchantingly.

I have all these foster people in my life—Emmy, who fills that maternal need, and then Lola, who is like the grandmother I never had. My parents are busy and distracted, and so I am very lucky to have these loving people spend time with me growing up, giving me good advice and helping me realize there is no limit to what I can accomplish. I feel so fortunate to have such guiding help from people who have my best interests at heart.

Dad sells his Alfa Romeo and is soon driving a gorgeous red-leather-on-black, four-door Jaguar Mark X sedan. His new toy for the moment, he drives it everywhere. It is so luxurious he can never get enough of it. One day we are heading home on Sunset Boulevard after he picks me up from school—I am six years old at the time—when suddenly we hear the sound of a bad blowout. We assume somebody's tire has blown.

"Boy, that'll be one unhappy amigo when they find out," Dad jokes.

Just as he says that, *kerthump, kerthump, kerthump.* The sound grows louder. Dad realizes the person with the flat is him. He is very unhappy about it, especially after just joking how some other poor amigo must have blown his tire.

"Wonderful!" Dad moans. "Just my luck."

We are near a blind curve on Sunset Boulevard. Dad quickly pulls over and jumps out. The left rear tire is flat. He walks back to my side of the vehicle, picks me up, and sits me down on the grass to play with my Hot Wheels away from the traffic while he jacks up the car to change the tire. Before doing so, he smartly grabs two emergency flares from the trunk. He lights them and puts them out in the middle of the street to alert drivers as he changes the tire in the face of oncoming traffic. With a speed limit then of twenty-five miles per hour, drivers have plenty of time to change lanes and go around us.

Dad is busy changing the tire while I am busy playing. Suddenly, he hollers, "Look out!"

Loud screeching of tires as Dad hurdles over the back of the Jag, lands and rolls, and ends up a foot from me on the grass. Then *Kablam*! It sounds like a bomb going off. We look up. Dad's Jaguar is suddenly in the middle of Sunset Boulevard. A small red MG convertible has plowed head-on into its trunk. The driver, who is racing another car down Sunset in the lane next to him, doesn't see Dad or his Jag until the very last second. By then it is too late. Meanwhile, the other car races right past us, never stops, never waits to see what happened.

Thanks to his swift reaction, my father avoids being sandwiched between the Jag and MG and emerges unscathed.

"Are you okay, amigo?"

I nod as Dad slowly rises to his feet and walks over to assess the damage.

"Yeah," I tell him as I start to stand up.

Dad's eyes nearly pop out of their sockets at what he sees. He throws his hands in the air as his voice goes up an octave like Desi Arnaz moaning, "Ay ay ay!"

Now buried inside the trunk of his expensive Jag is the MG, its back end sticking out where Dad's imported sedan once ended. Worst of all, the driver and his passenger are unconscious. Dad quickly says to me, "You wait here," and takes the flares from the curb lane to the middle of the street to divert oncoming traffic around the crash site so he can pull the drivers out of the wreckage.

"What happened?" the driver asks groggily.

"I was going to ask you the very same thing," Dad says. "Didn't you see my flares in the street?"

The man shakes his head and as Dad moves him, he winces in pain. He looks as if he hit his head on the dash and suffered a concussion.

"You okay?" Dad asks.

"No," the man says. "I feel as if I just went up against a three-thousand-pound gorilla and the gorilla won."

Just then, the passenger awakens. Blurry-eyed, he looks over at the driver as Dad finishes pulling him out. "What happened?"

The driver says, "That's what the man here is asking us."

The passenger's eyes get as big as saucers as he screams, "Oh my God, my MG!"

"Your MG?" Dad asks.

The driver says, "He owns the car and let me drive it."

"Amigo," Dad says with a laugh, "you just totaled my brand-new Jaguar Mark X and you are worried about your piece-of-shit MG?"

Under different circumstances, my father would have taken on both of them at once. Instead, he holds back as a police squad car pulls up behind them. An officer gets out and asks, "What happened here?"

My father smiles. "Ask them. That's what I've been trying to find out."

Within minutes, an ambulance is on the scene, and shortly after that two tow trucks come to haul off my father's Jaguar and the piece-of-shit MG that now really is, well, shit. The story has a happy ending. With his insurance settlement, Dad buys himself a new Jaguar XKE convertible but after that avoids that blind curve on Sunset Boulevard and is wary of MGs anytime he sees one on the road.

Every life has its changes, of course. Unfortunately, my changes are often extreme. After Mom divorces my father, the men come in and out of her life as though through a revolving door. We move around so often I change schools five times in eight years; it seems I am constantly leaving old friends and trying to make new. It is all very unsettling for a six-year-old who is seeking nothing more than normalcy in his life. As crazy as it seems at the time, it will prove good preparation for my career as an actor. And I believe it is why I become so reserved in my emotions, always ready to enjoy my life but without revealing much. But that's later; this is happening to a six-year-old child.

In December 1963, Mom separates from Christian, and in October 1964, she ends her unhappy four-year marriage to him. Mom claims he "showed no interest whatsoever in home or family life." As she says, "It was impossible to have a normal life with him." In the divorce, which is an ugly affair, the judge awards Mom the Pacific Palisades home where I grow up, plus $25,000 in $500 monthly payments and a percentage of his oil stock holdings.

During and after my mom's divorce, my friendships mean everything to me. My friends are my refuge, my solace from the tumult in my life. Most are regular kids in the neighborhood, including my first girl crush: Laurie Hayden, the daughter of well-known actress Eva Marie Saint and producer-director Jeffrey Hayden (who later directs me in a couple of *Falcon Crest* episodes). The couple also have a son, Darrell.

Laurie and I become friends due to the blossoming friendship between Emmy and the Haydens' black nanny, Bea. Emmy takes me to play with Laurie at the Hayden house while she and Bea gossip in the kitchen. Laurie, who is my age, seven, has the brightest red hair and the sweetest smile. I quickly develop a crush on her. We play in the pool out back, and I find her irresistible.

One day Bea brings Laurie with her to our place to play in the backyard tree house Dad helped me build. Laurie is a little scared as we climb up to the tree house. It is Laurie's first time, and so I help her up and then climb up after her. We sit next to each other and we play with my Hot Wheels and G.I. Joes. Suddenly I look at her. I feel this strong impulse to do something.

"What?" Laurie says.

Impulsively, I ask, "Can I kiss you?"

"Maybe," Laurie says coyly.

"When?"

"Not now."

"Well," I persist, "when?"

"I don't know."

Climbing down from the tree house, I wait for Laurie at the bottom, extend my hand to help her, and still hope to kiss her. I follow her around the backyard like a love-struck puppy. We meet at the swing set. She gets on a swing. I get on a swing. Now we are both swinging. Laurie stops after a while and gets off. She runs over and lies down on the grass under the huge maple tree. I run over and lie down next her. It is late in the afternoon. We have this epic view of the sky above. The sun is golden. Leaves sway on the branches as a cool ocean breeze ripples through them. Our heads are close together. Laurie suddenly looks over at me and says, "I guess it's okay for you to kiss me now."

I kiss Laurie on the lips. The kiss happens so fast and lasts only seconds. Immediately I feel tingly all over and think I am in love. I have no idea what love is, of course. I just know that kissing her feels right. The feeling is short-lived. We never kiss again but remain the best of friends after that.

In 1965, Dad and Esther finally move to a place of their own. They buy a tear-down at 11011 Anzio Road in Bel Air, damaged during the famous Bel Air fire of 1964. They purchase it for cash, and Bill Pereira, an architect friend of Dad's, then redesigns and rebuilds it. The finished property includes an Olympic-size pool out back, since both Dad and Esther (naturally) love to swim. Yet anytime I visit the house I feel like a guest. I never for a moment feel like part of the family. Esther, Dad, and her children from her previous marriage are "family" and I am just their houseguest.

Afternoons after Dad picks me up from school, he and Esther usually swim. It is all new to me, as I never remember them swimming at Lola's place. And I certainly don't remember the way they swim: completely nude. The first time I experience it, Dad says to me, "Go into the house and don't peek."

"Oh, okay," I respond.

As a seven-year-old kid, I know this is weird. On one level I understand, yet, on another, I know this is not something every kid should experience. Not until I grow up to become a parent do I realize how weird it really is.

I do as Dad tells me. I run back inside the house, grab a snack in the kitchen, and watch a little television while they swim naked in the pool. Curiosity finally gets the best of me. Like any kid, I do exactly the opposite of what I was told. I peek to see if they *really* are naked. After all, Dad said, "Don't peek," not "If you peek, you're in trouble."

I walk over to the living room window facing the pool, pull the curtain off to the side, and peer out. I cannot believe my eyes. Sure as shit, Dad and Esther are swimming in the buff. They are swimming laps as if they are training for an Olympic event, only naked. I find it too fascinating to stop looking. Next thing I know, Esther steps out of the pool *au naturel*. I cannot take my eyes off her. With her luscious, languorous locks of hair and curvaceous, robust figure, she is like a goddess standing there as she towels herself dry. Soon she disappears into their bedroom through a sliding-glass door off the patio, and my flirtation with the goddess is over as quickly as it started.

Next, Dad gets out. He is very much the man I imagine him to be, with a trim and athletic physique that complements his manly package. For a second, he looks my way. I shudder at the thought of him catching me. Fortunately, he doesn't see me. He picks up the other towel off the chaise lounge, dries off, and joins Esther in the bedroom for a very long time, like a half hour. I go back into the living room to watch television. It's getting close to dinnertime, and I'm getting hungry. In the meantime, I walk into the study adjacent to their bedroom and start my homework. The bedroom doors are still closed.

Suddenly, Dad appears right behind me. I turn and look. He is standing there naked with a huge erection. Never in my life have I seen anything like it. I am this seven-year-old kid, a guest in my father's home. Still learning the ways of the world. Still trying to figure things out. And now my father is standing there as if nothing is wrong, his corn dog sticking in my face as I try not to stare.

"Hey, amigo," he says, "you must be getting hungry."

I avert my eyes away from Dad's big salami. "Yeah, a little," I mumble. I've watched National Geographic specials and stared at enough pictures in magazines to know what penises look like. Dad's, however, is beyond my comprehension.

I add, "I was wondering when you guys were going to come out."

Dad carries on like we are having a normal conversation, as if nothing is out of the ordinary as his flagpole still stands at attention. "We took a swim, amigo," he says matter-of-factly. "Esther is taking a shower and then she is going to start dinner."

I can only think of one thing: "Wow, is that the way I am going to be? I hope so!"

The fact Dad is so well endowed makes me realize later why women loved him and put up with his shenanigans. As the years went on, I never mentioned the incident of the erection or its effect on me. I do ask once, much later, "Did you ever play around on Esther?"

And Dad says, "I never fooled around on Esther."

"Nothing ever stopped you before with other people."

"Well, with Esther, it's different," he admits. "She loves having sex and we do it a lot."

I laugh. "Oh, thanks, Dad."

"More importantly," he adds, "she treats me so well I could never live with myself if I did anything to hurt her."

It is a very mature thing for my father to say. Especially for the biggest corn dog in the studio system who, along with Douglas Fairbanks, had more tail than two of Gene Simmons of KISS fame. Simmons brags about how he has had two thousand women, but he has nothing on my father. Between his stardom in Argentina and glory days in Hollywood, my father had so much tail he easily eclipsed that mark.

As for Mom, now thirty-seven, romance blooms again and she is married for a fourth time, this time on Christmas Eve 1965, to Alexis Lichine, a prominent vintner and entrepreneur fourteen years her senior. They marry at Queen Forts House in Bridgetown, Barbados. His daughter, Sandra, who is a little older than me, and his son, Sasha, children from a previous marriage who continue to live with their birth mother in New York, are also on hand. Alexis, born in Moscow, USSR, seems like a fine fellow. He is refined, well spoken, well educated, and very ambitious, just like my mother.

In the beginning, Mom and Alexis maintain a bicoastal marriage. My sister, Carole, and I reside with Mom in Los Angeles while Alexis lives in two places: a beautiful Fifth Avenue two-story townhouse in New York and his lovely chateau at his world-famous vineyard, Château Prieuré-Lichine, in Margaux, Gironde, France.

I never really question the living arrangement Mom and Alexis have chosen. It is working, and of course, I love California, the beaches, and the weather so much I can never imagine leaving it, ever.

Despite marrying such a wealthy man as Alexis, Mom keeps pushing the envelope with her career. She writes a syndicated column that appears in some seventy newspapers and publishes a book on beauty care from a man's point of view, *Always Ask a Man* (the book soon has three studios negotiating for the film rights). In addition, she makes countless personal appearances at beauty clinics.

Not until I enter third grade do I realize Mom is a celebrity. In March 1966 she pioneers a completely new concept in television with a daily five-minute show called *Arlene Dahl's Beauty Spot*. It is broadcast on ABC affiliates between *Those Who Think Young* and *Where the Action Is*. She films sixty-five shows in four weeks and claims, "From now on I'll work six weeks in the fall and six weeks each spring on the show and take the rest of the year off."

Then I understand: My mom is famous. Then the reality really hits me: I will see even *less* of her now that she is. Later I am always happy that people ask for her autograph, but back then it has dawned on me that I have to share my parents with the world. They do not really belong to me.

TWO

Getting My Act Together

THREE YEARS AFTER I develop a close relationship with Dad, my whole world comes crashing down again when Mom announces in late spring of 1966, "We are moving to New York to live with Alexis."

I am slack-jawed, speechless over the news, and cannot believe this is happening. Not now, not at this critical time in my youth, not when Dad and I have bonded and become so close. It is a very painful time for me, as I dearly miss the daily contact I had with my father and the relationship we had built together.

Home for most of the year now becomes Alexis's beautiful Fifth Avenue two-story townhouse, easily worth two or three million dollars. In the summer, home is his spectacular chateau in France.

Everything that follows Mom's announcement is such a whirlwind that I barely get a chance to feel settled. In May of that year, I finish school, and then we fly to New York. Soon after, Mom ushers Carole and me onto a passenger liner bound for Europe to spend three months with Alexis, Sandra, and Sasha at the chateau in France. Sandra, Sasha, and I spend our summer vacation there like one big, happy family. I'm an eight-year-old kid getting my first taste of vineyard life, never knowing someday I will star in a television show about one.

The vineyards are sprawling and majestic, with grapes succulent to the touch and vines of strong, healthy stock. Most days a cloudless blue sky makes the perfect backdrop. The whole operation is so impressive. I remember watching with amazement as Monsieur Godin, one of Alexis's workers, makes wine barrels by hand. With his huge Popeye-like arms and hands, Godin cuts the wood, sands it, and fastens steel bands around both sides to form the barrels. He has worked with his hands his whole life and has absolutely no body fat, even though he's a man in his fifties. I find being around him nothing short of inspiring.

But then there's New York. I have spent my whole life in California, doing just about whatever I want, when I want. Living in New York is rough most of the time. It is all so depressing—the dreary, rainy, cold climate, the claustrophobic lifestyle of the city, the regimented school environment—everything. I am simply miserable. And the whole time I never see my father. The longer that goes on, the harder things become for me. I feel a tremendous loss in my life without him and the daily personal contact we once had.

Further compounding my frustration is a house servant who comes as part of the package with Mom's marriage to Alexis. Madame Lasaire is an angry, overweight, gray-haired old French woman. She moves in with us in California even before we relocate to New York. She and Emmy butt heads immediately and never get along. As a result, Mom unfairly fires Emmy, which breaks my heart.

Madame is no Emmy. It is absolutely horrible living with her. Anytime something goes wrong, she blames me. For some reason, she has it in for me; I am not sure why. But then one simple incident brings Mom to her senses: It's the night Madame makes lamb chops with string beans for dinner.

I love the lamb chops but hate the string beans. That night I merely pick at them with my fork, lift them up, look at them, put them down, but never eat them. In her thick French accent, the warden-like Madame says, "You will eat those string beans or sit here all night."

I choose the latter. I sit there, past my bedtime, until finally I fall asleep with my head on the kitchen table. There is no way I am going to eat those string beans. Anytime my eyes flutter open I still see them; the mere sight makes me sick to my stomach.

I wake up at two in the morning and sneak off to bed. Later that morning, I get up and go into the kitchen with my sister,

Carole, to have breakfast and then get ready for school. There on the kitchen table are those damn string beans, sitting cold and limp on my plate. They have not moved from the very spot where Madame left them.

Suddenly, as if she has a GPS tracker on me, the tough-as-nails Madame appears out of nowhere. "You will eat those string beans," she commands firmly.

The sight of them makes me want to puke. "They're gross and cold," I tell her flatly. "I am not going to eat them."

Madame snaps back, "You will not have breakfast until you eat those string beans."

"No, I won't."

The string beans and I have a staring match. Finally, I skip break-fast and go to school. That afternoon when I get home, the string beans—by now a cold, shriveled lump of green something—are *still* there on my plate. Madame pounces: "You will eat those string beans for dinner, then!"

"I will not eat those string beans"—I pause and look down at the mangy lump—"or whatever you call them."

Later, Carole is eating her dinner, and I have my string beans sit-ting in front of me, which I am not eating. I stubbornly refuse and go to bed. The next morning, I walk into the kitchen, and they are *still there*, on the same plate, now beyond recognition. Madame keeps insisting, "You will eat your string beans."

I stand firm. "I will not. They are disgusting."

Unruffled, Madame says, "You will eat these string beans or you will not eat another meal!"

"Fine, I'm not eating."

Mom, who never gets up before ten o'clock, rises early that morn-ing because she is on deadline for a project. She walks into the kitchen after hearing the commotion. She peers down at the putrid mass of green on the kitchen table and asks, "Lorenzo, what in God's name is that on your plate?"

I look up and explain, "Well, these are string beans from two nights ago that Madame Lasaire wants me to eat."

Mom goes, "What!" She then turns to Madame and asks, "Madame Lasaire, what is going on?"

Madame pushes out her chest proudly. "Well, Miss Dahl, your son is not eating his string beans. So he will not eat another thing until he finishes his string beans."

After two days of not eating, I am so famished that even those god-awful string beans are starting to look good. But bless her heart, my mom, for once in my life, sticks up for me. "Madame Lasaire, how dare you!" says Mom, outraged. "You will absolutely fix my son his breakfast, and you will never again make him eat food he does not want to finish. Is that understood?"

I cannot believe it. My sister cannot believe it. Never have we ever heard Mom raise her voice—ever. I keep looking at Mom and Madame Lasaire as they stare at each other without saying another word.

Taking a deep breath, Madame Lasaire explodes, "Well, I never!" She takes the plate, string beans and all, throws it into the trash, and storms out of the kitchen.

Mom smiles as she looks at me. "Well, I guess your mother is going to make you breakfast this morning."

I am so excited and thinking, "Yeah, thanks, Mom."

She makes me French toast. It is still the best French toast I have ever had. After that, I wish Mom would make breakfast more often. And she does, at least until she hires a replacement for Madame Lasaire.

But the series of nannies Mom hires to look after my sister and me cannot compensate for the void in my life left by Emmy, my father, and my California friends. Most days, I feel all alone and more frustrated than ever.

Mom never really addresses my pent-up anger and frustration. We never really talk about it. Instead, that fall she enrolls me in the fourth grade at Trinity School, an Episcopalian private school in Manhattan. It has a strict dress code: gray slacks, a blue blazer with the school crest on the pocket, a white button shirt, and a tie—every day. I am sure my mother hopes the change of environment will be good for me.

For some reason, Trinity does not bus students from the east side of town, where we are, to its campus, which is on the west side. In the morning, I either ride my bike to school or take the public bus, using the bus pass Mom has purchased for me. Getting there by bus is not easy. In fact, it takes two buses—catching the first near Seventy-eighth and Park Avenue and riding it down Fifth Avenue and then transferring to another bus that goes cross-town to school. But to get from the first bus to the second, I have to walk across Central Park, then a haven for heroin addicts and homeless people. These were the days when John Lindsay was mayor of New York, and you could not walk anywhere and feel safe. Even Forty-second Street and Times Square looked nothing like it does today. Back then X-rated movie houses dominated the real estate, and drug dealers peddled their wares on virtually every corner.

One morning, as I—a straitlaced, clean-cut, well-dressed eight-year-old—am walking my usual route across Central Park to catch the second bus, four older black kids suddenly jump me from behind. They push me and roll me to the ground, rough me up, kick me a couple of times, and pick me clean.

"What do we have in here, rich white boy?" the grungy leader says as he rifles through my wallet and plucks out ten bucks cash. "This all you are carrying?"

I stammer, "It's all I have."

After he and his gang of hoods work me over some more, they rip my bus pass from my shirt pocket, snatch my Samsonite briefcase from the ground, and run off. (Trinity required every student to have either a leather or Samsonite briefcase.) I am so scared I do not know what in the hell has just happened. Later I do: I just experienced my first New York mugging.

I hustle on foot to school, with grass stains on my trousers and the top two buttons missing from my shirt. My teacher immediately sends me to the principal's office for being late. I tell the principal why. Looking at me down the bridge of his nose from behind his glasses, he says calmly, "Okay, you should go home and tell your mom what happened. You should either take a cab to school from now on, or your mother should find some other way to get you here."

Obviously, it is not safe for me to cross Central Park. I will get mugged again—or something worse—if I do. I go home and tell Mom what happened.

"Oh, that's terrible," she says in a motherly tone. "Are you all right, darling?"

"Yeah, I'm okay, Mom."

I have a fat lip, so Mom says, "Let's put some ice on that."

I figure Mom has me covered. Tomorrow, she will give me cab fare to take a taxi to school. Seeing how badly beat up I am, there is no way she will put me on a bus again.

The next morning, I get up and have breakfast—a bowl of cereal. Mom comes into the kitchen and chirps enthusiastically, "It's a new day!"

"Yeah, it is. Can I have cab fare to go to school?"

"Oh, no, honey," Mom says. "You're going to have to take the bus."

Mom's lack of understanding flabbergasts me. "Mom." I pause. "That's how I got mugged in the first place. You have to give me money for cab fare."

Here we are talking about the safety of her flesh-and-blood son, but Mom classically says, "Oh, it's not going to happen again. Today's a new day. It's a new beginning."

I plead with her. "But what if those kids are still there?"

Mom says emphatically, "They are not going to be there, honey, because they know what they did was wrong."

Mom's words are stunning. "Give me a break!" I sigh.

In her usual chirpy voice, Mom says, "Off you go now." She ushers me to the front door to get my replacement briefcase and sees me off.

Without my bus pass, it costs me fifty cents to get to school that day. Mom soon buys me a new pass so I can take the bus to school every day, just like before. But from then on, so I do not look like such a douche bag and such an easy target, I carry my jacket and tie in my briefcase and pull my shirttail out over my slacks before walking across Central Park. My plan works brilliantly for about three months. Then another group of kids chases after me. I run so fast my legs feel as if they are gliding on air. I make it to the bus stop ahead of them. Fortunately, the bus is already there waiting for me to board. The driver—a big, imposing man who looks like a defensive lineman for the New York Jets who eats quarterbacks for breakfast—draws open the door. He spots the kids running up after me; he stands up, cracks his knuckles, and shouts at them in a deep, booming voice: "You kids go on, now! You leave this boy alone! Go on, now!"

The boys take one look at the hulk-like figure standing before them and scatter. Catching my breath, I hop on board and thank the driver as he returns to his seat. "Thanks so much," I pant. "I was mugged here about three months ago."

"No problem," he snaps back, "just get on the bus."

LIKE MY MOTHER'S PREVIOUS HUSBAND, Christian, Alexis never fully replaces my father. Much like my mother, Alexis is far too busy to be a parent, even to his own daughters. Dad and I are cut from the same cloth, from the same bloodline, and in my mind, no man ever comes close to his grandeur or ever will. Dad is not halfway around the world like he was when I was much younger, yet it feels that way most days, since I never see him.

In early 1968, Mom ends her marriage to Alexis, on good terms, after a separation. We continue to live in his Manhattan townhouse, and she and Alexis remain "good friends." Occasionally, they catch dinner together when he is town.

Even without Alexis in the picture, my frustration with my mom and living in New York starts to boil over. In fifth grade, I become this hard-to-manage eight-going-on-nine-year-old kid with no real compass, no real direction, mad at my mom and the world for everything that is wrong in my life. Finally, I lose control. I act out in frustration to get attention. One day, my classmate Nick Cassini and I take some M-80s to school, slip them in the locker room below and...well, you know what happens when you light a cherry bomb on a school property. The principal expels us both.

Mom tries to smooth things over with the principal, but to no avail. After that, she transfers me to another private school, the Dalton School on New York City's Upper East Side, for the remainder of my fifth-grade year. It's hard for me to talk to my mom about my feelings, since I don't think she will understand them anyway. So I simply bury them for the time being and stay out of trouble.

I finish out the school year, but for me, the summer of 1968 cannot come soon enough. I am so thrilled; I am spending my summer vacation with Dad! He invites me to join him on location in Almería, Spain, where he is filming *100 Rifles*, a 20th Century Fox western costarring Raquel Welch and Burt Reynolds and directed by Tom Gries. Dad flies me from New York and picks me up at the airport in Barcelona. Esther is also there, and it is like a family reunion. We pick up right where we left off. Dad and I laugh and joke. Dad tells more tall tales, offers more words of wisdom, and I again nod. As always, Esther is like a soul mom to me. She really takes the time to understand me and talk to me. I feel right at home again.

Dad and Esther and the entire cast are staying at a beautiful resort hotel in the city, complete with a spectacular swimming pool. I have an absolute ball swimming every day with Gries's kids, Jon and Cary. When on the set, we play games, including cowboys and Indians, because that is what the movie is about. One day, my black mustachioed father, in costume as General Verdugo, the career-minded military man he plays in the film, sees us playing and says, "Hey, amigo, why don't you take your friends to the wardrobe trailer, get yourself some cowboy and Indian outfits, and we'll put you in the scene."

We walk over to wardrobe and I tell the wardrobe lady what my father said. Before we know it, we are dressed in authentic cowboy and Indian outfits. The wardrobe lady even fits me with a just-above-the-shoulder black wig for effect. Just as Dad says, I appear in the scene with him. It is not a speaking role; I am just an extra. And Dad is nothing but affirming with me.

"Hey, amigo, you make a pretty good Indian," he says with a smile.

"Ah, Dad." I'm self-conscious.

"But we have to do something about that wig!"

In the blink of an eye, it's over. My first on-camera appearance as an uncredited Indian boy. Not a very promising start to a film career, even though becoming an actor like my father is the furthest thing from my mind at this point.

Burt Reynolds is not yet the number-one male box-office star; it's still four years before his now-famous nude centerfold on a bearskin rug, no less, in *Cosmopolitan* magazine. On the set, Burt is always very nice to me and calls me "kid." One afternoon during a break in filming, he teaches me how to throw a stage punch. We are fooling around and he says, "Hey, kid, come here."

I walk over.

"Let me see you throw a punch," he says. "I know your dad boxes, but can you throw a punch?"

Burt holds up his hand. I throw a punch as hard as I can. "That's pretty good, kid. Throw another one."

I throw another punch, harder than the first. Burt shakes his hand a little, blows on it, and smiles. Then he says, "Would you like to know how to throw a movie punch?"

"Sure," I say.

I cannot believe it: Burt Reynolds is going to teach me how to throw a movie punch!

"Okay now, kid, instead of punching straight into my hand," he says, "I want you to arc your punch like a windmill. Punch your punch, and come around wide."

I do it a few times.

"Great, kid, great! Let me show you how this works."

Burt demonstrates it for me, using me as the guy he's going to punch. "You're going to do that same thing. You're going to bring your punch around and come within a foot in front of my face with that nice swing that you did."

I do exactly what Burt tells me. Soon as I cross his face, he jerks his head back.

"Wow!" I shout. "That looked so real!"

"That's right, kid. You just learned how to throw your first movie punch."

Burt walks off with me. "You just might have a future in this business," he says jokingly and slaps me on the back.

Fast-forward eight years: I am sitting in a movie theater, now as a nineteen-year-old, watching Burt in his latest feature, *Smokey and the Bandit*. There is a huge knock-down, drag-out movie fight scene with his costar Jerry Reed, where the two of them bust through one set after another while fighting off their adversaries. I become a ten-year-old kid again and think, "Wow, I learned from the master!"

On the set, Dad also pals around with costar Hans Gudegast (who later changes his name to Eric Braeden and becomes famous on the daytime soap opera *The Young and the Restless*). Hans and my father have many things in common and become very close. Hans is a great soccer player, and Dad loves the sport. So between setups on the set, they fool around with the soccer ball, passing it back and forth. At times they draw quite a crowd. Hans, an excellent boxer in school, and Dad, a former welterweight, love to chat about boxing. After Dad and Esther move to Beverly Hills, he often has Hans and his lovely wife, Dale, over for a home-cooked meal. Other times, Hans and Dad head off to the Olympic Auditorium in downtown Los Angeles to catch the fights. They are just the best of buds.

It is such a blast being with Dad and Esther in Spain. Every night, we have dinner on the patio. What a life! Burt, Raquel, Hans, and other members of the cast often join us. They laugh and tell jokes. As a kid, I struggle to keep up with their intellect and humor. As the evenings grow late, I struggle to stay awake, but every night without fail, the candles on the table lull me to sleep. To this day, I cannot sit at a table and look at a candle for longer than five minutes before falling asleep.

Ever since she starred two years earlier in the British fantasy movie *One Million Years B.C.*, there has been no hotter actress—or no hotter woman, for that matter—on the planet than Raquel Welch. And this ten-year-old immediately takes notice of her. I have a monster crush on her from the moment I meet her. Anytime I am around her, I cannot take my eyes off her. She is drop-dead gorgeous, and everybody on the set is taken by her. If I manage to stay awake through dinner, I make a point to walk up to her, say good night, and stand there. She always starts it off.

"Well, good night!" she says, brightly.

"Good night," I say, softly.

Raquel, smiling, tries again. "Good night!"

I just stand there, my feet firmly planted. "Good night," I repeat.

Finally, Raquel starts to giggle. "Ahhhh, you want a hug, don't you?"

I nod.

Raquel walks over and gives me a big hug. I repeat the same trick every night, and it works like a charm. If I ever see Raquel again, I guarantee I am going to stand there and wait for my hug!

When it all ends, I am so sad and upset to have to go back to New York and my life there. I only wish I could stay in Spain and never leave. At the airport, I feel like the four-year-old I was when I visited Dad and Esther that summer in Italy. But saying goodbye is different this time; it's even worse. I can tell Dad understands how hard all of this is on me. As we hug, tears well up in our eyes. I am unable to muster the words, but Dad does: "Love you, Son. We'll be together again, very soon. I promise."

Dad lets go as I choke back tears. We embrace one last time. Regaining his composure, he then points to my plane. "You better be going, amigo. Your plane is waiting."

I take one last look at him and Esther. Esther reaches over, hugs me, and says, "Lorenzo, don't worry, your father and I will always love you."

I nod. "Me, too."

The afterglow of my summer vacation with Dad and Esther burns bright during the days, weeks, and even months ahead. On the plane ride home, I feel certain that if things are going to change this time, it will be because they will see to make sure it does. Until then, I remain hopeful and continue to pray that it will happen soon, and we will never be separated again.

The following year, my wish comes true. Mom moves us back to California and enrolls me at Paul Revere Junior High in Brentwood to start seventh grade in the fall. Coming from a New York private school, I place very high on my scholastic achievement test and am allowed to skip sixth grade.

I really love being back. I am eleven years old and living the dream again—seeing my friends, going to the beach, playing in the street until dark.

During the three years we lived on the East Coast, Mom rented out our Pacific Palisades home to Don Knotts, best known as Deputy Barney Fife on television's *The Andy Griffith Show* and *Mayberry R.F.D.* After returning, Mom is furious when she walks into her bedroom and sees a huge blob-like stain on the fancy fabric of her bed's headboard.

"Mom," I ask, stunned, "what is *that*?"

"Well, Mr. Knotts apparently uses hair pomade." With his Brylcreem or whatever, ol' Barney used more than "a little dab'll do ya," staining the headboard beyond repair.

Shortly after we move back, a television producer woos Mom and sweeps her off her feet. He is Rounseville W. Schaum, chairman of Western Video Industries, Inc. She is now forty; he is three years younger. In early December 1969, she quickly marries him in a ceremony performed by Dr. Norman Vincent Peale at Marble Collegiate Church in New York. He is her fifth husband (his nickname is "Skip"), and two years later they have a son, Rounseville Andreas. Skip seems like a nice fellow but so did Alexis, and before him, Christian, so I never get too comfortable with the idea of him sticking around for long either. Of course, none of those other husbands could ever measure up to my father. In my mind, he is irreplaceable.

My friends all have their own mini-trail bikes, so I have to have one of my own, specifically the new Honda Z50 Mini Trail. I wash cars, mow lawns, and save money, but never enough to buy one. A minibike is on every kid's shopping list. Finally, I wear my mom out and she says, "Lorenzo, if you have good marks and good behavior, you will get a minibike."

One day, Skip pulls his flashy white Mercedes into the driveway and pops open the trunk. "Your mother asked me to get this for you," he says.

Skip pulls it out for me. There it is, right before my eyes, my dream machine. Just as Skip is saying, "Your mother wants you to wear a helmet," daredevil me hops on and tears off. Before Skip can finish his sentence, I am roaring around the driveway with it. The feeling I have riding it is hard to describe in mere words, but let me try: the roar and vibration of the engine, the sense of freedom and adventure, the thrill and excitement, the speed and danger, the wind in my face. And I am not even out of the driveway yet! Having that bike unleashes a monster inside me. I know from that moment I am a biker at heart.

But the coolest thing about being back in California is being near Dad again. I see him three or four times a week when he picks me up from school. On December 31, 1969, Dad and Esther finally marry after being together eight years. It just happens to be the same month Mom and Skip tie the knot. Esther lives in total submission to my father—right down to honoring his wishes that her children can never live with them. In return, she is faithful and a good life partner who rarely challenges him, unless it concerns something really worth fighting over.

While my own mom is more detached and aloof, Esther is more mothering; she's how a mother should be, and I develop a close maternal relationship with her. I help her clean the kitchen, fold the laundry, and do the chores. Without fail, Dad picks me up from school; we hang out and have dinner together. Esther usually makes two dinners. The first is for the three of us; she serves at five thirty or six. The second one she takes later to her children, who live in Santa Monica with their father. After she gets back, Dad takes me home.

As dysfunctional as my life is, things settle into a nice routine. The pieces are finally falling into place. For the first time in a very long time, with Dad and Esther in my life, I start to feel part of a real family again. We are doing the kinds of stuff a regular family does. Everything is perfect—for now.

Any chance I get, I ride my Honda bike in and around the neighborhood. It is the closest thing to a motorcycle I have. On weekends, with more free time, I love to explore. One Saturday, I bike up the fire trail to the park near Will Rogers Beach. The terrain is rocky, rugged, and unspoiled, but I manage. Pumping the pedals as hard as I can, I get a strong headwind as I start to descend. Coming down the trail into the parking lot, I suddenly lose control at the bottom of the hill. With my bike carrying a bit of speed, the front wheel washes out and the bike buckles from under me. I land face-first, sliding on my stomach and knees across the hard black asphalt. Ouch!

I lie there in a daze until I realize what happened. With its misshapen frame and bent handlebars, my bike looks like an oversized pretzel. I feel fortunate that is the worst of the damage—until I stand up. My bloodied face has numerous cuts and scrapes and my elbows are bleeding. Then I look down to discover a huge gash across my knee with a large flap of skin folded over the gash. It has not yet started to bleed. When I pull up the flap, I can see the tendon and bone in my knee. I realize this cannot be good, even though I feel no pain at this point. Very quickly, my knee starts bleeding profusely. Within a minute, the whole bottom of my jeans is soaked in blood.

I am a mile from home. There are no cell phones then, not even a pay phone close by. I have no idea if my leg is going to work to get me home, but I give it a shot. I straighten the handlebars on my bike and hop back on. The pain is excruciating as I pedal a little with my injured leg. I pedal and coast, pedal and coast, and pedal and coast the whole way. It takes me twenty minutes, but I make it.

I walk through the front door into the entry hall, then the living room, and about twenty more feet to the dining room. Mom is busy working there on her astrology forecasts and her latest astrology book. I hobble into the dining room and stand there, bleeding all over the floor. I look at Mom and wait a second to see if she notices. She is so buried in her work, I finally say something like, "Hey, Mom, I'm sorry I'm getting blood on your floor."

Mom snaps her ahead around. She looks me in the face, then up and down, and screams, "Oh, my God, Lorenzo!"

At that moment, I pass out. My stepdad Skip happens to walk in. He rips the belt from his trousers, makes a makeshift tourniquet, and puts it around my leg to slow the bleeding. They immediately call for an ambulance.

I come to when the paramedics are loading me into the ambulance to take me to the emergency room at St. John's Hospital in Santa Monica. I remember asking the ambulance driver, "Can you turn on the siren?" just before passing out again.

In the ER, I wake up to see my jeans cut off and a pretty nurse standing over me, flushing chunks of asphalt out of the wound on my leg. She's holding what looks like a nailbrush and shoving it up near my shin bone to remove all the asphalt that's packed down in there. Fortunately, my tendons are okay. The only serious damage is to one of my main leg arteries, which is why there is so much blood.

Mom later tells me what the ambulance driver said to her as the paramedics loaded me into the ambulance: "Miss Dahl, I have never seen a leg as badly damaged as your son's—one that's still attached, anyway."

Had it not been for my stepfather Skip, I might not be here today to tell the story. He really saved my life by putting that tourniquet around my leg. I owe him more than mere words can say.

While we were living in New York, Mom got me a dog—a soft, floppy-eared, short-legged beagle I name George. I guess Mom hopes having the responsibility will settle me down. I love George like a best friend immediately, and he becomes a great companion for me. He is four years old by the time we move back to our California home in Villa Grove. He loves to run and play in the large backyard and enjoy all that open space, unlike in Manhattan, where the closest thing to grass is the nearest public park. George especially enjoys taking off into the Santa Monica Mountains for a day, but he always returns. Except for one day, when he doesn't. I whistle and call his name. I go searching for him. I stand out back, hoping for him to suddenly appear. Days go by; George never returns. Most likely, coyotes got him. I am just heartbroken. I miss him so much.

Every passing day, my life feels empty without him. I do nothing but mope around most days. Finally, Mom calls Emmy's stepsister Evelyn, a breeder who shows miniature poodles in dog shows, and says, "Can we find Lorenzo another dog?"

Evelyn is happy to oblige. "I'll take him with me to the next show," she says, "and we'll find him a new dog."

I love going to the shows with Evelyn and her son, Jeff, who sometimes shows their poodles along with her. At one show, after Evelyn and Jeff introduce me to a breeder of Great Danes, I fall in love with a crazy fawn-colored puppy and bring him home. Mom has a fit. "Holy smokes," she says, "look at the size of his feet. He's going to be huge!"

"Yeah, Mom," I explain. "He's a Great Dane."

"Couldn't you have found a *smaller* dog?"

"No, I really wanted him."

I just love Caesar—that's the name I give him—his expressive face and eyes, his friendly and energetic personality, and his strength and elegance. We instantly become best buds. As Caesar grows, Evelyn takes me along with her to dog shows where I show him in breed and win several blue ribbons.

At six o'clock on the morning of February 9, 1971, I am getting ready for school in my room when I suddenly feel a sharp jolt and then a rumbling under my feet. It intensifies with each second and grows louder, like a locomotive speeding through my room. My whole room starts to rock and sway. My bed begins to shake. My books fall from their shelf, while my toy Batman collection starts doing the mambo on my desk. It is an earthquake—and not an ordinary one. This feels like a major tremor. Caesar immediately dives under my bed. Meanwhile, my stepdad Skip rushes into my room.

"Lorenzo," he orders as the ground beneath us shakes violently, "we have to get out of the house right now!"

My room has a door to the backyard. I tell Skip, "Okay, cool!"

I grab Caesar's leash and attach it to his collar but cannot get him to move out from under my bed. He is trembling and shaking and will not budge.

I shout, "Caesar, come! Caesar, come!"

Caesar is unresponsive. He is a year old now and weighs about one hundred pounds. With all my might, I keep trying to pull him out as I hear Mom scream, "Everybody out!"

My family runs out the front door of the house as everything around them shakes and rattles out of control. As the force of the quake builds to a crescendo, I finally pull Caesar out by the collar instead of the leash. Like a wild horse, he races out my door into the backyard, pulling me along with him. After coming to a quick stop, we end up on the grass. The tremor finally subsides, and the ground stops rumbling and shaking. At that moment Skip comes into the backyard and demands, "Where were you?"

I point to the ground on which I stand. "Right here."

Skip is clearly agitated. "I told you to come out the front door."

"I never heard that," I explain. "I had a door and just went out the door."

Long story short, everybody is safe. The only serious damage is to a sliding-glass patio door that shattered. As it turns out, the earthquake is a magnitude 6.6 centered in the San Fernando–Sylmar region of Los Angeles and felt throughout Southern California and into western Arizona and southern Nevada. Aftershocks occur for several months, but the original quake causes widespread damage to many older buildings in nearby Beverly Hills and the surrounding suburbs of Burbank and Glendale. Because of structural damage to highway overpasses, roads, and bridges, and concerns over more aftershocks in the area, schools close for the day, including mine. I am oblivious to it all. With no school, my friends Bill and Dave and I go hiking up the Santa Monica Mountains for the day. Only later do I discover just how lucky we really are.

Later, during my eighth-grade year at Paul Revere Junior High School, I start running around with a bunch of crazy guys doing those crazy things eighth graders do. I'm trying to be part of the in-crowd, to be "one of the boys." Some stunts we pull I know are dead wrong, but I do them anyway, so the kids will say, "Hey, Lorenzo's crazy. He's okay."

The leader of the group comes up with a stunt sure to get every-body's attention: set the school lockers on fire. I go along with the idea. It sounds cool. Everything goes as planned. Except for the part where they catch us and expel us, including yours truly—overall the third school to give me the boot. Mom finally steps in to put an end to my shenanigans.

"You're going to military school," she announces.

"Military school? What's that?" I ask, dreading the answer.

"You'll see," she says.

As long as I can still see Dad and my friends, I figure everything will be okay. I love everything about California, especially its glorious sunshine, sandy beaches, majestic mountains, and, yes, all its pretty girls (although they do not yet know I exist). I simply can't imagine living anywhere else. It is home. My father, my friends, and every-thing familiar to me are there. Mom, of course, has other ideas. She enrolls me in a school as far away from my father and my friends and California and as close to her as possible: Admiral Farragut Academy, an all-boys military school, in New Jersey.

Mom ships me off to the academy before moving back to New York to promote her cosmetic company, Arlene Dahl Enterprises, with its new line of wigs she'll market through Sears Roebuck and its Manhattan advertising agency, Kenyon & Eckhart. She and Skip take the whole family to live there—my sister, Carole, and little step-brother, Steven—while sending me off to Farragut. Before I leave, Mom tells me, "You have to give Caesar away."

I am too heartsick to do it myself. Mom calls Evelyn, and she finds a home for him. It is not as bad as I fear. I know the people who are taking him because I see them at the dog shows all the time and have a crush on their daughter. Mom is heartened by that fact. "Oh, he's going to a nice home, Lorenzo," she says happily. "Evelyn tells me you even like one of those people."

"Yeah, Mom," I confess, "but that's not the point. Caesar's my dog. Can't you keep him so I can see him when I come home?"

Once again, Mom never puts herself in my shoes. "We're so busy, Lorenzo," she says. "We can't possibly keep him."

I never feel as if Mom puts my needs before hers, and this latest incident only deepens that feeling. I have so much trouble saying goodbye to Caesar the day the people come for him. I give him a long, hard hug as tears well up in my eyes. Then I give him a simple command: "Go, Caesar."

Caesar goes to his new owners. As they exit out the front door, he stops, lingers for a second, and looks back at me one last time. Working through my tears, I find the strength to command him one final time, "Go, Caesar, now." The big lug turns and lumbers out the door as I collapse on the floor, crying my eyes out. To this day, I can see his furrowed brow creasing his forehead and that puzzled look in his deep-set brown eyes as I bid him goodbye. I still choke up just thinking about him.

The following day, Esther drives me to Los Angeles International Airport. Fighting back tears, I gulp hard as we say goodbye and I board the 747 bound for New York. Seconds after, the airplane cabin door closes shut. It is like a jail cell slamming in my face. The only thing missing is the standard-issue prison jumpsuit, because that's what I feel like, a prisoner.

New Jersey seems like the end of the world to me—and is. I loathe it as much as I did New York when Mom moved us there before. I hate every minute and am just heartsick over not seeing Dad and my friends. Most of all, I am angry with Mom for sending me there, for keeping me from my father and my friends, and for moving us away from them now for the second time. My inner radar, however, tells me, "Lorenzo, get your shit together." I know that I am a young man in need of saving regardless of how deeply upset I feel.

It is no small task to grow up in the shadow of a famous father. From his larger-than-life persona to his grand presence as an actor, he has big shoes to fill. At times, as a boy, I think I will never measure up. Entering the academy is no different. I am this overweight, out-of-shape, chunky twelve-year-old kid who looks more like Buddy Hackett's son than Fernando Lamas's. What's more, I'm hardly what you'd consider a jock. My father, on the other hand, is this giant of a man in tip-top athletic shape, someone who can do just about anything physically.

Military school is the hardest thing I have ever experienced. Nothing but guys, bunk beds, lots of marching, and no girls (not even one!). It all seems so extreme. I just want to go back to California.

Yet even though the disciplined environment is grating, eventually I come to appreciate it. In the end, it is all good for me. The lessons I learn there have a lasting impression on me.

All freshmen at the academy, including me, are classified as "plebes," the lowest class in the U.S. Naval Academy, actually no rank at all. All incoming freshmen are required to take the Marine Corps physical fitness test. It's a series of drills designed to teach self-discipline and maintain a high level of physical fitness, all pillars of "the Marine Corps way of life." Standard dress is green-on-green T-shirts, shorts, socks, and running shoes. No deviation. The test is composed of three events: pull-ups, abdominal crunches, and a three-mile run, all conducted in a single session.

Most of the guys run rings around me. They do the pull-ups, the crunches, and the three-mile run with ease, unlike the aforementioned overweight, out-of-shape, chunky twelve-year-old who looks like Buddy Hackett's son. I fail the test miserably. I cannot do a single pull-up. I cannot do a crunch (does a *Nestlé's Crunch* count?). I am so down on myself sitting at my locker afterward I want to quit. Suddenly, I feel this presence and look up. It is Stan Slaby, the coach who administered the test.

"Hey, Lamas," he says, "what's going on? Why the long face?"

"Coach," I confess, "I just feel horrible, you know. I can't do a push-up or a pull-up."

What the coach says are just plain, simple words, but the fact they come from someone who has probably seen a thousand kids in my situation throughout the years means more to me than he can know. "Stop feeling sorry for yourself," he says gruffly, "and get on a team."

After that, Coach mentors me. My junior year I get on a team as he suggests—well, three teams: first track, then wrestling, and then swimming. In a few years, I have a much different image of myself. Coach is a big reason for that.

Another guy I look up to back then is my company commander, Tom Coffey. Like Coach, he pushes me to be better than I am and, most important, to lead through my actions.

"Lamas, if you are *ever* lucky to become an officer of your own company," he barks at me as if he is giving an order, "don't take your privilege for granted. Don't treat anybody less than you would want yourself treated. The best way to lead is to be an example for the others to follow."

"Yes, sir!"

During my four years at the academy, I really buckle down. I abide by the school's rigid rules of forced responsibility; I take things more seriously. Until attending the academy, I admit cracking the books or studying hard never turned me on. But now I study hard and my grades reflect it. I possess a keen interest in animals and nature, and so I set my sights on going to vet school after I graduate. My goal is to become a veterinarian and work with animals for the rest of my life.

I earn varsity letters in track, wrestling, swimming, and football after honing my athletic skills, and become more confident in my abilities and in myself. Taking notice of my exemplary behavior and results, the academy promotes me to battalion staff second lieutenant; I'm in charge of 250 cadets.

Even Esther notices my amazing transformation during one of my summer breaks back in California. "Military school is the best thing for you," she says.

Esther, of course, is right. Because of that experience, I am a much different person today—more disciplined, more focused. And I'm grateful to Mom for stepping in when she did.

Who are you calling chunky now?

During summer breaks in California, I'm like a regular kid again and enjoy quality time with Dad. We go to soccer games, swim in the ocean, and hang out together a lot. My first summer home I work as a gas station attendant to earn extra money. It is not something I would recommend on a long-term basis, but it works for me. To my friends' amusement, I would say, "I have a job with the Royal Dutch Shell Group." It sounds better than saying, "I work at the Shell station in Brentwood."

The summer of my junior year with Dad and Esther, I land a job as a lifeguard at the Jonathan Club, a prestigious private Santa Monica beach club that's been in existence since the late 1920s. Dad gets me a car through Bucky Norris, his well-connected friend and former minister-turned-insurance-salesman and longtime drinking buddy at the Cock'n Bull. It's the first time I drive legally on the streets of California as a licensed driver: a smoking, brand-new, kick-ass-under-the-hood Ford Falcon. Between lifeguarding a bevy of hot-looking babes and driving that beauty around, I feel like the coolest guy on the planet. After getting the Falcon, I end up calling my first childhood crush, Laurie. It feels like forever since we last saw each other. I get her number from Emmy and dial it. She answers on the first ring. After exchanging pleasantries, I ask, "I'm working today at the beach until five or six tonight; can I come by and see you?"

After a slight pause, Laurie says, "What do you think, silly?"

That means "yes" in my book. I pick up Laurie on time in my fancy Ford Falcon. She is instantly impressed as I whisk her off on our date. She has the same beautiful bright red hair and sweet smile I remember. It is so great to see her. Like me, she is entering senior year that fall. We catch up on things, relive old times, and end the night with a kiss. It is as if no time has passed, even though our lives are totally opposites—with me living on the East Coast, and her on the West. We stay in touch after that even though our lives go in separate directions.

Not until I start lifeguarding do I really begin to think seriously about girls. Being overweight as a kid had affected how I saw myself. I doubted any female could be attracted to me. That changes after I get in the best shape of my teenage life and work as a lifeguard. Suddenly bikini-clad girls are swooning over me and coming up to me for no other reason than to ask, "What time is it?" I am too naïve to realize they are coming on to me. Never in my wildest dreams do I imagine they are there because they are interested in knowing me—yes, me, the kid with the chunky past.

THREE

Making the Right Choices

AFTER GRADUATING from Farragut in June 1975, I return to California and live with Dad and Esther for a year. My living arrangement, however, is rather unconventional. In his marriage to Esther, Dad has this rule prohibiting the children from another man and marriage living under the same roof with their mother (his spouse). It is a staunch, traditional belief of his. Esther's children never stay with them, even for one night. Dad is a very proud, macho, chauvinistic, and obstinate man. But he also is fair. Therefore, he cannot very well allow me to stay in the house with them either. Putting myself in the mind-set of my very proud, macho, chauvinistic, and obstinate Latin father, I understand and accept what he decides: I will live and sleep in a special space he makes for me in the garage.

Esther goes along with the whole idea. "Since my kids aren't allowed here," she declares, "Lorenzo can stay in the garage."

It is hard for me to imagine doing that to my own kids. Yet I forgive my dad for many things, and this is one of them.

That summer, I quit my job at the Shell station to work two part-time jobs: as a ticket taker at Avco Embassy Theatre in Westwood and as an order taker at McDonald's. I make shakes, burgers, fries, and Egg McMuffins for six months at McDonald's before they put me out on the counter. Father loans me a car to get to and from work until I buy my own first vehicle that summer: a white Dodge Tradesman 200 delivery van. It's just a shell inside, no paneling, no carpeting, nothing; I pay $300 for it. Dad helped me shop around, but he made sure I bought it myself. Personal responsibility is, after all, the essence of how he raised me. He could easily buy a car for me; he certainly has the money. Yet he knows the importance of my fending for myself. He never wants to hear anyone say, "Oh, it's easy for Lorenzo because his dad did it all for him."

After buying the van, I want to spruce it up and make it something very cool chicks will love. Dad offers to help me install wood paneling. "Let's go to the lumberyard," he says.

"Cool."

I am there right alongside Dad as he drives us to Koontz, his favorite hardware store in West Hollywood, to buy the necessary paneling I want in eight-by-twelve-foot sets. With its cylinder-shaped interior, laminate is the best choice. It is pliable enough to follow the curves and be quickly installed and fastened in place.

When we get to the lumberyard, I tell Dad, "Great, they have the laminate sheets I want."

Dad says, "Lorenzo, we're not getting that."

"No, Dad," I counter, as I walk over where the laminate sheets are to show him, "this is what we need to put in the van because it bends. You can't put real wood paneling in a van."

My father famously says, "Yes, we can. Laminate wood is so expensive, but this other wood is cheap. Let's just use this other wood."

I explain, "Dad, real wood is much heavier and won't bend."

My father narrows his eyes and says, "Do you want me to help you or not?"

I reluctantly concede. "Okay."

Dad has the last word. "Besides," he says, "I'm paying for it."

Dad marches off and buys the real wood paneling, just as he wants. We drive back to the house. Dad gets out his tools and cuts the paneling to size to fit. When he goes to install the sheets, however, he cannot bend them to catch onto the wood screws to attach them to the frame of the van. The harder my muscle-headed, short-fused father pushes to bend them, one by one the panels break and splinter in his hands. I can tell my father is quickly losing patience for the task. He mutters something in Spanish as his temper starts to get the best of him.

I explain, "See, Dad, this is why I wanted to get the laminate wood paneling. Because it bends!"

Dad throws the hammer down. We are both sweating. It is the middle of summer and a hundred degrees inside the van. In a flash, he storms out and screams, "You're an asshole!"

"Why am I an asshole? I wanted to get the laminate wood. You wanted to get the regular wood that doesn't bend."

Dad is fuming at this point. "You can fuckin' do this all by yourself. You're an asshole."

Now I am an eighteen-year-old asshole for wanting to get the right wood paneling all along even though my father does not see it that way.

We get out of the van and Dad wants to box me he is so pissed. "C'mon, let's go!" he says, angrily, as he puts his fists up, ready to box my socks off.

I'm thinking I'm a big strong kid now but no match for a trained fighter with ham hocks for fists and a Latin temper. So I try to talk Dad out of it.

"C'mon, Dad," I say in my defense, "do you really want to do this?"

Dad is unwavering. "You're an asshole and I'm going to teach you a lesson."

"I'd rather be an asshole."

I storm off down the brick path that goes by the kitchen window, on my way straight to the pool to cool down from sweating my ass off. I need a break from all this. Esther is standing at the sink doing dishes or something as I walk past her with a full head of steam.

"Hey," she hollers after me, "what's going on with you two?"

I stop dead in my tracks. "Dad called me an asshole," I tell her.

"He did?" she asks. "Why?"

"I don't know." I explain the whole story. "The wood paneling Dad bought isn't working. I wanted to get a different kind of wood."

"Wait a second," Esther says, "let's figure this out! Come back around the front of the house."

I walk to the front of the house where the van is. Now the three of us are standing there and Esther is doing all the talking. "Fernando," she asks, "did you call Lorenzo an asshole?"

Still fuming mad, Dad says, "Yes, because he is an asshole. He abuses me for not buying the stupid wood."

I get a word in edgewise. "Dad, I said if we had gotten the other wood, you wouldn't be getting frustrated trying to bend wood that won't bend."

"You see, Esther," Dad counters, still with anger in his voice, "he's an asshole."

Esther says, "Fernando, first of all, Lorenzo is not an asshole. He's the son that you love."

Dad rolls his eyes. "Yeah, right, sure, whatever."

Esther persists. "Lorenzo is not an asshole." Then to me she says, "Lorenzo, you are not an asshole."

"You're right, Esther, I am not."

Then Esther says to my dad, "Fernando, you have to try to be a little more patient with this van situation because I know it is important for both of you to get this done. Please try and work together with a little more harmony."

"Fine, okay."

Esther has the last word. "Come on, make up, you two."

Dad gives me a hug, just enough to please her.

In the end, we cut so much wood that it takes five times longer than if we had used laminate paneling. My van looks like a patchwork as a result. It is not quite the chick mobile I had hoped for but, hey, at least we get it done without Dad calling me an asshole again.

At night, I sleep on a mattress in the back of my van, parked in Dad and Esther's garage. Under our arrangement, they never give me a key to the main house. They keep the front door and the door off the kitchen locked, and instead leave the back door open so I can use the half-bathroom (toilet only) off the kitchen and laundry room as needed. Without access to a shower or bathtub to clean up, I hop out of bed in my van around seven o'clock every morning and jump into the pool instead. Dad and Esther are never up before nine o'clock, when they come out for breakfast on the patio, so I have the pool to myself.

As a frustrated, single eighteen-year-old living in a parked van in a garage, with no shower, no kitchen, no freezer privileges, and no girlfriend, I also wake up every morning with an erection. Usually it goes away when I jump in the pool. This particular morning, however, it is not going anywhere. I do what most frustrated, single eighteen-year-olds living in a parked van in a garage with no shower, no kitchen, no freezer privileges, and no girlfriend do. I take care of business myself.

I am doing my thing. It is just me, the pool, the beautiful view, not a soul around. Right in the middle of it all, Esther opens the sliding-glass door to the upstairs terrace and steps out, wearing a robe over her nightgown. She has gotten up early. She takes in the spectacular view, inhales the cool, fresh morning air, and then looks down and sees me jerking off in the pool. I have no idea she is watching. I haven't seen or heard her.

Quietly, Esther turns on her heels and walks back inside. She never utters a word. Instead of keeping it to herself, however, she tells Dad: "Fernando, I cannot tolerate this! He's your son and you have to do something about it."

I finish, get dressed, and go to work my shift at McDonald's. When I return home that afternoon, I find a note written in capital letters and underscored in parts and posted on the garage door. It reads:

LORENZO,
HOW DARE YOU!!! YOU MASTURBATING IN THE POOL??
I'M ASHAMED!

Obviously, the note is from Dad. Sensing his anger and humili-ation, I am just dying inside as I read. I am so embarrassed. Dad and Esther are not home at the time. Even if they were, I probably should not go knocking on the door right now. But how can I? That level of shock and anger is coming from my father, a man who has the biggest penis on the planet, a man who should understand that sometimes you have to take care of things.

Grabbing some clothes from the closet in the garage, I end up driving back to McDonald's and parking on the street and living there in my van. I work my regular shifts every day and then later at the theater, taking tickets. I go to Santa Monica Beach and use the public showers. During this time, I never hear from Dad or Esther. They never even call me at work to see if I am okay.

A week goes by. I am sitting at a table on my break at McDonald's, munching on a tasty Big Mac, when I see Dad pull up in Esther's Mercedes. I slink down in my seat and mutter, "Shit! Fuck!"

I badly want to disappear but have no place to hide.

Dad enters the restaurant and, from behind his sunglasses, spots me. He is very melodramatic: "Oh, there you are!"

He walks over, sits down at the table next to me, and says, "Lorenzo, we need to talk."

I sheepishly say, "Okay, where?"

"In your van."

We get up, walk out of the restaurant, and I open the van door. Dad enters ahead of me. We are sitting in back—Dad is on the bed next to me. It is the middle of summer and it feels like a fucking furnace inside. Dad says, "Lorenzo, I understand about the need, you know, and I don't have a problem with your need. But, for Chrissake, your sperm is going to ruin the filter!"

I say, "What?"

Dad clarifies: "Your sperm is going to burn the motor out in the filter."

I cannot believe this is the total sum of my father's anger. I respond, "Oh."

"Yes. You know how much it costs to replace the motor in the filter?"

"Oh, I'm sorry, Dad. I didn't think of that."

Dad shrugs. "Besides, Esther probably does not need to see it."

"Oh, okay, I understand."

Dad stays around long enough to deliver the message. He stands up and gives me a big hug. "Okay, see you tonight."

Dad climbs out of the van, puts on his sunglasses, looks around suspiciously like a mobster just concluding a big drug deal, and briskly walks toward the Mercedes. He hops in and gives me a quick wave as he tears out of the parking lot. I can only shake my head as I ponder what he said: "Your sperm is going to ruin the filter!"

I start laughing my head off as I head back to work from my break. I can assure you after that I never jerk off in the pool again—at least for Esther's sake, if not the filter!

Many nights after working at the movie theater until around midnight, I come home very hungry. Esther keeps a freezer in the garage stocked with whatever she wants to make for guests; she and Dad entertain from eight to twelve people a couple of times a week. Because

I cannot simply go into the kitchen to get myself a snack whenever I want, I do what any frustrated, single, starving eighteen-year-old living in a parked van in a garage, with no kitchen privileges, would do: I raid the freezer every night. I figure anything edible—mostly desserts Esther has saved to serve her guests—is fair game. I do not care that they are frozen. I eat frozen pound cake, chocolate cake—whatever I can stick my fork into.

Esther warns me a couple times that the freezer is off-limits. "I will try to leave something on the back counter for you to eat," she says, "but please don't go into the freezer because those things are for company."

After I raid the freezer yet again one night and polish off another pound cake, Esther informs Dad. The next day he feels out the situation with me. He understands I am a frustrated, single, starving eighteen-year-old living in a parked van in a garage, with no kitchen privileges, but he bends to her will this time to keep the peace between the two of them. Esther browbeats him into finally padlocking the freezer. Thus, my pound cake days officially end. To this day, if I see a pound cake anywhere, that cake is history. I will eat that cake just out of spite. Now Esther and Dad have locked me out of not only the house but also the freezer!

After beating my brains out studying for four years at Farragut to become a veterinarian, I apply to veterinary schools at many major universities and colleges. Three accept me: the University of Miami; the University of California, Santa Barbara; and the University of California, Los Angeles. In the end, I choose UCLA since it has one of the best veterinary science programs in the country.

Four weeks before starting classes that fall, I think, "Do I really want to do this?" Yes, I love animals, but I have a hard time envisioning myself fifteen years from now standing in my office with a white smock on, swabbing down some beagle's ear. As a little boy, people would often ask me, "What do you want to be when you grow up?"

Many times before I answered, they would say, "You want to be an actor like your daddy, don't you?"

I would reply with something silly like, "I want to be a plumber." Or, "When I grow up, I'm not going to be an actor. I'm going to be a *fireman*." Then later . . . "a highway patrolman."

Striving to become a veterinarian suddenly no longer makes sense to me. I also keenly understand I do not have the grade point average or scholastic aptitude to go through six years of veterinary school. My junior and senior years at the academy, I managed to get up to a 3.4 grade point average. Back then, however, you really need a 4.0 combined with an SAT score of over 1200. My SAT score is around 1150 or something. It is foolish of me to entertain the vet school idea further.

The whole time I'm living with Dad and Esther, I keep up my physical exercise regimen: swimming and surfing. After growing six inches into a muscular 185-pound, six-foot-two-inch frame, I remember saying to myself, "Now that you have a new body, what are you going to do with it?"

For the life of me, I cannot make up my mind. So I enroll that fall at Santa Monica City College (now called Santa Monica College), mostly so I can join the swim team. The school is a two-year, public junior college. I take enough classes there to qualify to try out for the swim team. Their acting classes look like a breeze, so I sign up for theater. I also take police science. Up until then, I had never really thought of getting into acting or drama; it was the furthest thing from my mind. Yet as things play out, taking drama becomes a turning point for me, although not immediately.

Between working two jobs, going to school, and swimming on the swim team, I have little time for much of a social life. I really want what every eighteen-year-old wants—to date girls, party, have fun, and sow some wild oats (since I can no longer do that in the pool!). Because of my strange living situation, I never date. I mean, how can I? It is no place to bring a young, hot-looking girl back to after a date. No way to impress a lady.

"Where's your room around here?" she'll ask.

"Uh..."

"Is it this way?"

"Uh..."

"You do have your own room, don't you?"

"Uhhhhhhhhhh!"

I cannot *wait* for the day I can afford my own place.

Of course, I barely make enough money to pay for a date, much less pursue a serious relationship with anyone. Admittedly, I know little of what it takes to have a meaningful and successful relationship; my understanding, as they say, is a "work in progress."

Eventually I start dating some girls from work and school. Dad gets a kick out of me bringing a different girl to the house. In fact, he encourages it and sees it as something healthy. Esther is equally encouraging. They feel I should date as many girls as I want. Even before I start taking them out, my father readily shares with me his philosophy of women, including his particular tastes.

"How are you going to find the person of your dreams unless you date?" Dad says with his usual dramatic Latin flair. "You've got to make the scene and you've got to dance and find out what love's all about."

Lisa Monte, one of the girls I date (and have a serious crush on), is a cute, petite blonde who works at the theater box office with me. I bring her home for dinner a couple of times. After the second or third time, I say to Dad, always wanting his approval, "What do you think of Lisa, Dad?"

"Yeah," he shrugs, "she's okay."

"But did you *like* her?" I ask.

"She's kind of quiet and a little intimidated," he says, "and she's very small."

"I kind of like them small."

"You do? Why?"

"I don't know," I explain. "It kind of makes me feel like I'm a bigger guy."

I have never forgotten my father's response: "Let me tell you something. Women cost the same whether they are tall, big, short, or skinny. They cost the same. You should get more for your money. Go with the *tall* ones!"

Then one night, to my surprise, Dad informs me, "Esther and I are going to Palm Springs the third weekend of this month."

I reply, "Great, Dad, I hope you both have a wonderful time," while thinking, "*Awesome!* I will finally be alone in the house!"

I throw a party that weekend, a big Saturday-night bash. I invite my closest friends and buddies from the swim team, and, of course, Lisa. Every time I go to school or to work, I invite another person. "Why don't you come to the house, man? I'm having a party. I'll have beer. We have a huge pool with great views of the city. It will be a blast." (The house has a magnificent view of downtown Los Angeles and the Pacific Ocean. It is just magical, especially on a clear night when the city lights below sparkle like small diamonds.)

Excited, my friends high-five me. "I'm there, duuuude!"

My mind is working overtime planning the party and all the things I want to do while Dad and Esther are gone, including showing Lisa the inside of my cool chick-mobile van with *real* wood paneling.

Friday comes. Dad and Esther are finishing packing the Mercedes (Esther makes Dad buy her one after selling the Mustang and moving to Beverly Hills). They'll be flying to Palm Springs from Los Angeles International Airport and are very excited. When they're ready to go, I see them off.

"Have a great, great trip," I tell them. "See you on Sunday." Turning to Dad, I ask, "Can I have a key?"

"Key?" Dad asks with a quizzical expression on his face. "Key to what?"

"The house...Can I have the key to the house? So I can have my friends over to my party." Dad and Esther know about my plans to have a party because I have told them ahead of time.

"Ohhhhhhh, no, amigo," he says firmly, "there will be no party in the house."

I cannot believe my ears. "But, Dad, I told everybody that there will be a party tomorrow night. Everybody is coming."

"Fine. They can come. They can use the garage. They can swim in the pool. We'll leave the back door open for the small bathroom. But they can't go into the house, Lorenzo."

I feel as if blood is going to spurt out of my eye sockets any second; I cannot believe this is happening to me. My own father, my own flesh and blood, denying me this one small favor. It's vanishing, this one opportunity to have a little fun and impress my friends.

"Oh, my God, Dad, are you serious? What am I going to do with all the beer?"

"You can use the cooler," Dad explains, "but they are not coming into the kitchen."

"Geez, Dad, really? Are you serious?"

"Do I look like I am joking?"

Dad and Esther speed out of the driveway in Esther's new Mercedes like two young lovers going on their first romantic weekend, while I stand there slack-jawed and embarrassed and, as usual, locked out. I can just imagine the reaction of my friends when they come over: "Are you sure you live here?"

And I really want Lisa up to the house, to impress her with the pool and the inside of my van, if I am lucky. I decide, Screw it! I am going to have the party anyway.

About ten friends show up. They park down the street from the house. As they arrive and realize that my living in a garage with a huge house I cannot get into is embarrassing to me, they are cool. Everybody seems to enjoy the party—the cooler of beer, the heated pool, and the groovy tunes blasting from my ghetto blaster. If they need the bathroom, they can use the small one. Everything goes better than I had even hoped.

As the party gets into full swing, Lisa shows up along with another cool girl from the college swim team I really like, but only as a friend. She's Amy, a beautiful brunette in a stunning orange bathing suit. My heart belongs to Lisa, a girl I'm sure I want to marry. I really think the world of her.

Everybody is having a good time. Amy and I are chatting while Lisa is talking to friends from the theater. Suddenly Amy jumps into the pool and I join her. We are splashing around together, joking and carrying on. I look off to see where Lisa is. She's gone. I ask my friend Newman, a fast-as-lightning freestyle swimmer on the team, "Do you know where Lisa went?"

"I think she went toward the garage," he says and points.

I dry off and walk over. As I enter, I see Lisa sitting in the bed in my van all alone, crying. "What are you doing?" I ask.

"I thought you really cared about me," she says between sobbing and sniffling.

"What are you talking about?" I counter. "Of course I care about you. You're the most important person in my life."

"Well, that's not the way it looks," she says, holding back tears. "The way you were swimming with that girl."

I explain, "She's Amy. She's just a swimmer. Just a friend. We go to college together. There's nothing going on between us."

Lisa jumps to her feet in a huff. "Well, I'm going to leave and you can never, ever talk to me again."

"Are you kidding me? Please don't leave. Come on. Let's go swimming."

"No, I don't want to go swimming," Lisa says, pouting. "I don't want to do anything with you ever."

With that, Lisa drives off in her Toyota Celica GT, which, by the way, I am dying to drive. Back in 1975, the Celica GT is the bomb. Compared to the Datsun 280Z, it is no contest.

Lisa speeds off in the Celica-of-my-dreams. After she screeches to a stop at the stop sign down the street and her brake lights go off, I think, "Fuck, I guess I'll never get a chance to drive that car."

I return to the party and jump back in the pool. Amy and I have a great old time. Seriously, Lisa leaving like that, her not wanting to see me again, saddens me. I really wanted to get serious with her, but it's just not meant to be.

BETWEEN WORKING AND TAKING CLASSES at Santa Monica City College, I feel rudderless most days. No clear goals, no clear objectives, eighteen years of age and frustrated, most nights sitting there wondering, "Damn, where is my future?"

I still really do not know what kind of career I want to pursue. I rack my brain for days trying to think of some other profession. With my military academy background, I keep thinking more and more about just going back into the military.

Then, out of desperation, I become an actor, never considering what I am getting myself into or how Dad and Esther will react. They've always been supportive of whatever I do, so I figure they will be this time as well. My plan is to first tell Dad of my intention to go into the military and then hit him with my second choice: acting.

But then as Father opens the door, the first thing out of my mouth is, "I want to be an actor."

Running his hand through his gray-streaked hair, Dad shouts, "Oh, shit!" I never thought for a second Dad would say that.

Father walks me inside and calls Esther into the room. She comes into the living room and we exchange quick hellos. Then Dad gets me back on track.

"Acting, huh? Lorenzo, only 5 percent of professional actors earn a living."

I look around me, impressed. "You, Mom, and Esther have done all right. How can you, with a Mercedes and Rolls-Royce, argue against acting?"

Dad gives me a good, hard look. He knows I am right but tests me to see just how serious I am. "Why don't you go to college and study real estate? Get a real estate license and sell properties."

"Uh, I don't know," I mumble. "I've come to the realization I need to try it. I don't know what I'm going to do."

Dad looks me straight in the eye and says, "Well, okay, you want to be an actor, here's what we're going to do. I'm not going to have you go out there and embarrass me. I'm going to see if you can act first."

Dad ushers me outside. "Think of an event, a scene you want to play," he says, "totally improvisational."

From taking drama at the academy, I know a little bit about that. He brings Esther into the mix to play with me in this scene I am about to come up with on the spot.

"When you come back in," he says to me, "knock on the front door."

To Esther he says, "Answer on my cue." Turning to me, he adds, "She is going to improvise with you," and he goes in and shuts the door in my face.

I am like, "Shit! You just have to open your big fucking mouth, Lorenzo, and say you want to be an actor."

I stand outside and think of a scene: *I've run over a dog on my way up to the house. I have the dog in my trunk and don't know what to do with it since the owner is nowhere in sight.* It needs a little work. I change it to "a stray dog" with no collar. Perfect!

I ring the doorbell. Esther answers right on cue. "Lorenzo, what's wrong? What happened?"

"Esther, something terrible."

We walk into the living room. She sits me down on the couch to console me. We play out the scene together. Esther is right there with me. We get into the scene for a good ten minutes as my stern-faced father looks on. I tell her what happened, that I killed this poor dog and then I start bawling.

Waa-waa-waa. "I just ran over a dog." Waa-waa-waa. "Come see for yourself." Waa-waa-waa.

Esther starts crying, too. "But, Lorenzo…" Waa-waa-waa. "…I'm sure you…" Waa-waa-waa "…you didn't mean to." Waa-waa-waa.

"I was driving…" Waa-waa-waa. "…and then…" Waa-waa-waa. "I didn't see it." Waa-waa-waa.

Now really sobbing, I say, "I don't know…" Waa-waa-waa. "…what I'm going to do." Waa-waa-waa. "Should I take it to the beach…" Waa-waa-waa. "…and bury it in the sand?" Waa-waa-waa.

Esther and I are like two sissies, bawling our eyes out, the whole time. Finally, Dad throws up his hands. "Okay, forget it, enough of this nonsense. You can act."

Esther speaks up on my behalf. "Fernando, if you don't support Lorenzo, I'm going to."

"Okay," Dad says, "you two crybabies win."

Dad turns to me and in that thick accent, parsing out each word dramatically like he is performing onstage, says, "Son, if that is what you want, I will support you, too!"

Esther and I laugh so hard we start crying all over again. Waa-waa-waa.

After that first reading, Dad never questions my heart's desire again. Even though he is ambivalent about my pursuing an acting career, he realizes that I have never been so serious about anything in my life.

"Well," he sighs, "we better find you a good acting school."

In January 1976, Dad enrolls me in a beginning acting class at Tony Barr's Film Actors Workshop in Burbank. It's a great acting school, and Dad called Tony himself, a CBS executive who runs the school on the side, to get me in. It is one of the few times my father lifts a finger to help me.

"Send the kid over," Barr says.

Working my other jobs by day, by night I attend acting school twice a week, three hours each session. Over the course of eight weeks, I learn the basic techniques and am really enjoying the whole experience. It feels as if my destiny is in my hands.

FOUR

Just Call Me Lucky

HE IS THE EPITOME of fifties biker cool: free-spirited, dark hair slicked back into a high pompadour, dripping in masculinity in his black leather jacket as he leans against his iconic 1949 Triumph TR5 Trophy motorcycle. He sports a twisted grin on his face, wanting to be noticed. His motorcycle is his first love, his pride and joy. Everything else he keeps at arm's length because his bike monopolizes his attention. I am speaking, of course, of Arthur Herbert Fonzarelli, better known as "The Fonz," brilliantly portrayed by Henry Winkler in one of my all-time favorite sitcoms, *Happy Days*. After watching The Fonz in action every week, I imagine how cool it would be to fulfill my childhood dream of owning a motorcycle, and having what he has, a virtual chick magnet.

I have to have one. Right after I start taking acting classes, I sell the Dodge Tradesman 200 van and use the money to buy myself a Honda 500. I drive it everywhere; I'm getting my Fonzie on; I am somebody. And chicks love it, too. They cannot resist my biker cool.

Nothing compares to the thrill and sense of living in the moment I feel when I'm on my new two-wheeled, macho, chick-attracting machine. The whole experience continually fans the flames of my passion for riding. Every time I don my retro shades and hop on that black leather seat, I become cocky, fearless, and the epitome of biker cool, just like my hero, The Fonz. I'm completely in touch with the world, on a journey of self-discovery, seeking experiences that feed my soul and the daredevil in me—and never thinking of the consequences or risks involved.

On a cool, brisk spring afternoon in 1976, I am roaring down Laurel Canyon and really showing off, popping wheelies all over the city. That afternoon, a Porsche suddenly stops next to me at the light. I take that as a challenge and decide to race it down Laurel Canyon. I figure my two-wheeled, macho, chick-attracting machine can beat his four-wheeled, overpriced import any day of the week. Bending forward with the chilled air against my face, I twist the grip and accelerate to a high speed. I start gaining on him as we come to a tight curve; I make it through.

I'm now almost neck-and-neck with his piece-of-shit import when we come to a second curve. "Come on, baby," I tell her as I pat the side of her, "let's roll."

With the Porsche on my left side, I start to inch past. As the road curves, the corner is tighter than I imagine and I make one big miscalculation: His four-wheeled Porsche is more stable in tight turns.

As I hit the bend, I suddenly lose control. My bike spins and scrapes against the curb, jumps and flips high into the air, and then crashes hard upside down. The full weight of the bike—all 496 pounds—lands on top of my head. In the process it tears off my cool Fonzie shades, rips my black leather to shreds, and knocks me unconscious in the middle of the street. With no helmet laws then, I am not wearing any protection. A few feet from me is what is left of my two-wheeled, macho, chick-attracting machine—a misshapen heap of painted metal and shattered glass and spilled fuel. I lie there motionless. I remember nothing after that but total darkness.

Out of the darkness, I suddenly see a bright light. I sense some kind of commotion as I become conscious, unsure if I am alive or in some otherworldly place. Someone is moving around, touching me, talking to me. As my eyes focus, I stare uncomprehendingly at a man crouching over me. An incandescent glow encircles his face like he's an angel. He is talking faster than I can comprehend. As I struggle to focus, with a loud piercing sound ringing in my ears like a siren, I discover he is human and very real. He is an emergency medical technician in the back of an ambulance with me.

"Easy, son," he says.

I struggle to move my head and body but feel nothing.

"You've fractured your skull, so take it easy," he adds. "We've strapped you to a gurney to immobilize you for your own protection."

Just as the EMT says that, my head feels as if a ten-thousand-pound elephant is sitting on top of it. The pain is so sharp and excruciating it is hard for me to keep my eyes open, much less talk and remain conscious. My eyes grow heavy and the man looks fuzzy.

"Where am I?" I ask groggily.

The EMT says, "We're rushing you to Children's Hospital. They have the best trauma center in the area."

"Shit," I moan, "my dad's going to kill me. How's my bike?"

Before the EMT has a chance to answer, I pass out. I remember nothing about the EMT reassuring me, the ambulance ride to the hospital, or the accident—until the next morning after waking up in my room in ICU. Hovering over me is a brown-haired nurse checking my vitals, feverishly writing something down on my chart. I try to speak to her. She keeps writing. I try again. It is futile. Finally, she looks over. It is a battle for me to string words together or speak coherently. Anything I say comes out jumbled.

"Don't try to speak," she says in a comforting voice. "You need your rest."

As I lay my head back against the pillow, the sharp, throbbing pain is debilitating. I close my eyes and wonder what is wrong with me. For the first time in my life, I am truly frightened out of my mind.

Unbeknownst to me then, Dad had rushed to the hospital as soon as he was notified. He conferred with the emergency room doctor and got my prognosis. I did fracture my skull but I also have severe swelling of the brain that developed overnight. The doctor told Dad, "We are not certain with a brain injury such as your son's how fast his ability to speak will come back, if it comes back at all."

For days, my condition is touch-and-go. I show little progress and the doctors remain unsure what the future holds for me. The first time Dad comes to see me later that next day, tears well up in my eyes from the fear and frustration I feel trying to form words to speak to him. He is nothing but comforting.

"Son, you have a serious head injury," he explains. "The doctors are doing everything possible."

Every day without fail Dad comes to the hospital to boost my spirits as I lie there scared shitless, not knowing if I will ever speak again. Dad immediately senses my fear.

"You have nothing to worry about, Son," Dad says. "You should see the other guys."

According to my father, when the ER staff was trying to restrain me to examine me—I was this strong son-of-a-gun back then—I fought them off and even put one of them into a headlock. I was totally out of control and in no state to know what I was doing.

Dad breaks out laughing. "They never knew what hit 'em."

It is a miracle how the brain responds to injury. Sometimes the injury is so severe the brain never recovers and the patient loses all ability to talk and function normally; other times, the opposite happens. Four days after the accident, I wake up to discover I can speak normally again. I do not recall what my first words were, but know I broke down crying, relieved that I could talk. I continue to make progress, and the hospital discharges me a week and a half later. I realize how truly fortunate I am. I may not be so lucky next time.

The only time I ever live with Dad and Esther in the house is during my recovery. I stay with them for about a month. Even though I have my own little apartment, Dad insists I be with them. Esther goes along with it; she knows I am in no condition to live by myself. They put me up in the study, with a fold-down Murphy bed to sleep on. I stay there for a month, taking it easy. The doctor says firmly, "Don't raise your blood pressure. No working out for a couple of weeks."

Following my recovery, I resume acting school and working my two jobs. I had already completed the beginning acting course before my accident, and now I successfully complete the school's intermediate and advanced professional classes. One week we learn how to do scenes onstage, play in front of a camera, and hit our mark in a scene; the next, how to shoot and work behind the camera and how to light a scene. I have never worked a day in my life as an actor, and the workshops are providing me with a solid foundation to build on. I have so much fun that I decide acting is what I want to do as a profession.

Ever since the accident, Dad frequently expresses his deep concern about my ever getting back on a motorcycle again. He offers to buy me any car I want, but I don't take him up on it. Dad is insistent about my next vehicle, saying, "Promise me, Son, you won't ride another 'murdercycle' [as he calls them] again."

I feel bad about what I put him through and tell him, "Well, okay, I promise," crossing my fingers behind my back as I say it.

In the months following my accident, I ride a bicycle to work at the theater and gas station until I can buy myself a new set of wheels. Knowing that another motorcycle will never fly with my father, I settle on buying a black Benelli moped at a local Yamaha dealer. I hope this might warm him up to the idea of me eventually getting another motorcycle. It may be great on gas, but the moped is hardly what you call a chick magnet. I doubt Fonzie could ever feel cool riding one. In no way is it the bike of my dreams. So come hell or high water—and the wrath of my father—I know I will someday get back on a motorcycle again.

In the meantime, I don't try to sneak the moped past Dad, figuring there is a huge difference between a moped and a motorcycle. I ride it when I go over to the house for dinner one night, and right away he is upset.

"I thought you promised me you would not buy another motorcycle?" he says, infuriated.

"This is a moped, Dad."

He is naturally suspicious as he examines it closely. Although it looks and smells like a "murdercycle" to him, he starts to see the difference as I explain, "It's made in Italy"—I figure the fact he and Esther lived there, that would impress him—"and like a two-stroke scooter. Just powerful enough to get me where I need to go."

"Well." Dad pauses. "I guess it's not really a 'murdercycle.'"

"You're right," I tell him. "It's not."

For the moment, Dad seems satisfied. I ride it around in the rain and whatever else for months. Yet Dad continues to disapprove of it. He's concerned for my safety, of course, and the Italian-made vehicle simply reminds him too much of a "murdercycle."

So I sell it and buy something with four wheels to appease him, even though I cannot afford anything decent. From a local body shop, I acquire a $300, three-on-the-column stick, gas-guzzling, primer green Ford Panel Wagon. But not just any Ford Panel Wagon. This one is special. It has more Bondo (auto repair putty) on its body than the manufacturer allows and an exhaust that spews huge plumes of smoke every time you drive it. It is like something out of a Cheech and Chong movie. My friends and coworkers know I'm coming when they hear the loud chugging sound it makes and see the endless clouds of smoke belching from its tailpipe—and from every place else. It is embarrassing to drive it, even though it gets me where I need to be. But if I really want to snag some chicks, this thing will have to go!

On July 4, 1976, in my own declaration of my independence, I move out of Dad and Esther's garage and into my first apartment, 320 N. Oakhurst #8 in Beverly Hills. It's a nothing-fancy, $100-a-month cracker box studio—one room with a Murphy bed, bathroom, hot plate, and Igloo icebox. It is not much, I admit. But it is mine. I have run out of excuses—and "uhhhs"—to give any girl I've asked out who wants to go back to "my place." For too long, I've needed my own pad—and now I have it.

Coinciding with the move, I decide it is high time to get my biker "cool" back and buy myself a Harley. More than a guy thing, it is a fulfillment of my childhood fantasy. I've wanted to own a Harley ever since I watched the TV drama *Then Came Bronson*, starring actor Michael Parks as disillusioned newspaper reporter Jim Bronson, who takes to the road on his Harley. I want to be just like Bronson.

Naturally, I do not have the cash to buy one. Instead, I call Mom for help but never mention what my real purpose is. "Mom, I need some money."

"What for?" she asks.

I think fast. "Uh, I'm going to go for a second semester at Santa Monica City College."

"How much do you need?"

"Twenty-five hundred dollars."

A short pause and Mom says, "Okay, Son, I'll send it to you."

Mom sends out a check for $2,500. Of course, I never do a second semester that fall. Instead, I cash the check, go straight to the Harley-Davidson dealership in downtown Marina del Rey, and plunk the money down on my first Harley, a year-old 1976 Sportster. The dealer is already selling the 1977 models.

I keep the bike a secret from Dad. I sell the three-on-the-column stick, gas-guzzling, smoky, Bondo-envy-of-the-world Ford Panel

Wagon back to the body shop where I bought it. Man, do I love having a Harley! Every time I come home from work, I roll the bike into the garage, take a rag to it, and polish it up. It is a dream come true.

One day, I cruise up Doheny Drive in Beverly Hills. Then roaring north down Doheny to Sunset Boulevard, I come to a stop at the light. There on the opposite side of the street in Esther's Mercedes, waiting for the light to change, is my father. I think, "Oh, shit! He's going to see me."

I am not wearing a helmet and he, obviously, does not know I have a new "murdercycle." There is no way he will *not* see me or hear me, because Harleys are very loud. Just then, the light turns green. I ease out the clutch and keep the idle low, trying not to make too much noise, and inch my way along, hoping that a car will pass between us so Dad will not see me. Murphy's Law, right? Anything that can go wrong will. It does.

Dad gets about even with me in the intersection. Suddenly he looks over at me and does a double take. I look over just as I am opposite him. He thrusts his middle finger into the air and yells, "Asshole!" Then he speeds off.

My cover is blown. Not only did I break my promise to Dad, but I lied to Mom to get the money. After that, Dad won't take my calls, no matter how many times I try. Every time I do, Esther answers and says, "He doesn't want to talk to you," and hangs up. This goes on for a couple of weeks. Then, one day, I receive a handwritten letter in the mail from Dad that reads:

> *Dear Lorenzo,*
>
> *First, I am your father and I love you. I have to tell you how disappointed I am with you. Not only because you made a promise to me, but your mother called me last week asking me how your new school year was going at Santa Monica City College. I put two and two together and I figured you lied to your mother in order to get the money to buy the motorcycle. This is true. IS IT NOT? A man is only as good as his word. If you ever want me to trust you again, or ever want me to be your friend again, you will have to sell your motorcycle and show me the pink slip. Proof!*
>
> *I will always love you.*
>
> *Dad*

I have a sick feeling in the pit of my stomach the entire time I'm reading it. Like part of me is dying inside. The part *or ever want me to be your friend again* really tears me up. I am heartbroken for days. What a dilemma: sell my bike or lose my father. My father's friendship means more to me, naturally, and I choose him. I march down to the Harley dealer and they give me the money back, minus a couple hundred bucks. I send the money back to my mom and show Dad the pink slip.

After that, I honor Dad's wishes by not buying another bike—for now.

One night in late summer of 1976, after the advanced class, my teacher, Laura Rose, comes up to me and says, "You're ready, Lorenzo, you should go out and audition."

BESIDES *HAPPY DAYS*, my two favorite sitcoms are *Chico and the Man* and *Welcome Back, Kotter,* both produced by James Komack. The latter stars a young actor by the name of John Travolta. Every week while watching *Kotter*, I have a yellow legal pad at my side and write the following (figuring that by putting my actions into words they will come true): "I will succeed as an actor. I will have my own television show. I will be as successful as John Travolta."

By then, I have quit the movie theater job to work as a trainer at Jack LaLanne's Health Spa. On days when business is slow and I only have one or two clients, I ask the floor manager if I can use that time for personal business. He lets me. Taking longer breaks in the break room, I look through the casting listings published in *Hollywood Reporter* and *Variety*. I am shameless when calling the casting agents to introduce myself: "I'm Lorenzo Lamas. You don't know me, but you probably know my parents."

Every week I call about twenty casting agents and maybe get one person who is serious about meeting with me. I keep doing this for maybe six or seven months, getting nowhere.

I am between girlfriends at this time, and I find out that a very attractive older woman—for the sake of anonymity, I'll call her Jenny—who works with me at Jack LaLanne's has her eyes on me. I cannot imagine why she is interested in a dumb eighteen-year-old like me who trains people and works out. She is ten years older than me, really out of my league.

One day at work her boss and head instructor, B.J., a big, funny black guy who smokes like a fiend (at least two packs a day), is working out with some friends before we open for business. He is bench-pressing something like 350 pounds. In between sets, he lights up a cigarette. I am not into smoking then, so I do not understand the attraction.

"How can you breathe and smoke cigarettes?" I ask.

B.J. laughs. "Easy, bro, I breathe and smoke just a little bit at a time."

B.J. takes a few more drags of his cigarette, then goes back to working out. During a break, he approaches me. "Hey, man," he says, "Jenny likes you."

I do not think anything of it. "That's cool."

B.J. shakes his head. "No," he says with added emphasis, "Jenny *likes you!*"

Again, I am just a dumb eighteen-year-old kid who trains people and works out. "What does that mean?" I ask.

"Brother, are you stupid? She wants a piece of your honky ass."

I am just dumbfounded. "She does?"

Suddenly, B.J. is coaching me on how to approach this hot cougar. "Yeah, but take it easy, bro," he suggests. "Don't go in there like some excited, stupid kid. Play it cool, man. Go in there and get her phone number, for Chrissake."

It takes me all day to get my nerves together before I actually go to see her. I am sure she is wondering what is taking this dumb eighteen-year-old kid who trains people and works out here so long. Later that day, I walk into her office and introduce myself to her. "Hi, Jenny."

"Well," she responds in a deep, sexy voice, "*hello.*"

"Hey," I continue, now that I have my nerve up, "would you mind going out with me sometime?"

"Sure," she murmurs in anticipation.

Jenny gives me her address. She lives three blocks from the gym. Later that night, we meet. I go to the apartment complex where she lives, climb the stairs, and knock on her door. I see the door is already open. I crack it open wider and shout, "Hello!"

Jenny hollers from somewhere, "Just make yourself comfortable, I'll be right out."

I walk inside and take a seat in the living room. Immediately a mélange of fragrances, like incense, overwhelms me. I don't know what to expect.

Suddenly, Jenny walks out of the bathroom. She is not ready to go to dinner. She is not even ready to go to the movie afterward. She is wearing something so frickin' sexy she could never wear it in public. To say it is sheer is an understatement. This cougar is ready to pounce.

Jenny saunters over and sits across from me on the couch. Her beauty and sensuality overpower me. I am star-struck in her presence.

"Can I get you something to drink?" she asks. "Are you thirsty?"

Looking at this beauteous creature before me, I figure I can use a little fortification if I am going to keep up with her. "Yeah, do you have a beer?"

"Yes, I think so," she says as she rises to her feet. "I'll get you one."

Jenny gives me an eyeful coming and going that leaves nothing to my imagination about what lies beneath her scanty outfit. As she returns, she sits next to me with a cold, wet one in her hand. I know I need to say the right thing, not something stupid, so I do not fuck this up. I speak from the heart.

"You look beautiful," I admit, as I ogle her up and down. "Not exactly the kind of thing you can wear to work. I don't think."

Jenny laughs. "That's a good one. Yeah, yeah, not exactly. That's good, Lorenzo."

She flashes a seductive smile as she stalks her prey. "How would you like to get comfortable? I have a bath drawn," she says in a breathy and whispery voice.

I gulp. "You have a bath drawn?"

"Yeah, I do."

In my mind, I am thinking, "Oh, my God, this is not happening."

Jenny adds slyly, "Why don't you go into the bathroom, get yourself comfortable, and I'll come in and join you in a minute."

I decide the beer can wait!

I walk into the bathroom. Surrounding me is an array of elegant, lit fragrant candles that first sent my sinuses over the edge when I arrived. I take the bait, get out of my skivvies, slip into the tub, and get ready for Jenny. There's barely enough water to cover what is going on just below the surface.

Jenny walks in. Sashaying out of her scanty nightie, she looks heavenly as she glides into the tub, wraps herself over my thighs, and faces me. "How's the water?" she asks.

Before I can get out the word "Amazing," Jenny reaches down with her hand and grabs colossus. Suddenly, we are having an amazing time. We never make it to the restaurant or the movie. We have our own movie going on in the bathroom of her apartment.

Our one night of ecstasy ends, but this cougar is far from finished. At work, we are platonic with each other. We never kiss and we just do our jobs. At night, it is a different story: She is on the prowl, ready for more. Jenny is just amazing.

Then after a night together, I show up at work the next day to find Jenny is not there. I never see or hear from her again. It turns out she transferred to another Jack LaLanne's out of the area. I realize I should not expect more out of her. After all, she got what she wanted and so did I. Besides, cougars need to roam.

At last, I find the girl of my dreams, someone I dated before on the college swim team, a beautiful, brown-haired, blue-green-eyed, buxom, and slender former timing girl, now a wannabe children's book artist: Debbie Bishop. I'd gone out with her a few times before I got serious with Lisa. Debbie is unlike other girls. She is sweet, attentive, easy to be around, and, above all else, eager to make me happy. We start seeing each other again. I want to take things slow, however, especially after my experience with Lisa. Instead, we become seriously committed on our first date, right after seeing a terrible Bernardo Bertolucci film that we both laugh off. We consummate our relationship that night in the back of her Volkswagen van.

I have no idea our passionate kissing is going to lead to you-know-what. We start by making out. Next thing I know, Debbie has her top off and my shirt off. Into the moment, she slips out of her jeans, then her panties, and then I'm out of my pants and boxers. I am so excited, imagining just how amazing our first time is going to be, like fireworks going off. Debbie is amazing and pushes all the right buttons, but I am so nervous I cannot relax and have trouble finishing.

Debbie puts me at ease right away. Suddenly, we pause. Debbie asks, "You okay?"

"Yes," I claim, despite being nervous about not performing as well as I should.

Debbie flashes a warm, seductive smile. "I could do something else."

Debbie does that something else and it works like magic. After that, we are boyfriend and girlfriend. Even my hard-to-please father approves of her. After inviting us over for dinner, he tells me he likes everything about her, for the same reasons I do. She and I develop a wonderful, loving relationship I hope never ends.

FOLLOWING IN THE FOOTSTEPS of my famous father is more difficult than I imagine. When stardom doesn't comes fast enough for me, I decide to give my acting career a lift by posing nude for *Playgirl* magazine. One day at Jack LaLanne's Health Spa, this photographer, Norbert Jobst, a client I train, walks in and recruits me. "How would you like to make three thousand dollars?" he asks.

Three thousand dollars was a lot of money back then, especially to a young struggling actor, especially to one working three jobs. Besides working as a health spa trainer, I also park cars at Stear's for Steaks restaurant on La Cienega's famed "Restaurant Row," for a guy named Stavros Niarchos, who trains horses at Hollywood Park during the day. Still living in the same $100-a-month cracker box and still driving that three-on-the-column stick, gas-guzzling, smoky, Bondo-envy-of-the-world Ford Panel Wagon, I am now making a combined income of $125 a week. Norbert's proposition sounds like a great idea: Take pictures and make three thousand bucks.

"Yeah, I'm interested. The only condition I have"—because I know the pictures are for *Playgirl* and he is a photographer for them—"is that you let me bring my girlfriend along and be part of the pictures."

I do not want to come across as a homosexual.

"Fine, bring your girlfriend along."

Prior to taking the pictures, I ask my mom what she thinks. I never ask Dad because I know he will never want me to do it. I call her on a break from parking cars at Stear's for Steaks.

"Mom, I got a chance to take some photographs," I tell her. "They're naked photographs for *Playgirl* magazine. What should I do?"

After a brief pause, Mom says, "Well, Lorenzo, you should be proud of your body. You've worked so hard at it. You should go for it. Go ahead."

We do the photo shoot. Norbert rents a house in the Hollywood Hills that has a sparkling pool in the back. He takes pictures of my girlfriend, Debbie, in a two-piece bikini and of me in much less, around the pool. Afterward, Norbert says, "You have a very good chance of winning the top male model of the year with these pictures," which then was like a $10,000 bonus.

"Holy cow," I reply, "that's fantastic!"

Playgirl plans to publish the spread six months later. Then what happens is like something straight out of a Hollywood script. Two to three months later, I am offered a job by Jimmy Komack, the producer of *Chico and the Man* and *Welcome Back, Kotter*, whose work I admire, to play a supporting role in a television pilot he is producing for a new series called *Whatever Happened to Dobie Gillis?* Reuniting the original cast, it is an update of the classic 1959–63 comedy series *The Many Loves of Dobie Gillis*. It's been in development since 1974 by the show's original creator, Max Shulman. This is, like, huge!

I receive the contracts. Then, before signing them, I notice they contain a morals clause. In essence, that prevents me from doing any other job deemed offensive to the show or its properties. Suddenly I have a huge dilemma. What about my nude photo shoot?

Anytime I have questions about contracts or anything, I always go to see the old man. I call and tell him, "I need to talk to you about this contract."

Dad is very happy I am doing the Jimmy Komack–produced sitcom. It is a *big* deal to him. "Wonderful! I'll be here."

I run over to the house with the contract. "Dad, I have a big, big problem."

"What's the problem?"

"Uh, well. I took some pictures that might conflict with this morals clause."

"How many pictures did you take?"

"Well, I did a photo shoot for *Playgirl* magazine."

Long pause. "You did what?"

"I did a photo shoot for *Playgirl* magazine and Mom said it was okay."

Father's eyes widen and his nostrils flare as the mere mention of Mom's name sets him off. "Oh, that's fantastic, Lorenzo! Your mother said it was fine and you go ahead and take pictures that only homosexuals see. You do know that?"

"Well, Dad, actually, women also see this magazine."

My proud, macho, obstinate Latin father, with his hard-core old-world values and convictions, is not buying my argument for one second. "Lorenzo, there are no women who see that magazine—only homosexuals. Okay? Are you proud of yourself? You happy? You're going to be the poster boy for homosexuals."

What seemed like such a grand idea on my part suddenly feels like it is not so grand after all. "Dad, I wasn't really thinking about that," I explain. "I was only thinking about the money."

"How much money they pay you?"

"Three thousand dollars."

Dad says, "You're going to give it back."

"What? No." I reason, "I can't give it back."

My father is emphatic. "You're going to give it back and we're going to get those pictures back."

"Dad, they're going to go to print in like two months," I counter. "There's no way you're going to get those pictures."

"Oh, yeah," he says with a fiery determination in his eyes. "We're going to call Francesca Daniels. We're going to get those pictures back."

Back in the day, Francesca Daniels was a high-profile, high-powered attorney with offices in Century City. She was a friend of my father and Esther's. We are still good friends to this day. Then in her midthirties, she is like this Italian firebomb, at the top of her game. Dad calls her and she says, "No problem. I'll have a talk with this Norbert Jobst." The poor fucker does not know what is about to hit him.

I give Francesca his phone number. "Do you want me to go with you?" I ask.

"No, Lorenzo. Your father wants me to take care of this," she says. "I'm going to take care of this."

Francesca does exactly that. She not only stops *Playgirl* from publishing the photos, but she also gets the contract back that I had signed and all of the negatives. I never saw the pictures. I do not know if my father ever saw the pictures. This past year, I asked Francesca, "Do you know what happened to them?"

"They're gone. History!"

I realize now I did the photo shoot for all the wrong reasons. First, I did it for the money. Second, I had this warped sense that after *Playgirl* published the photos I would be famous. I was so naïve then. Those photos would have made me famous but in the wrong way.

My father's reaction should not surprise me. A man of deep moral convictions, anything that is not masculine he thinks is not cool. Homosexuality is one of them.

When I was seven, Mom let a gay hairdresser—whose real name I'll withhold but for the purposes of this story we'll call John—come live with us in Villa Grove in a room adjacent to the attic, far removed from the main living quarters. He's out of work, but she takes him under her wing. Mom is not married at the time; it is after her divorce from Christian. She gives John some handyman work to do around the house—paint my room and dresser and install molding around the ceiling, stuff like that. It never bothers me that John is there in the house. But it really bothers my father.

Now and then, John stumbles home very late at night. Once time, Mom is talking on the phone with Dad when he does. "You should not have him in the house," he tells her. "I don't want him around Lorenzo. He just shouldn't be there."

Another time, John is so drunk he starts breaking stuff in the house. Mom calls Dad, who drives straight over. Dad runs up to John's room off the attic. John is standing there, crying. "Don't throw me out, Mr. Lamas."

Dad is in no mood for it. "Your ass is out of here!"

My father grabs John by the collar, drags him down the stairs, and physically throws him out of the house, with his suitcases after him. Mom feels terrible afterward. "You sure that was necessary?"

"Yes!" Dad exclaims. "It was. He is a danger to you and Lorenzo."

Mom is very generous when it comes to helping the downtrodden, as am I. Another time, she befriends another gay man, who lives with us for a while in both Los Angeles and New York. I like him. He is really cool and I consider him a friend. Sometimes he helps me with my homework and stuff. After we move to New York, Dad lives too far away to do anything about it, whether he likes it or not.

Dad is unrepentant in his treatment of gays. One time when I'm riding with him on Sunset Boulevard, Dad spots two gay guys in T-shirts and short shorts. He slows down the convertible to a crawl and hollers loudly, "Darlings, why don't you kiss each other? Come on, give each other a kiss."

Suddenly, in one quick motion, Dad flips them off and screams, "Fucking faggots," and drives off.

Dad thinks it is funny. As a kid not knowing any better, I get into it a little bit with him. I holler a slur I considered innocent, "Yeah, down with fags."

At Farragut Academy, they would single out kids who were gay and harass them unmercifully in front of others by calling them names. It is horrible and I am ashamed of myself for participating in it. And that's where I differ from my father. We should treat everyone fairly regardless of race, color, creed, and—of course—sexual orientation. I am proud that I am open-minded enough to see people for who they are, without passing judgment like my father.

IN LATE 1976, we tape the *Dobie Gillis* pilot at CBS Studios on Beverly Boulevard with Dwayne Hickman (Dobie Gillis), Bob Denver (Maynard G. Krebs, still his friend), Sheila James (Zelda Gilroy, now Dobie's wife), and Frank Faylen (Dobie's father), all of whom starred in the original series. The premise is they are gathering to celebrate Dobie's fortieth birthday. In this new version, I play Lucky, a friend of Dobie's son, George. The first day the cast reports to rehearsals, I tell Jimmy Komack how much it means to me being in one of his shows and thank him for the chance.

"Think nothing of it, kid," Jimmy says. "You have what I'm look-ing for."

We rehearse the pilot all week in an empty rehearsal hall, know-ing that people are coming later to watch the taping. Never having performed before, not even in a high school play, I come off pretty green, nervous, and easily rattled. It marks the first time I ever perform in front of a live audience and my first experience with stage fright. Walking out onto the set for the first taping, I just freak out. I get through it, but I am just awful. Jimmy takes me aside before the final taping and gives me a pep talk.

"I know you can be good," he says, "and I have faith in you."

Jimmy's encouraging words do the trick. I relax and go out and give a good performance, enough to get a thumbs-up from Jimmy afterward.

I have always been a strong believer in circumstance. Some people call it fate. A fortuitous sequence of well-timed events happening at such lightning speed will produce a positive result. Filming the *Dobie Gillis* pilot feels just like that, despite intense behind-the-scenes infighting between Jimmy and the Dobie Gillis creator, writer Max Shulman. Finally, Jimmy fires Shulman for not "understanding the characters" (strange, considering Shulman actually created them!).

With a Jimmy Komack pilot to my credit, I feel confident that career opportunities are going to finally open up. I call on more casting agents, informing them of my recent success but, surprisingly, with little to show for it. Frustrated and tired of never making ends meet, I go back to my original plan: to join the military.

That December, I walk into the Marine Corps recruiting office in Santa Monica with my graduation papers and all of my credentials, including naval sciences courses I completed at the academy, and announce, "I want to enlist."

The recruiter shuffles through my papers. He sees how I was a yeoman chief by virtue of a correspondence course I had completed through the U.S. Navy. He looks up and says with a wide grin on his face, "You have great officer potential, recruit."

"Yes, sir," I say.

Before I can change my mind, the recruiter quickly signs me up. He then sends me downtown to take the officer training candidate test. I score very high on it. Before I know it, I receive my report date to Camp Pendleton to become a marine. I ship out in a month. Naturally, I still have to tell my father.

Two weeks before I ship out, I break the news to him.

"Like hell you are!"

"Dad, I've already signed. I'm fed up."

My father classically says, "Lorenzo, don't be an asshole. You've only given yourself a year. What do you expect? That somebody is going to walk up on the street and say, 'You're a good-looking kid. Let me make you a star'?"

"Well, it happens, doesn't it?" I ask.

"It happens to other people, Son," he says. "You have to be realistic."

My mind is set. "I think it's too late, Dad," I explain. "I've already signed."

By the look in my father's eyes, I can tell he is hatching a plan. "No. We'll get you out."

"How?"

Dad says, "You had a motorcycle accident six months ago where you fractured your skull. I'm going to get you a medical excuse from Dr. Omar." Dr. Omar Fareed, who formerly served as the physician for the U.S. Olympic tennis teams in 1964 and 1968, is my father's private doctor.

Dad asks Dr. Fareed to write a letter on my behalf to the Marine Corps recruiter. I really doubt he can get me out of going because I have signed on the dotted line and technically am considered "government issue." My father and Dr. Fareed march in with me to the recruiting office. The recruiter recognizes me right away.

"Hey, Lamas," he says with a grin, "are you getting ready?"

My father does all the talking, and I keep my mouth shut. "Sir, we have a problem," Dad says.

"Who are you?" the recruiter asks sternly.

"I'm his father," Dad says, and then points to the man next to him, "and this is Dr. Fareed."

Without saying a word, Dr. Fareed hands the recruiter the letter. Because of my skull fracture—or cerebral hematoma—and the resulting swelling on the brain, all of which took months to heal, the chance for residual effects from the injury is very real. If I suddenly have a seizure when dealing with firearms or explosive charges, I could cause harm to myself and those around me.

The recruiter puts the letter down on his desk. Shaking his head, he looks up at me and says, "You were such a *good* prospect."

With that, my days as a marine thankfully end. And for that, I can thank my father, for helping me be more patient and give my acting career a better chance.

STARTING IN 1976, Dad began moving behind the camera, taking on fewer acting roles in favor of directing many popular shows, including *Starsky & Hutch*, *The Rookies*, and *S.W.A.T.* In January 1977, he signs on to direct an episode of *Switch*, another hit series by producer Glen A. Larson, starring Eddie Albert and Robert Wagner. Dad is a strong believer in me making my own way, just as he did as an actor. Yet understanding the difficulties I am facing finding parts, he gives me a helping hand. It's only the second time he does so in my career, even though he could have many times. He gets me a guest shot on *Switch*, which will officially mark my acting debut (it will air before the *Dobie Gillis* pilot).

Most people think actors simply stand up and read their lines, but there is far more to it than that. My dad has had rigorous training and extensive experience, more than most. He makes me realize acting is, or *can be*, an art. For my age, however, I have only a little camera presence and just a modicum of acting ability—two things that work against me while filming my guest spot on *Switch*. Canadian-born director Gerald Mayer is directing the episode, called "Eden's Gate," in which I play a hit man, Tony, who is supposed to take some guy out. My appearance amounts to a walk-on. In my only scene, I tell my gangster boss—I am in this phone booth, talking on an old-style rotary phone—that I was not able to take the guy out. Of course, I am in deep shit. I have only one line: "I didn't get him, boss. I'm sorry."

Standing in that telephone booth, I am just petrified trying to get that line out. I am great at dialing the phone number fast, but my mouth feel likes it is full of marbles when it comes to saying my line. It takes something like ten takes.

Mr. Mayer yells, "Cut!" Then he motions to me. "Come here, kid."

I walk over and he says, "Take it easy, slow down, this isn't a race, you know. What's the line?"

I repeat it to his face: "I didn't get him, boss. I'm sorry."

"See how you just said that?"

"Yeah."

"Say that in the phone booth after I say, 'Action!' Now say it again."

I repeat the line: "I didn't get him, boss. I'm sorry."

"Perfect. Now just say the line."

Mr. Mayer hollers to the cameraman, "Roll cameras. Action!"

The assistant snaps the clapboard containing key identifying information—the studio name, production title, director's last name, date, scene number, and numbered take. The camera starts rolling. I quickly dial the number on the phone in the booth as Mr. Mayer eagerly waits, as does the crew, for me to deliver my now famous line. I draw a blank and for the life of me cannot get the words out.

"Cut!"

"Come here, kid." Mr. Mayer pulls me aside again. "Look, I know your dad. Your dad and I are really good friends. So just say the line."

"Yes, Mr. Mayer," I say.

"Call me Jerry."

"Yes, Jerry."

"Say the line!" Jerry barks again, "Roll cameras. Action!"

Finally, I say the line as written: "I didn't get him, boss. I'm sorry."

"Cut! Print it!"

Jerry and the crew stand and applaud. I smile sheepishly; I am so embarrassed. Despite Laura Rose having all of this confidence in me to send me out to audition, I never think for a moment I have what it takes to be an actor. Later, I realize I put a lot of unnecessary pressure on myself that day because I just wanted to make my father proud.

On February 20, 1977, the episode of *Switch* premieres on ABC. Despite my father's generosity, I keep struggling to find regular work as an actor. By now, I am holding down four jobs—training clients at Jack LaLanne's Health Spa and parking cars at Stear's for Steaks by day, working as a security guard three nights a week at a local Budweiser brewery, and parking cars at private parties on weekends as well. After seeing other actors my age enjoying huge stardom on *Happy Days* and *Welcome Back, Kotter*, I get discouraged.

"What am I doing wrong?" I wonder.

In March of that year, Mom asks me to escort her to the 49th Annual Academy Awards in Los Angeles. It marks my introduction to the world of glamour and exclusivity. Mom has always been involved in the Academy of Motion Picture Arts and Sciences. To many members, including myself, it is a measure of achievement and exclusivity, afforded to a select few. Every branch of the motion picture business is represented. Actors, directors, writers, editors, costumers, production design, and so on are all included in this very special group.

Back to the story: Mom takes me that year. It is just the two of us. We are still on good terms with each other. The "cold war" that Esther and Fernando have started with her has not yet taken its full effect on me. I have a few television credits to my name at this point, but nothing significant enough to warrant the kind of attention my mom is trying to stir up with the press as we walk the red carpet together outside the Dorothy Chandler Pavilion, where, in less than an hour, the Oscars will be broadcast, live, around the world on ABC.

"This is my son the actor!" Mom yells out to the press and paparazzi. "He's in a pilot called *Whatever Happened to Dobie Gillis?* He's Lorenzo Lamas and he's coming to a TV near you!"

Honestly, I am surprised, if not a little bit embarrassed by the commercial my mother is doing for me on the red carpet. All for a good cause, I'm sure, to give my acting career a boost she feels only she can give.

Once inside, I am completely floored and humbled by the sheer pageantry, not to mention the star wattage that is so close you can reach out and touch them. Our seats are ten rows from the stage. Gregory Peck, a friend of my mom's, stops by to say hello. She introduces us. Then there is Kirk Douglas, his son, Michael, and their wives sitting close by, along with Karl Malden, Liza Minnelli, James Coburn, and Roger Moore. *Rocky* wins best picture that year, and at the Governors Ball after the show, Mom's friend, famed Hollywood columnist Shirley Eder, introduces me to Sylvester Stallone. I smile and shake hands with him. I feel then I am in the presence of greatness. It is clear he is a very talented actor, writer, and director, and *Rocky* is proof. I want to pinch myself. It is so cool to be there among the true legends and up-and-comers in the business. That night convinces me to continue to knock on those casting doors and try to nail every audition I am put up for. Shirley Eder also introduces me to Allan Carr, who is soon to give me the biggest career boost yet.

He is executive producer for *Grease*, the movie musical currently in development for Paramount Pictures.

Never in my life do I feel more encouraged and more supported by my mother than I do that night. She may have been gone a lot when I was growing up, but she is there for the important moments when they count, and this night is one of them.

After a delay, CBS finally premieres the hour-long pilot for *Whatever Happened to Dobie Gillis?* in early May of that year. Without Shulman's hand, the result lacks the flavor of the original series, as a critic for the *Los Angeles Times* writes, "combining the worst of the old and new." Consequently, CBS decides not to pick it up as a series. To say the news is devastating to me is an understatement. With a genius like Jimmy Komack behind it, I figure, how can it fail? I mean, this is Jimmy Komack! Meanwhile, the only guy zooming to worldwide superstardom later that year, after unleashing his disco-dancing prowess in the mega-movie hit *Saturday Night Fever*, is Travolta. If only I had Travolta's agent!

FIVE

"Grease" Is the Word

AFTER *DOBIE GILLIS* FLOPS, Dad calls his friend Don "Red" Barry, a famous cowboy-and-western star and then head of his own talent agency, to represent me. After signing me to my first agency contract, Barry assigns me to another agent, Mike Rosen. Just when things look their bleakest, a bright glimmer of hope suddenly dawns on the horizon. Producer Allan Carr remembers me from the Academy Awards I attended with Mom. That summer, he calls Mike with an offer for me to audition for a supporting role in the movie *Grease*, soon to start production.

"There's probably not a chance you'll be one of the T-birds," Mike says when he phones me with the news. The T-birds—or Thunderbirds—are cronies of Travolta's in the movie. "You should go meet Allan Carr because if it doesn't work out for this, it might work out for something else."

Polite, impressionable, and eager to please, I am this rather naïve nineteen-year-old nouveau actor with nothing to lose. I meet with Allan and the film's director, Randal Kleiser, and read for a scene as one of the T-birds. Allan tells me right after, "Lorenzo, you're very interesting. I want to try and find something for you."

As I leave the audition, I feel maybe, just maybe, things are finally going to break my way. Two days later, Steven Ford, President Ford's son, bows out of the production. He is Allan's original pick to play Olivia Newton-John's dim-witted football jock boyfriend. But Steven decided that after doing a prerehearsal sock hop scene and rehearsing other scenes with the rest of the cast on the Paramount lot, he would go back to his career as a rodeo rider. Allan immediately calls me back to screen test for the role and offers me the part on the spot. "You're the perfect all-American jock," he says.

I call Dad, Mom, Debbie, everybody I know, and tell them the news. After landing the role, I move out of my $100-a-month cracker box studio into a larger one-bedroom apartment in Santa Monica. A few months later, I ask Debbie to move in with me.

From the very first day of filming at Paramount, the set is unreal, like a party atmosphere every day. It is an open set, with people dropping in and out all the time. Delicious catered food, compliments of the studio, is trucked in to the set daily, and some folks bring in their own homemade goodies. It *is* like being in high school—the best one ever.

Every minute I am on the set, I'm absorbing the experience fully, and when I'm not in a particular scene, I mix in the background with my fellow costars Barry Pearl, Didi Conn, Susan Buckner, and the late Jeff Conaway (whom I stayed close to through the years). Every second I'm there I keep my nose to the grindstone and never goof off. I want to make my father proud.

I have no lines but am seen prominently as the rival to John Travolta for Olivia Newton-John's affections. My first day on the set, Allan comes up to me (because of my resemblance to Travolta back then) and says, "We're going to have to change the color of your hair."

I kiddingly ask, "How much am I getting for this role again?"

Allan says, "Seven hundred and fifty dollars a week."

When I was working four jobs, I didn't earn that in a month. So I tell Carr, "For that amount of money, you can dye my hair green. Or would you like purple?"

Allan laughs. "Blond will do."

I dye my hair blond, wear walking shorts, and act sort of vapid— completely different from how people think of me in real life and a stark departure from my previous roles. Playing the character is a real trip for me, as is costarring in my first major Hollywood production.

From the very first day of filming, one thing is clear: John and Olivia are the stars. The movie becomes a perfect showcase of two super talents who can do it all: act, sing, and dance. Travolta is so busy I never interact with him. I am just flattered to be in the same film, much less on the same set, with him.

Of course, what guy does not have a crush on Olivia Newton-John? I happen to be one of the legions of hormone-raging young boys and teens who do. My buddies and I have listened to every one of her records. What a voice! The voice of an angel that goes so well with that blond hair, sugar-and-spice look, and leggy figure of hers. In person, she is just as beautiful and so down-to-earth. Unlike some stars, she never puts on airs. She is genuine and real.

One day, I get up the nerve to introduce myself to Olivia. I walk up and knock on her trailer door. I am fully expecting Olivia to come to the door, but her beautiful sister Rona (who later marries Jeff Conaway) answers instead. Again, I am so naïve that when Olivia does not answer, I just stand there like a stooge, as if I have marbles in my mouth. It feels ridiculous.

Finally, Rona smiles and says, "Did you want to say something to Olivia?"

"Yes...yes, please," I stammer.

Rona exits, giggling. Seconds later, Olivia, in all her beauty, pokes her head out. She is a foot away from my face.

"Oh, hi, Lorenzo, how are you doing today?"

"I just wanted to say something."

"Yes, I know," she says sweetly. "What was it you wanted to say?"

"Um." I pause to think of something to impress her. "Give me a minute." Then I say the first thing that pops into my head. "I think I wanted to ask you if you wanted some, uh, orange juice."

"Oh," she says with a developing smirk on her face, "aren't you a dear."

Olivia turns to her sister. "Rona, he wanted to ask me if I wanted some *orrrrange* juice."

You can hear Rona in the back of the trailer laughing her head off.

"Actually, Lorenzo, that's *very* sweet," Olivia says, holding back her laughter. "I would like some coffee, though. Would you mind bringing me two cups?"

I barely get the words out. "S-s-s-ure. Anything else?"

Olivia flashes that megawatt smile. "You're such a dear. Thank you."

Olivia closes the door. As I walk off, she and her sister break out laughing so hard they cannot stop. I do not know how I get to craft services to get them coffee because my mind feels as if is not even attached to my body at this point.

What was I thinking? "*Orrrrange* juice?"

As an actor, you easily become attached to the people you work with while making a film or television series. You develop close friendships with everyone in front of and behind the camera, almost like you're all an extended family. For many us, making *Grease* becomes exactly that: a close-knit group with friendships that last for years. The day filming wraps is like a high school graduation. Everybody cheers, laughs, and sings silly songs like the Rydell High graduates the movie is about. The studio even issues us yearbooks to pass around and sign. Like the pretend high schoolers we are, many of us (except for John and Olivia) pledge to meet again for five-year and ten-year reunions (and most of us keep that promise).

Now that I have gotten a little taste of success, I, unfortunately, become rather conceited. It is not something I am proud of. I start treating Debbie like Dad does Esther. He's my role model, after all, and so I put more and more demands on her. Debbie is there for me every step of the way. She puts her life on hold and responds to my every whim. She makes me steak dinners. She drives me to auditions. Whatever makes me happy, she does it.

While filming *Grease*, I become friends with the Barbi Twins, fraternal twins Shane and Sia, after meeting them as extras on the set. This is the same blond-haired, blue-eyed, voluptuous pair that later enjoy record-breaking success in the 1990s for *Playboy* magazine. We hang out together. Sia and I start crushing on each other during the shooting. We kiss a couple of times in my dressing room and on the set. We start a physical relationship.

After finishing *Grease*, the twins and I stay in touch. Debbie knows we are friends and considers our relationship purely platonic. And in the beginning it was.

As a waitress at Marie Callender's, Debbie usually works the lunch shift or dinner shift until closing. On those days, unless I have an audition or acting job, I hang out at the apartment for a while. One sunny fall afternoon, while Debbie is working, I go to the beach with Sia and Shane. I meet them there in my green Chevy Caprice (I had ditched the crappy Ford Panel Wagon) with my surfboard in the back. Not exactly a muscle car, but getting close. I invite my friends Albert and Robert Roche and their girlfriends to join us for a little sun and surf until dusk. We'll watch the sunset, light a bonfire, and enjoy a few six-packs of beer together.

It is getting late. The bonfire is working its magic, crackling and shooting tiny embers that flame out into the nighttime sky. As the night wears on, the physical attraction between Sia and me gets harder and harder to deny. We excuse ourselves and take a walk down the bend in the dark, lay a towel down on the sand, and start kissing. As things get hot and heavy, I suggest, "Let's go to my place."

Grabbing Shane, we say goodbye to our friends and leave. We get back to the apartment around eleven o'clock; Debbie is due home around one-thirty. We waste little time continuing where we left off. Sia and I go wild on top of the bed and Shane joins us. Sia is naked, I am naked, Shane is naked. Suddenly, we have this amazing *ménage à trois*. I am kissing Sia, Shane is touching and rubbing me. Now I am kissing Shane and Sia. Shane is into it.

"You guys are so beautiful," Shane purrs with affection. "I love you together."

The whole time I am not thinking about Debbie. The twins and I are so into the moment I lose track of time. Finally, I look up at the clock in the bedroom: It is one o'clock.

"Guys." I pause. "We got to go in the living room because Debbie will be home any minute."

Like thieves in the night, we hurry to cover our tracks, get dressed, and try to look presentable before Debbie walks in the door. We'll be sitting and chatting as if nothing happened. At exactly one thirty, Debbie opens the door and enters. She sees us and says hi to Sia and Shane, goes straight into our bedroom, and closes the door.

The three of us hang out in the living room a little longer. Finally, I say good night to Sia and Shane as I walk them to the door. Sia whispers, "Lorenzo, I don't feel right about this."

I know what Sia means but I brush it off. "Why? It's cool," I say calmly. Sia says, "Okay."

I kiss Sia and Shane goodbye. Afterward, I do not feel guilty at all. In my twisted and sick narcissistic mind, I figure Debbie is so into me she will be supportive. What I want is Sia, and now that I have Sia, Debbie will go along with it.

I go to bed; Debbie is fast asleep. When we wake up the next morning, the first thing she says is, "Did you have fun?"

"Yeah, it was really fun." I change the subject. "How's work?"

"It was fine." Then Debbie asks, "What did you do?"

I tell her, "We went to the beach. We partied with Robert and Albert and their girlfriends."

She says, "Well, what did you guys do *here*?"

I do not lie. I tell Debbie the truth: "Everything."

Debbie turns ghostly white as her heart breaks right in front of me. Folding herself up in a chair, she breaks down sobbing and choking on her tears. I am surprised by her reaction, I guess because my relationship with her has always been about me. In my youthful ignorance, I am stupid enough to think Debbie is okay with me being with Sia because our relationship is all about my happiness. Seeing her sobbing uncontrollably, I feel so ashamed. I realize how wrong I have acted. How I never put her first—her dreams, her desires, her feelings. At that very instant, I want to roll up and die. Here is this pure and loving woman, who has done everything to make me happy, to create a happy and loving life together, and I drive a stake right through her heart.

I feel tremendous remorse. In my heart, I know I really, really love Debbie but am unsure what I can do now to repair what I have broken. I reach over to put my arm around her and tell her, "I'm so sorry."

Debbie says nothing. She cannot speak or look at me. Instead, she immediately puts her hands up like, *Don't touch me!*

I know it is over between us and I am the cause. I never forgive myself after that. Debbie moves back in with her parents. We don't speak again for years.

When Sia and I sit down and talk, I really understand the extent of how badly I hurt Debbie, and I sob in her arms. I am just one confused corn dog who does not really understand how to be a man. With all these conflicting examples in my life, including my father, I think to be like Dad is how a man is supposed to be.

Many times, I try finding Debbie to make amends, but it proves pointless. I lose track of her and never find her. In the meantime, I drift in and out of relationships but never, ever cheat on any woman again. It takes some real growing up on my part before I become my own person. For a very long time, I carry the burden of our breakup. It haunts me and is something I never get over.

Twelve years later, in 1989, I am in Las Vegas at a trade show in the Hilton Convention Center to promote *Self Defense Workout*, a self-defense video I made for Congress Entertainment. I am busy signing autographs at the booth when the next person in line moves forward. I cannot believe my eyes. It is her. It is Debbie. "Oh, my God, Debbie," I say. "I've thought about you so much for the last twelve years."

Debbie looks at me and says, "Do you have a moment?"

"Of course."

I leave the booth and join her. We sit down at a table in the cafeteria. Immediately, I tell her how glad I am she is here.

Debbie looks at me with her beautiful blue-green eyes and smiles warmly. "I know. I saw that you were here promoting your video. I am so happy for you, now that you are having all of this success."

"Thanks," I say. "What are you doing here?"

Debbie removes a book from her purse. She sets it down in front of me. I look down. It is a children's book she did all the illustrations for; she is at the trade show to promote it.

I tell her, "I'm so glad you've realized your dreams."

"Thanks," Debbie says. "I've been married now for almost six years."

"Really?"

"Yeah, I've actually been doing really well." Debbie pauses and says, "I also just wanted to tell you, Lorenzo, that I forgive you."

It takes everything on my part to hold back my emotions. To forgive me for doing that horrible thing to her means the world to me.

I walk over, hug Debbie, and tell her quietly, "I love you."

We cling to each other for a second. "I love you, too," she whispers.

Debbie is on her feet at this point. "Well," she says in a business-like manner, "I have to go."

I thank her again. "Debbie, thanks for coming. You being here means everything."

Flicking her shiny brown locks of hair off her shoulder with her hand, Debbie says simply, "Likewise."

We hug again. Debbie walks off. As she does, she smiles back at me for what becomes the last time. Within seconds, a mass of convention-goers crowding the lobby swallow her up, and she disappears from sight as I linger there for a moment. It becomes a nice ending, one I hang on to and carry with me, always.

DESPITE HAVING LANDED A PART in a major motion picture, I am still this naïve nineteen-year-old nouveau actor trying to find his way. Getting work, even as the son of a famous actor, proves elusive. But then in November of 1977, I am offered a second stint on the television series *Switch*. The episode is "Thirty Thousand Witnesses," and it airs after Christmas. I play the soccer star son (Sobranski) of a mother held hostage over an international incident.

Dad directs me in this one. It is the first time I ever have to cry on television. In the scene, the hostage takers are threatening to kill my mother or something. As soon as Dad yells, "Action!" I cry right on cue. Once the floodgates open, however, I cannot stop. The pent-up feelings I have in my father's presence, the desire to make him so proud of me, just boil over. Finally, Dad yells, "Cut!"

In anger, I pound my first right through the locker there in the scene and keep crying for about another five minutes. Father clears the room of cast and crew: "Okay, give the boy some space."

Dad comes over and puts his arm around me. "That's good, amigo," he says. "Let it out."

For what should have been a simple emotional scene, I simply overdo it in my attempt to win my father's approval. Dad does the right thing: He lets me work through my emotions.

"Okay now?" he asks after a bit.

I nod, wiping the tears from my eyes.

Dad calls everybody back, and I film the scene without any further disruption. My father and I never speak about the incident again. It is over and past. Although Dad never says it so much in words, he knows I am really trying and he gives me the time and space I need to figure things out on my own.

Although I have wanted to give up many times, I always remember my father saying, "Pay your dues, work hard, keep your nose clean, be a good boy, and good things will happen."

After *Grease* premieres nationwide in June 1978, Father is so right. Not only does it become the highest-grossing movie and musical of its time (surpassing the previous box-office champion, *The Sound of Music*) and receive eight Academy Award nominations, but after my big-screen debut, my luck also starts to change in dramatic fashion. Producers sign me for one television and movie role after another. Many see the same thing, a young actor with tremendous promise, all because of *Grease*.

I do a second pilot for Jimmy Komack, a half-hour comedy called *Ship Shape*, a cross between Don Rickles's *C.P.O. Sharkey* and *Happy Days*. It's about life on a Navy relocation base but dies in the ratings after CBS airs it that August. I also get a single guest shot on producer Glen A. Larson's short-lived NBC series *Sword of Justice*, which premieres in September. Then in December, I fly to Connecticut to film a small supporting role for director Jerome Heller in a movie with Marsha Mason and Kathleen Beller called *Promises in the Dark*. After that, I work on two independent films: *The All-Americans*, filmed in Pittsburgh and Dallas, and *Take Down*, an American Consortium and Disney release shot entirely in Utah. In the latter, producers cast me as a high school wrestler boyfriend to my pretty and talented costar Maureen McCormick (best known as Marcia on TV's *The Brady Bunch*). It's my first starring role in a movie; I play a bitter, poverty-stricken high school wrestling star, Nick Kilvitus. I guess the producers felt I was perfectly suited for the role because I worked as an instructor at Jack LaLanne's Health Spa.

Working on the film with my costar Ed Herrmann is a great experience. He takes me under his wing and teaches me a lot about acting. In celebration of my twentieth birthday, the whole crew throws a party for me (which I think Ed had something to do with).

Released nationally in April 1979 through Disney's Buena Vista Distribution company, *Take Down* becomes Disney's first PG-rated film; it's still five years before the studio expands into the "adult" market with the launch of Touchstone Pictures. In November 1978, months before its national release, the studio test screens *Take Down* in Salt Lake City and in other major cities. Three months later, it previews for an entire week at the Director's Guild in Los Angeles. Judging by the reaction, the movie looks destined to become an immediate hit with teen audiences.

After a New York preview, Mom takes me out to Charley O's in downtown Manhattan to celebrate. She is very happy over the turn of events in my career. "Pardon a mother's pride," she tells a reporter, "he's a very good actor."

That same month, *Take Down* previews at the United Artists Theatre in Westwood. It is a very big moment for me because Dad attends. He has never acknowledged seeing anything I have done up to that point. He never saw anything I acted in—no television shows or movies, not even *Grease*. This is the first time he actually *comes* to something in which I star. Our dear friend Lola Leighter, then on portable oxygen and suffering from emphysema, joins us. In spite of her failing health, she tells me, "There isn't anything in the world to keep me from seeing you in your movie."

Dressed in a blue turtleneck and sports jacket (I really loved wearing turtlenecks then), I am both excited and nervous, especially with Dad there. During the screening, he gives no indication of what he is thinking or feeling, like a poker player playing his hand close to the vest. Esther, on the other hand, shows her emotions freely. She smiles at me and squeezes my hand during many of my major dramatic scenes.

After the movie ends, we walk out of the theater together. My father still has said nothing to me until finally, when we're outside, he looks over at me with that familiar grin and says, "Well, kiddo, you have it!"

It means more to me than anything in the world. The bottom line: Dad is finally proud of me. I have done something he can say he is proud of. It is not a small role in a movie or just a part of an ensemble cast—it is my own film. It is a big, big night for that reason alone.

I am so glad I have stuck it out. After the success of *Take Down*, I am finally able to make my living as an actor and can quit my job at Jack LaLanne's Health Spa. There might have been a time when I could not handle the success or money or all those things that come with being a celebrity, but this is not one of them. I am just happy for the success, for the publicity, and the groundswell of popularity building in my career.

Back in November 1978, on the strength of my performance in *Take Down*, I audition for—and land—a role as a devilish ladies' man surfer in my first weekly television series for CBS, *California Fever*. It is a teen comedy in the style of *Happy Days*. It is the perfect fit for me: a beach bum at heart who loves surfing as much as—in real life—I love motorcycling. The show is a romp set in Southern California, filmed entirely on the beaches of Venice. It stars Kristy McNichol's brother Jimmy, Marc McClure, who plays Jimmy Olsen in the first *Superman* movie with Christopher Reeve, and Michele Tobin as a cute, redheaded teenage rocker chick. We run a surf shop and have a big Jeep outfitted with a stereo and a boom box.

But I almost don't get to film the series.

One afternoon, I go down to the beach to surf. I take along a young neighbor with me to show him how. When we go out into the waves, he loses control of his board. Suddenly it flips and slashes the upper left side of my face with its fin. Immediately streaks of blood start pouring down my face. I have a hard time seeing out of my left eye. I am really, really scared.

I am rushed to the nearest hospital, where the ER doctor stitches me up. The injury requires sixteen stitches, and after examining my eye, he says, "You may permanently lose vision in your left eye."

But I do recover, and fortunately, my vision fully returns without any impairment, although the injury leaves my left eye slightly smaller than my right.

Medically cleared, I return in time to begin filming *California Fever*. In making the series, I earn more money than I ever have for anything. For a guy who once worked four jobs a week to eke out a living, suddenly I am making like $15,000 per episode. That's a six-figure annual income, great money in 1979, especially for a twenty-one-year-old single guy. My father always handled money well in his life, made solid investments, and never squandered what he earned. He used to say, "I learned very early in the movie business that the important thing is not how much you make, but what you do with what you make." In the 1940s and 1950s, while making big money, he kept putting it into land and real estate in order to build a solid foundation for the future. Later, his investments paid off for him, providing the kind of financial security in his life that never would have been possible had he stayed in his native country.

"Here's what you do, kid," Dad suggests. "You go buy a house with that money."

I quiver at the thought. "But, Dad," I nervously tell him, "I don't know if the show's going to get picked up."

Dad lays it all out for me in the clearest possible terms. "Look, you're making $15,000 an episode guaranteed for ten episodes," he says. "That's $150,000 before taxes. You take $40,000 of what's left and put it down on a house. I'll help you. You take the other $40,000 and put it in the bank."

It was good advice. I am only sorry my dad did not live long enough to keep giving me that good advice. I ended up spending every dime I ever made.

Dad helps me find a little one-bedroom A-frame cottage up in Laurel Canyon for $105,000. Just as he says, I put $40,000 down. With high interest back then of 11 ¾ percent, I have an $1,100-a-month mortgage payment on like an $80,000 loan. Nutty, huh? I keep that house for a long time, continuing to rent it out even after later buying and moving into my second home. It becomes one of the smartest investments I have ever made (thanks, Dad!).

Exactly three years after honoring my father's wishes that I never ride another "murdercycle" again, I give in to the temptation and buy myself a 105-horsepower, six-cylinder street bike, the Honda CBX. The biggest bike manufactured in the world, it is like my mini-trail bike revisited. Only this one is a beast on the road. Its smooth, precision handling, euphoric acceleration, and raw power end up making it the envy of bikers for more than a quarter of a century. I purchase the new CBX right off the showroom floor, using money I make acting in a supporting role in Detour to Terror, a Columbia Pictures feature starring O.J. Simpson, Anne Francis, and Arte Johnson. Because I had made that promise to Dad, however, I keep the bike hidden from him.

I finally get up the nerve and ride the CBX up to the house to show him. By then, because of my accident, I am sporting a helmet. I park the motorcycle outside, put it up on its center kickstand, and hang the helmet on top of the gas tank so Dad will surely see it. I ring the doorbell and stand aside so when he opens the door, he can see the bike and the helmet. Dad swings open the door, steps outside, looks at the bike and then me, and, fuming, says, "You fucker, you did it!"

"Dad, look," I say, "I've got a helmet."

"I suppose you just have to have the biggest fucking 'murdercycle' they make. You couldn't just get a little 'murdercycle.'"

"No, Dad, it's the fastest street bike on the planet."

"Wonderful!"

I try to steer the conversation back where I started. "But look, Dad, I've got a helmet."

My father famously throws up his hands. "What am I going to do with you? You and your 'murdercycles.'"

Exasperated, he storms off and slams the door behind him.

Because I am my own man at this point in my life, my father eventually resigns himself to the fact this is something I really want and need. He knows it is part of who I am and will never change.

After buying the Honda, I fulfill another dream: buying a Harley and building a chopper out of it. I do the work with Mike Liakos, a grip and good friend from *California Fever*. We start going on bike rides and eventually talk about customizing my bike into a more original style, something I had been reading about in magazines and wanting to do for a long time. We also talk about and do many other things together, including dope. One thing leads to another and I find myself getting high. It is a feel-good thing—talk motorcycles, drink beer, smoke pot, get a little high.

The first time I tangle with the Peruvian marching powder, otherwise known as cocaine, is on the set of *California Fever*. I do not recall who introduced it to me or who gave me my first hit (and probably would not tell you if I did). I remember it is late on a Friday. We are shooting night scenes at eleven or twelve o'clock. I am just exhausted. We have been up since eight o'clock that morning, working and filming straight through. The further in the week a show gets behind, the later the schedule gets pushed out to finish. By Thursday and Friday, when that happens, you are into overtime and working well into the night.

Hanging out at the coffee machine, I tell the property master, "I'm fuckin' beat, man. This coffee is just not doing it."

"Come on up to the truck," he says as he waves for me to follow him. "I'll give you a bump."

"Oh, that's cool; they call it a bump"—that's what went through my mind. *Okay, I'll give it a try.* I follow after him.

I am this adventurous twenty-one-year-old who's not thinking about anything else, really, other than "I'm doing a little cocaine with the big boys." I hop up into the property truck, do a line of coke, and do not feel a thing. Nothing is happening. I tell the property master, "I don't feel anything."

He chuckles. "Give it a few minutes."

I go back to the set. All of a sudden, I am walking around and talking to everybody at hyper-speed, totally unaware of how I am acting. Finally, one of the crew goes, "You okay, Lorenzo? How much coffee you have?"

I laugh and say, "A lot."

I am flying and loving it. Coke becomes something I do on occasion and then more than occasionally, even at the risk of losing everything I have worked for. More about that later.

For years, Dad and Esther brainwashed me into believing my mom never really wanted me. That she did everything to cast me aside, right down to putting me in military school. Hear something long enough and it creeps into your soul. You begin to believe every word. I do. In 1979, I cut myself off from Mom completely, even stop talking to her.

One day that year, Laura "Larry" Mako, a friend of my mother's who served as the matron of honor at Dad and Mom's wedding, and someone I've remained close to for years, calls me to tell me Mom is in town. Although Larry knows I am not on speaking terms with Mom, she says, "She wants to see you, Lorenzo. I really think it is important that you at least return your mother's call."

I call Mom and give her my address; I'm still living in my A-frame house on Laurel Canyon. She is delighted to hear from me, as always: "How nice of you to call, Lorenzo."

Our conversation is cordial but brief. I have become very close to Dad and Esther; they are always there for me, while my mom is not. They support me in my decision to become an actor. They help me find that house. They are up there every weekend to help me clear the brush around the house after the fire marshal issues a warning. They are a major part of my life. They have become my family. Conversely, Mom, who still makes her home in New York, is far removed and less of a force in my life, which is her choice, of course.

I agree to see Mom, but unfortunately, Dad and Esther show up at the house the very day she is to arrive. I am mortified. Oh, man, what am I going to do? I feel such intense loyalty to both of them that this is like a bad dream ready to happen. They hate my mom. I hate her. I can just hear my father saying, "What is *she* doing here?"

Built on stilts, my house has a carport on the first level and a walk up to the front of the house, with a sliding-glass door for my front door. There's a long dirt-and-gravel driveway. I know Mom has arrived the moment the tires of her limo crackle against the hard gravel.

Opening the slider, I walk down the steps through the carport to meet the car in the driveway. By then the driver has jumped out to walk around and open the door for my mom.

"Don't bother!" I shout.

The driver is so stunned he stops short. The passenger window rolls down, Mom sticks her head out, and asks, "Can I see you?"

"No," I say flatly and start walking off.

After that, it is all downhill. I smash the hood of her limo with my fist and shout to the driver, "Take this piece of shit and get it off my fucking property right now!"

The driver jumps back into the limo, backs up, and speeds off, kicking up a cloud of dust behind him. Everything I have heard over the years from Dad and Esther about my mom bubbles to the surface. I am no longer in control of my emotions. Finally, flailing my arms and making a big scene, I scream after her, "Get out of my life!"

Storming up the stairs, I slam the sliding-glass door shut, feeling conflicted and confused. This is my mom. She has come all this way to see me, and I slammed my door in her face. Finally, I break down crying. Putting his arm around me, Dad comforts me, "That's okay."

"Well," Esther says in a harsh tone, "she had it coming."

Ashamed, I am just sobbing. "Well, I guess."

Only many years later do I realize that Esther is so insecure about my mom because not only is Mom beautiful, but my father is still so much in love with her. Esther can never quite come to terms with that. She picks on my mom mercilessly and wears my dad down to the point where he no longer defends my mom. Eventually also I realize that my mom is not the bad person they have led me to believe she is. My coming to terms with that and then mending my fences with Mom does, fortunately, happen, but not until after I experience an awakening with help from my first wife, Victoria.

AFTER ITS PREMIERE, *California Fever* soon vanishes from the airwaves. CBS announces its cancellation after nine episodes. The December 11, 1979, broadcast of the tenth and final episode becomes the lowest-rated show for the week, watched by only 13 percent of the television viewing public. In their attempt to capitalize on the popularity of *Happy Days* and *National Lampoon's Animal House*, our producers went bananas with the show's concept, turning it into an unrealistic representation of how teenagers actually live. The fact that we have to compete with *Happy Days* in the same time slot does not help. Viewers, I think, were looking for something more than just another *Happy Days*.

I get the news of *California Fever's* cancellation in a strange way, to say the least. The day before, I receive my call sheet to report to the studio the next morning at nine sharp. We are to shoot interior scenes on a sound stage at Burbank Studios, now Warner Bros. I drive to the studio the next day, park in my usual space on the lot, get out of my car, and walk to the sound stage. The stage doors are wide open, which is strange because on filming days they are usually closed. I walk inside and nobody is there. Just a lonely janitor sweeping up with a push broom. Suddenly I have an eerie feeling in the pit of my stomach: *Oh, shit, they're at the beach today and nobody's called me.*

"Hey, brother," I call out to the janitor still sweeping up, "where is everybody? I have a call time of nine A.M. here."

"Oh, man," he says, sweeping the whole time, "they didn't tell you?"

"No, what?"

"The show was canceled yesterday."

"What?" I ask, stunned. "Nobody called me."

"God, bro, it's been canceled."

I am holding the call sheet in my hand. "But it's on my call sheet."

"Sorry, dude." He continues sweeping.

I am beside myself. I glance down at my call sheet again. As clear as day it says in beautiful black and white, "Call time: 9 A.M." I keep thinking, "This is a joke! Something is wrong here."

I drive back to my apartment and call my agent, Mike Rosen. "Hold on, let me get back to you," he says.

Mike calls the executives at CBS. They apologize to him for not letting me know. "They say they're sorry, Lorenzo," Mike tells me. "I wish I had better news."

Back then, I was more like number twenty-one rather than number one on the list of people to call. It becomes a harsh reminder of how temporary things are and of the cold realities of the business. It can be harsh. It can be cruel. It is not all fun and games. When you are twenty-one years old and you enjoy a certain level of success, it does not hit you as hard as when you are thirty or forty after working nonstop, bouncing from one show to another. Overall, I learn a very valuable lesson about the ups and downs of the trade—something my father himself often preaches to me. The business is very transitory, and if you take things like that personally, you are in big trouble.

My change in attitude is largely the result of my study of Tae Kwon Do that same year. By acquiring skills of speed, power, and coordination under the instruction of oriental grand master Jun Chong, I become more self-confident while overcoming my fears. The workouts do more than teach me deadly moves and self-defense. I also learn the importance of preparation and mind control. From torso-twisting leaps to power-controlled thrusts of martial arts, I reshape and whittle my body down to a lean 175 pounds, unburdened by even an ounce of flab. After going to the dojo to study for an hour and a half, my focus and thinking become clearer and sharper as well.

Because of my athletic build, producers, fortunately, keep casting me mostly in sports-oriented roles, and I have little difficulty filling them. I never worry too much about repeating myself by doing such roles as long as the characters I play have an underlying sensibility. Producers typecast my father as a Latin lover for twenty years, and he did well for himself and made a lot of money. I am perceptive enough to understand that my success depends on what roles the public will accept.

In 1980, between accepting roles in two features, *The All-Americans* (in which I play a sensitive jock football star) and *Promises in the Dark*, I sign on for a costarring role with the young and beautiful Linda Hamilton (later of *The Terminator* movie fame) in a second television series, CBS's *Secrets of Midland Heights*. It is a well-paying gig for a small role; I play a boy-next-door football jock. Unlike my first series, I stay hopeful that this one will finally boost me to a level of stardom I have only dreamed about.

My mother, Arlene Dahl, and Dad pose for the camera after marrying in a Las Vegas chapel in 1954. *Courtesy: Lorenzo Lamas Private Collection.*

Baptized, at almost three months old, into the Church of Religious Science in Hollywood in 1958. On hand are Dad and Mom, my godmother, Laura Mako (far left), and my godfather, architect William Periera (far right); and (in the background) Dr. Ernest Holmes, the church's founder, and Dr. William Hornaday, who officiated the ceremony. *Courtesy: Lorenzo Lamas Private Collection.*

With my father and mother in this May 1960 photo that accompanied the wire story that reported their marriage was "succeeding," only for them to divorce shortly thereafter. *Courtesy: Lorenzo Lamas Private Collection.*

Dad waterskiing with Esther Williams (whom he later married after divorcing my mother) in a scene from her 1960 hour-long NBC special, *Esther Williams at Cypress Gardens*, watched by more than half of all television sets in use in the United States during its premiere. *Courtesy: Lorenzo Lamas Private Collection.*

"The Two Guys" together for the first time in 1962 at Ostia Beach in Italy since my parents' divorce two years earlier. *Courtesy: Lorenzo Lamas Private Collection.*

At age four, sitting on the ridge of the black leather top to my father's Alfa Romeo convertible in a photo taken by him. *Courtesy: Lorenzo Lamas Private Collection.*

At the airport in Italy with Dad before my sad flight back home to the United States. *Courtesy: Lorenzo Lamas Private Collection.*

Dad gives me tips on picking up girls at my fifth birthday party at Lola Leighter's estate in Brentwood in 1963. *Courtesy: Lorenzo Lamas Private Collection. © Globe Photos, Inc.*

My first professional photograph, at age six, by famous glamour photographer John Engstead.
Courtesy: Lorenzo Lamas Private Collection.

Sharing with Dad our love for the sea on Jonathan Goldsmith's boat off the coast of Marina del Rey in 1966. *Courtesy: Lorenzo Lamas Private Collection.*

May 1966: On the passenger liner *France*, with Mom and my sister, Carole, bound for Europe to spend three months at the chateau of my mother's fourth husband, Alexis Lichine. *Courtesy: Lorenzo Lamas Private Collection.*

Who are you calling "chunky"? Well, I was before Mother shipped me out and shaped me up two years later. From my eleventh birthday party in 1969 dressed as Aquarius. (Mom had all the kids she invited dress as their Zodiac signs.) *Courtesy: Lorenzo Lamas Private Collection.*

From my first film appearance with Dad— as "uncredited Indian boy"—in the 1969 20th Century Fox western *100 Rifles*, after my father cajoles the director into putting me in costume and in the movie on the spot. *Courtesy: Lorenzo Lamas Private Collection.*

Attending with Dad and Esther the 1972 Los Angeles premiere of the movie *The New Centurions*. *Courtesy: Lorenzo Lamas Private Collection.*

"Atten-hut!" Graduating in June 1975 as a lieutenant after getting my act together as a cadet at the Admiral Farragut Academy after Mother sent me there to straighten me out. *Courtesy: Lorenzo Lamas Private Collection.*

Escorting my mother to the 49th Annual Academy Awards in March 1977, my introduction into the world of Hollywood glamour and exclusivity. *Courtesy: Lorenzo Lamas Private Collection. © Globe Photos, Inc.*

On the Warner Bros. studios back lot with Dad, wearing a fan-made T-shirt bearing my nickname as a child and the shortest shorts to attract girls, in front of his Rolls-Royce Shadow between takes of his costarring in the comedy feature *The Cheap Detective. Courtesy: Lorenzo Lamas Private Collection.*

With Dad and Esther going to a special event in 1979. I loved wearing turtlenecks then, lots of them. *Courtesy: Lorenzo Lamas Private Collection. © Globe Photos, Inc.*

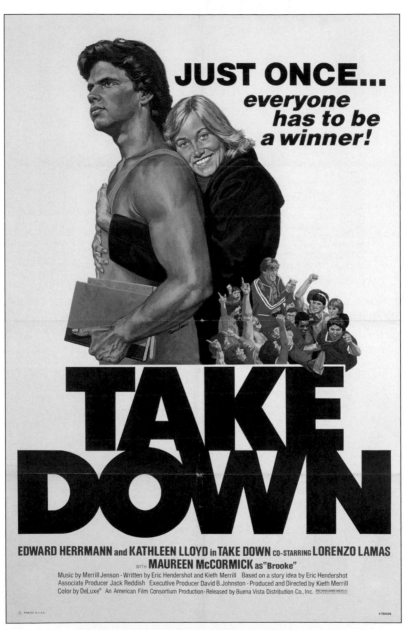

My first starring movie, *Take Down* (1979), with costar Maureen McCormick (of TV's *Brady Bunch* fame) that landed me my first television series, *California Fever* (1979). *Courtesy: Lorenzo Lamas Private Collection. © American Film Consortium, Inc.*

As a devilish ladies'-man surfer (center) with my fellow cast members (left to right)—Jimmy McNichol, Michelle Tobin, and Marc McClure—from my first starring television series, *California Fever* (1979–80), on which I learned a hard lesson about the realities of the business. *Courtesy: Lorenzo Lamas Private Collection.*

Now tell me, what does Travolta have over me? With my first Harley-Davidson chopper I built with my friend Mike Liakos in 1979. *Courtesy: Lorenzo Lamas Private Collection.*

In 1981, at Studio 54 in New York for my twenty-third birthday with my mother, Arlene, and my first wife, Victoria, who, unfortunately, mixed like oil and water with my father. *Courtesy: Lorenzo Lamas Private Collection.*

With the matriarch of the Channing family and my maternal guide on earth after my father's death, screen legend Jane Wyman, in front of the famous vineyards in Napa Valley as seen on the hugely successful CBS series *Falcon Crest. Courtesy: Lorenzo Lamas Private Collection.* © *Lorimar Television.*

With the cast of *Falcon Crest*: (front, seated) Jane Wyman; (first row, left to right) Robert Foxworth, Jamie Rose, Ana Alicia, Susan Sullivan, and Chao-Li Li; (second row) William R. Moses, Abby Dalton, me, and Margaret Ladd; and (back row) Mel Ferrer, Laura Johnson, and David Selby. *Courtesy: Lorenzo Lamas Private Collection.* © *Lorimar Television.*

Like old times for Dad, reunited with my costar Jane Wyman on the set of *Falcon Crest* to direct the episode "For the Love of Money" in one of the last photos taken of us together before his death in 1982. *Courtesy: Lorenzo Lamas Private Collection*

"I'm on top of the world, Ma!" On my return visit to New York in 1983 as part of a whirlwind publicity junket for *Falcon Crest. Courtesy: Lorenzo Lamas Private Collection.*

With my second wife, Michele, and our baby son, A.J., after his birth in December 1983. *Courtesy: Lorenzo Lamas Private Collection.*

With the legendary Gina Lollobrigida when the producers of *Falcon Crest* tried developing a younger man–older woman romance between our characters, including my giving her an on-screen kiss, which I flatly rejected. She acted icily distant toward me after that as a result. *Courtesy: Lorenzo Lamas Private Collection. © Lorimar Television.*

With Patty Kotero (better known as Apollonia) in a romantic dip in the pool in an episode of *Falcon Crest* in 1985, two years after having a real-life romance together in Del Mar where we spent little time seeing any actual horse racing. *Courtesy: Lorenzo Lamas Private Collection. © Lorimar Television.*

Celebrating my first major victory in the celebrity division of the Long Beach Grand Prix in 1985, months before my horrific race car crash at Riverside International Speedway. I was fortunate to survive. *Courtesy: Lorenzo Lamas Private Collection.*

My relationships with women after my first two ex-wives became like that of my on-screen alter ego, Lance Cumson, one of entrapment and wondering whether the baby was mine. *Courtesy: Lorenzo Lamas Private Collection. © Lorimar Television.*

On the set of *Falcon Crest* in 1987 with my costar and ex-fiancée Robin Greer, who made me realize after our breakup that I had a little more of Fernando in me than I realized. *Courtesy: Lorenzo Lamas Private Collection.*

Demonstrating a high kick after black belting in karate in 1989. *Courtesy: Lorenzo Lamas Private Collection.*

In 1989, making my marriage to Kathleen Kinmont official during a formal wedding ceremony at Lakeside Country Club in Burbank, California. *Courtesy: Lorenzo Lamas Private Collection. © Globe Photos, Inc.*

The hunk-on-a-hog look responsible for my biggest individual starring success on television for five seasons, as the motorcycle-riding bounty hunter Reno Raines in *Renegade. Courtesy: Lorenzo Lamas Private Collection. © Cannell Entertainment.*

With Kathleen, my son A.J., and my daughter Shayne, in 1993. *Courtesy: Lorenzo Lamas Private Collection.*

With costars my third wife, Kathleen Kinmont, and my dear friend and brother-in-arms, Branscombe Richmond, in a cast photo for *Renegade. Courtesy: Lorenzo Lamas Private Collection. © Cannell Entertainment.*

Heading out on assignment on the bike that chicks loved in a scene from *Renegade. Courtesy: Lorenzo Lamas Private Collection. © Cannell Entertainment.*

In 1994, directing my first episode of *Renegade*, "Sheriff Reno," with my former *Falcon Crest* costar Ana Alicia. *Courtesy: Lorenzo Lamas Private Collection.*

In April 1996, walking down the aisle with my fourth wife, former *Playboy* model Shauna Sand. *Courtesy: Lorenzo Lamas Private Collection. © Globe Photos, Inc.*

As the pilot–undercover agent Rio Arnett from my sixth starring television series, *Air America*, in 1998. *Courtesy: Lorenzo Lamas Private Collection. © Fremantle Corporation.*

After getting my pilot's license, I bought my own planes to fly wherever I wanted, including a Piper Mirage I flew from Los Angeles to Vancouver to film my seventh starring series, *The Immortal. Courtesy: Lorenzo Lamas Private Collection.*

Out on the town with my fourth wife, former *Playboy* Playmate Shauna Sand, and our three daughters, Alexandra, Victoria, and Isabella. *Courtesy: Lorenzo Lamas Private Collection.*

As Hector Ramirez from my four-season run as a regular, beginning in 2004, on the popular daytime soap *The Bold and the Beautiful. Courtesy: Lorenzo Lamas Private Collection.*

At home with Alexandra, Victoria, and Isabella. *Courtesy: Lorenzo Lamas Private Collection.*

At the cast reunion for the *Grease* Rockin' Rydell DVD Launch Event in September 2006. *Courtesy: Lorenzo Lamas Private Collection.*

Playing the role of the king, with Broadway actress Rachel deBenedet as Anna, in a theater production of *The King and I* at the Ogunquit Playhouse in Maine in 2007. *Courtesy: Lorenzo Lamas Private Collection/Ogunquit Playhouse.*

In August 2008, celebrating Mom's eightieth birthday at Swifty's Restaurant with (left to right) her husband, Marc Rosen, my brother Stephen, and my sister Carole. *Courtesy: Lorenzo Lamas Private Collection.*

With Shayne, A.J., my ex-wife Michele, and Shayne and A.J.'s half sister, Dakota Pike, in a publicity photo for the short-lived reality series for E! *Leave it to Lamas* in 2009. *Courtesy: Lorenzo Lamas Private Collection/E! Entertainment.*

Dancing the salsa with my partner Milagros Michael on Argentina's television version of *Dancing With the Stars* in May 2010. *Courtesy: Lorenzo Lamas Private Collection.*

In May 2011, sealing our marriage with a kiss, with my lovely wife, Shawna, at our wedding off the coast of Cabo San Lucas, Mexico. *Courtesy: Lorenzo Lamas Private Collection.*

At the Paley Center for Media's *Falcon Crest* thirtieth anniversary reunion in October 2010: (back row) Me with creator Earl Hamner and David Selby; (front row) Jamie Rose, Susan Sullivan, Margaret Ladd, Ana Alicia, Abby Dalton, and Robert Foxworth. *Courtesy: Lorenzo Lamas Private Collection.*

Back to my first love, motorcycles (or as my dad called them, "murdercycles"), as a custom bike builder of my own brand of cycles, Lorenzo Cycles; pictured with the Patriot FXR model. *Courtesy: Lorenzo Lamas Private Collection.*

With Shawna and my daughters Victoria, Isabella, and Alexandra on the episode of ABC's *Celebrity Wife Swap* in 2013. *Courtesy: Lorenzo Lamas Private Collection/ABC.*

With Chase Rogan in a scene from the fake reality series *The Joe Schmo Show* for SPIKE television in 2013. *Courtesy: Lorenzo Lamas Private Collection/SPIKE.*

On the red carpet with Shawna, Isabella, Victoria, and Alexandra at the premiere of Disney's *Planes* in August 2013. *Courtesy: Lorenzo Lamas Private Collection*

SIX

Mixing Oil with Water and the Perfect Vintage

ROM THE TIME of my breakout role in *Grease*, studio publicists began packaging and selling me as this tall, dark-haired playboy with smoldering good looks, an easy smile, and rippling muscles, a man who has all these girls on a string and a series of broken hearts a mile long. It made me very uncomfortable, as I was much less the playboy than they made me out to be. Besides, playboys are heartbreakers, and I am not like that. Heartbreak is never any fun, especially when a woman's heart is broken. I know this much: I hoped to find that special someone and shower her with lots of love and attention rather than spend my time running from girl to girl and not knowing any of them.

At the age of twenty-two, I am still learning who I am. Admittedly, I do not have the same personality and personal polish as I would later in my peak acting years, but I have a good idea then of the person I think I am. It is then, as I'm coming into my own, that I lay my eyes on a woman who leaves me breathless: Victoria Weston.

In the fall of 1980, I am coming back home from the beach on my new Honda 900 street bike. I had acquired it in trade for my CBX; I also own another bike, a big twin Harley Super Glide. As I am about to turn into the driveway, this stunning, blue-eyed, thick wavy-haired blonde in a tight tank top and satin shorts zooms past me on roller skates. I turn to look as she whirls by me. Our eyes find each other and I just clamp on the brakes. The look of this woman leaves me spellbound. Making a small turn, she skates to a stop and looks at me with her alluring ocean-blue eyes. I throw the bike into a fancy skid, turn around, and pull alongside her.

"Hi," I blurt out. "Do you live around here?"

"Yeah, I'm in Carole King's house down the street," she says.

"Cool," I tell her. "Maybe I'll see you sometime."

"Probably will," she says with a smile, "we're neighbors."

From the moment our eyes meet, I feel this connection to Victoria. In my heart, I know I am going to see more of her. Victoria smiles and skates off as I park my motorcycle. Later that day, I walk over to Carole King's house—a beautiful two-story, six-bedroom Tudor-style home with a large swimming pool in back. I knock on the door. Victoria answers. She stands there, stunned. "What a surprise!"

I laugh. "I said I'd be over."

Victoria welcomes me inside. We engage in some small talk and hang out. She tells me all about herself. How she met Carole in Telluride, Colorado, and lived and toured with her. Then how she married a musician and they had a son, Shile, and now at thirty-four years of age she is divorced. Victoria's beauty defies her age. Twelve years older than me, she looks much younger; I never would have guessed her age if she had not offered it.

After the visit, we start seeing each other. Victoria comes down to the house with her son. He loves playing there, especially climbing up the ladder to the loft of my A-frame like it's a big tree house. Victoria and I really start to bond. I hang out at her place, too, often in the pool. We laugh and have a great time.

During a visit with my father, he wants to know all about Victoria. I tell him, "Well, she's a model from New York."

I explain how Richard Avedon, the famous fashion photographer, took pictures of her and how she had a successful modeling career in New York before giving it up to move to Telluride and live a commune lifestyle with Carole King and her band mates for about a year. Victoria is very much a flower child of the 1960s; she's into the whole astrology and *I Ching* thing. My mom has been into astrology my whole life, but I have never taken it too seriously. Yet I never hold it against anyone who does. And Victoria is very much into it.

After I mention Victoria's commune lifestyle past, alarms immediately go off in my father's well-coiffed head. "This is going to be a woman with an opinion!" he says, thrusting his finger into the air to make his point.

Right away, Dad has a sneaking suspicion Victoria is not the right person for me. He is always this very realistic, highly grounded person—something he senses Victoria is not. She is very spiritual, very much in the moment. Because my dad has this old-world view where a woman's place is at home taking care of the man, the last thing he wants for me is to have a woman who considers herself my equal. He never minds a woman being independent and paid the same amount of money for the same job a man does, but "their real job is to be at home like Esther is." Esther quit her career to be my father's wife. He loves that she did so and wants the same for me.

Sure enough, when I bring Victoria to the house for dinner to introduce her to Dad and Esther, it's a disaster. Victoria and my father mix like oil and water. Later, my dad and I actually have words over his treatment of her. But that evening, I put up with his third-degree examination of her and his usual flair for theatrics.

Knowing how much older she is than me, he frankly asks her, "What do you do?" and "How do you support yourself?"

"Well, you know," she answers, "I do a little painting and I take pictures."

"Oh, I see, I see," says Father. "Are there any places where we can see your paintings? Are your pictures published anywhere?"

"Oh, no," Victoria confesses. "I kind of do it for myself."

More alarms go off. I know what my father is thinking: Here is a woman who is attaching herself to a young kid who is on a network television series; she'll use him to pay her bills. That is the way my dad thinks.

"I see," he says. "Do you have any long-term goals?"

"Yes, I want to direct."

Dad is a very good actor but I can see it in his eyes: This woman lives like a vagabond, formerly in a commune doing God knows

what, paints a little, takes pictures, and with no experience whatsoever, she wants to direct!

"Wonderful, you want to direct. What exactly would you like to
direct?"

"Well, I love television but I would do motion pictures."

"Marvelous." Now Dad is really patronizing her. "Have you ever
trained? Have you ever studied anything like technique or been inside an editing room?"

"Oh, no, I haven't."

The incredulous look on Dad's face speaks volumes. I'm hoping
dinner will end *soon* so I can take Victoria home, but he's just warm-
ing up.

"Well, that's interesting about your goals, but you have no training to do the work," he says. "I've directed television for twenty years
now and I have to tell you, Victoria, it's not as easy as you think."

Dad's Spanish Inquisition wears thin. Victoria, reaching her limit,
rises to her feet. She thanks Esther for "a wonderful dinner" and in
one fell swoop asks me to escort her home. The happiest person in
the room is my father, who just cannot—will not—warm up to her.
From then on, I find myself in the middle of a battle royal between
the two people I love the most. I try everything I can to make things
work and to please everyone.

Another member of Victoria's family I should mention is Saluki,
her beautiful long-haired, thin Egyptian greyhound. Saluki is
quiet, calm, affectionate, and very sociable, especially compared
to my Doberman, Nails, who is naturally aggressive, impetuous,
and dedicated to one person—me. While Victoria and I are dating, we make every effort to include the dogs as part of the family.
I first set eyes on Nails in 1979 at my friend Eddie's house in Simi
Valley, the place where Mike and I got parts to build my Harley-
Davidson chopper. Eddie has something like $100,000 worth of
parts in his garage.

Eddie has two male Dobermans, Sam and Nails, that he chains up
by the garage to keep intruders from stealing parts. They viciously
bark and bare their teeth anytime anyone comes remotely close. It
is clear they do not like each other, and it is only a matter of time
before one of them kills the other. Feeling sorry for them, one day I

ask Eddie, "Look, you only need one Dobie to protect your backyard. Just get a longer chain. Can I have one of your Dobies? I have a house now and have room."

"Take Nails," he says.

I take Nails. In a short time, he becomes my constant companion. I take the big guy everywhere with me, to work, even into my dressing room. I just love that dog. Dad loves him, too. Nails is everything Dad loves in a dog—one hundred pounds of pure masculinity and brute strength. Anytime I call to go over to the house, without hesitation, Dad says, "Bring Nails."

Victoria and I bring Saluki and Nails along in the Suburban every time we go to the beach so we can let them run. Saluki is so fast there is no way Nails can ever keep up with her. It is so much fun to watch them run.

In January 1981, after it flounders in the ratings, CBS cancels *Secrets of Midland Heights* after only eight episodes. The show fails on the same basis as *California Fever*: an unrealistic depiction of how teens live. Also, it has so many characters at the beginning of each episode, if you miss one, you lose any idea of what the show is about. Not long after CBS dumps us, my agent, Mike Rosen, calls.

"Lorenzo," he says, "I've got a role I think you're perfect for."

Hearing that twice before, with two failed series to show for it, I am admittedly skeptical. "What is it?" I ask, less than enthusiastically.

"It's for a pilot for a new series that's in development," he says. "It's called *The Vintage Years*."

Great, I'm thinking, another pilot. Been there, done that. "What's the job?"

"Well," he says, pausing to look over his notes. "It's a wealthy grandson of a matriarch who runs a vineyard in Napa Valley."

Now, what Mike is talking about is something I like hearing. I know something about vineyards after spending summers in my youth in Bordeaux, and also about what it is like being a wealthy grandson living a life of privilege. I can channel some of that. I can channel some of those summers.

"Sounds good, Mike," I tell him. "I'll go and read for it."

Mike arranges everything. I know little about this new series other than that Earl Hamner (of TV's *The Waltons* fame) is executive producing this for Lorimar. I've been asked to read for the part because Earl remembers me from my previous television work. The show is to have a Gothic look, with the vineyard as a principality run by a tough-as-nails, manipulative baroness who's the matriarch of a traditional Italian family. To add a little spice, Earl wants an actor to play a young dark prince, Lance Cumson, a dashing figure akin to something out of a romantic novel, and a young fair prince, Cole Gioberti, who is like Italian royalty. I am Earl's choice from the very beginning to play the dark prince.

But I am a little reluctant to try out for and maybe play such a mean character. The first time I read the script, I think to myself that this guy is strictly an S.O.B. with no redeeming qualities whatsoever.

When I show the script to Victoria, she says, "Lorenzo, an opportunity like this does not come along that often."

Re-reading the script, I realize that even though my character is evil, he is not one-dimensional. I decide to do it.

After starring in two canceled television series, I dearly hope this time will be different. I read for the part, unaware how much Earl really wants me. At the audition, I read for Lance opposite another actor who reads for Cole: a good-looking actor, early twenties, wispy blond hair, warm inviting smile: Billy R. Moses.

I meet Billy for the first time at casting. They pair up four other sets of Lances and Coles for the same audition. Billy and I decide to memorize our scenes together. We are not going to have the script pages in our hands when we audition. For twenty minutes straight, we work on it. Sometimes actors are selfish and will not work with the other actor; they'd rather do it on their own. Then if they get the job, they can say they did it all by themselves. For some reason that day, Billy and I are simpatico. We fast become friends and work together as a team.

The scene we do—actual dialogue from the pilot script—is very combative and very heated. It involves the mean family's grandson (me) and the good family's grandson (Billy) giving each other shit over which one will inherit the vineyards someday.

"I'm getting the vineyards."

"No, you're not going to get the vineyards. We're going to get the vineyards."

"Well, you can't do this."

"Well, yes, I can."

The anger and tension between us is palpable. The casting people in the room like something else about us as well. They see two guys who could be friends if there were not so much history between them. In fact, they probably could be best friends. That's how we come across in doing the scene, without even thinking about it.

After the reading, they call us back to read the same scene in front of CBS executives. Beforehand, Billy and I make a pact with each other.

"We're going to do this, Lorenzo," Billy says.

"Yep, it's you and me, brother, all the way. Let's get this."

We walk in and read the scene for the network mucky-mucks. We just kill it. We nail the scene. Earl hires us both. Later, Earl tells me why: "Beneath that sweet face of yours I sense a skein of downright meanness, which is exactly the quality we want for the character."

In March and April of 1981, we shoot the pilot for *The Vintage Years* in beautiful Napa Valley. Before production commences, the producers recast two of the roles: Robert Foxworth replaces Clu Gulager, and Susan Sullivan takes over for Samantha Eggar.

Napa is gorgeous any time of the year, except March. During February, March, and the first half of April is typically when Napa gets its heaviest rain of the season, with daytime highs in the fifties and nighttime lows plummeting into the forties. The day we start filming, it is just pouring outside. And because it's the off-season, not a single grape is on a single vine anywhere. The fall is harvest season, when Napa Valley is at its zenith with beautiful foliage colors in brilliant shades of green and gold. Consequently, Lorimar trucks in seven- to eight-hundred pounds of fake grapes to dress the set. You cannot have a show set on a spectacular vineyard without grapes!

We all stay at the Holiday Inn on Route 9. It is about twenty minutes from Spring Mountain, the working winery where we film the pilot and the series. All along Route 9 are spectacular views of the vineyard and the vines that lay dormant. I'll never forget Susan, Robert, Billy, Margaret Ladd (who played Emma), and me—everyone except for Jane Wyman, who has a private driver—heading down Route 9 in this nine-passenger van to the winery the first day of filming. We are talking about the hotel, what we did the night before (catching a band playing at the Holiday Inn), what time lunch is—everything but the show—when Margaret suddenly pipes up from the back of the van: "Anybody know what all these trees are?"

Susan speaks up. "Margaret, those are called 'vineyards.' We're doing a show about them."

Everybody cracks up. Margaret, bless her heart, is the sweetest, dearest person you will ever meet. Just like the character she played, she has something otherworldly about her. We all got a kick out of her because she would say the most innocently entertaining things all the time.

Personally speaking, my relationship with Victoria continues to move forward. In fact, we become very serious, despite my father's disapproval. In the spring of 1981, I film "Julie's Tycoon," a two-part episode for ABC's top-rated fantasy series *The Love Boat* on a cruise to the Greek islands. I play a wealthy entrepreneur; the episode is for the series's 1982–83 season. Victoria accompanies me on the trip. We have a wonderful time enjoying magnificent ports of call and the crystal-clear, blue-watered coast and beaches. We're shooting the episode off the island of Mykonos and have an overnight stay there. Taking advantage of it, I go bar hopping with the show's camera operator, drinking ouzo from one place to the next. Mykonos is an island that embraces the alternative lifestyle. Back then, more so than ever, it seems every flamboyant person is hiding out there, partying and celebrating their lifestyle without inhibition.

We end up in a bar that has a jewelry store out front, specializing in reduced-cost silver jewelry. Having consumed probably a fifth of ouzo at this point, I am already seeing double. We walk into the place and my buddy wants to get his ear pierced. A discussion ensues about which ear to pierce. One side signifies you are homosexual, the other that you are straight. To make sure we get it right, we decide not to ask anybody around us. They might tell us the wrong ear! Somebody in the bar who is straight suddenly shouts, "The left side is straight, the right side is…"

Today, the issue would not matter as much but decades ago, it did. Back then, I worried about sending the wrong signals.

Drunk enough, I get my ear pierced, too. But we are so plastered afterward that we have trouble finding our way back to the dock. We need to get back to the cruise ship before it shoves off at 5:00 A.M. We get to the dock with minutes to spare, but none of the little dinghies you can charter that take passengers to the ship are there. They all have already set out with passengers for the ship. Even as drunk as I am, I know we are in *big* trouble.

Luckily, I find a grizzled old fisherman who is getting ready to cast off. He has a little dinghy with an outboard motor. Climbing aboard, I hand him a few drachmas. "Can you take us to our cruise ship?"

"Yes," he says. Not yet seated, the man starts motoring out of the harbor.

"Wait a second," I holler at him. "Do you know where you're going? There are three cruise ships out there."

The man gives me a look. "Aw, there's *one* cruise ship."

No more ouzos for me; I'm seeing three.

The waves are choppy, the ride even choppier as we chug across. The ouzos I drank are taking their toll. I am not only seeing triple, but I swear a bevy of beautiful mermaids just waved at me.

We reach the cruise ship as the last call goes out for passengers to board. Neither of us is in any condition to run, walk, or stand. Somehow, my buddy and I make it back on the ship, but not before I make a promise to myself: next time, one less ouzo.

The next day, I report to makeup, and the producers get wind of my ear-piercing adventure. Let's just say they are not very happy with me. They are upset for an obvious reason: I pierced my ear but I still have scenes to film. They discuss it with the director and decide to film me only from the right side of my face for the balance of the episode. Fortunately, the producers of *The Love Boat* never hold the incident against me. They call me back for a third appearance—four years later!

After completing the pilot for *The Vintage Years*, CBS never airs it. I start thinking, "Here we go again."

One day, Lee Rich, then the head of Lorimar, says to Earl, "The title 'The Vintage Years' makes me think it's a show about old people." Earl subsequently renames the show to something more fitting, *Falcon Crest*, after the fictional vineyard in the pilot. The series, despite the finished pilot, is also retooled. In the original, Jane Wyman has snow-white hair. Her character, as one critic writes, is also "a rather ancient crone who ruled the family vineyard with a furious frown." Now, besides changing her hair color to auburn brown, producers glamorize her character with a love life, while keeping her as a powerful and wealthy woman with whom to reckon. Without airing the pilot, CBS picks up the series for a full twenty-two episodes right out of the gate. Back then, networks gave an order for twenty-two with an option for four or six more. We make twenty-eight episodes altogether that first season.

Meanwhile, the situation between Dad and Victoria does not change. Every time we go to Dad and Esther's for dinner, Victoria comes home in tears and gives me an earful. "Your dad is a male chauvinist. He has no respect for women. Esther's a doormat." Blah-blah-blah-blah.

I always end up defending my father. "Well, if you would try and understand where he is coming from; he is not a bad guy." Blah-blah-blah-blah.

Then anytime I see Dad and Esther, they give it right back to me. "Victoria is using you. You have no business being with her."

Dad reminds me every time, "She's twelve years older than you. Have an affair but don't get married."

So what do I do? I marry Victoria. In October 1981, we drive up to the quaint coastal town of Carmel and are married in a little chapel in Big Sur. Victoria, now thirty-five, never wanted to marry but I push her into it. In hindsight, knowing how much my father disapproved of her, she was right. I just did not see it back then.

When I share the news with him after, Dad is very disappointed. "I can't believe you married *that* girl."

"Dad, I love her," I proclaim. "I don't think I could love anybody more."

In my father's case, there is no bridging the divide. "Give it time," he says, arching his eyebrows.

In retrospect, I should have listened. I was too much in love and committed to Victoria and her son, Shile, to see it.

Dad feels slighted as a result. Because I went against his wishes, he and Esther stop inviting us to dinner. Suddenly, he is not talking to me because of "her." The divide between us only widens. A rift develops in our relationship I am unsure will ever mend.

To make matters worse, I give Nails away after Victoria grows increasingly concerned that he is going to attack Saluki or worse. In confined spaces, Nails and Saluki do not get along. After growing up always chained, even in his bed, at Eddie's house, Nails definitely does not want Saluki to bother him. But Saluki wants Nails as a friend. She goes over, sniffs him, and every time, Nails snaps at her. This happens over and over. I never think it is an issue, but Victoria does.

Finally, one of them has to go—Saluki or Nails. I get chills thinking of giving Nails away, but because Victoria has had Saluki longer, in fairness, I know Nails is the one to go. I love Victoria and do not want to break up over that. I find a home for Nails. The following day, I go to Dad's house. The first thing he asks is, "Where's Nails?"

I tell him, "I gave Nails away."

"Oh, my God!" The look on Dad's face is as if I gave him the worst possible news, like there'd been a death in the family. "You gave away the dog because of that skinny bitch you are married to?"

"Dad, please don't. Don't talk about Victoria like that."

Dad becomes incensed. "I am so disgusted with you. I am so disgusted how you let that woman treat you."

"Dad," I explain, "she does not control me. Nails was going to kill her dog."

"That would be a good thing."

"That wouldn't be a good thing, Dad. She has had her dog for like five years."

Dad raises his voice to the point he is shouting at me. "That's the way it is going to be? She says, 'Jump,' and you say, 'How high?'"

"Geez, Dad, it's not like that."

I feel terrible about it. The incident with Nails only adds to the perception my father has that Victoria is wrong for me. I wish I could convince him otherwise. I feel terrible about the whole situation. No matter how I explain things, I will never win that argument with him. In my father's mind, the die has been cast and there is no bringing it back, regardless of how much I try.

FALCON CREST PREMIERES in early December 1981, landing in sixth place in the weekly Nielsen ratings. It becomes the highest-rated new program of the season. It consistently ranks in the top fifteen and becomes one of the most-watched prime-time soaps of the decade. It airs Friday night right after *Dallas*, and the two shows become a powerful one-two punch, watched by millions of households each week. They overwhelm the competition and become lucrative enterprises for CBS.

Enjoying the kind of meteoric rise to fame and fortune few actors realize, suddenly I am recognized the world over, everywhere I go. At the local supermarket, beautiful women and adoring fans mob me to sign my pictures in the latest tabloids or pose for photos with them. It is all great fun. I never want it to stop.

With the tumult in my marriage and personal life, *Falcon Crest* becomes my salvation. I really grow as an actor while making the series. I am happy for the steady work and, most of all, for the chance to work with actress Jane Wyman.

Jane's friendship with my father goes back many years, including the day I was born. Next to my parents, she is the most influential person in my young career. Playing this ruthless baroness on-screen, she is very maternal around me and willingly shares her craft with me. Thanks to her, I learn how to work in front of the camera, and even if I make many mistakes, I always learn from them.

I'm a young actor, still learning, still struggling with pages of dialogue, still trying to make an impact. One day on the set Jane walks over to me, flashes that grandmotherly smile of hers, and says, "You're really making too much out of it. It is just words on a page. Just know the words and say them."

Simple but profound. I owe so much to Jane for the impact she has on me.

Jane had not been the first choice to play Angela Channing. The producers originally want four-time Academy Award–nominated actress Barbara Stanwyck, best known to television audiences as the matriarch in the western series *The Big Valley*. Then in her early seventies, Barbara looked at the pilot script and figured that if she was on a weekly television series, she would not have a life. She told the producers, "I just can't do this."

They offered the role next to Jane, and she said, "Well, thank you very much, I will."

Divorced four times, Jane, then single, is living in a beautiful condominium on Ocean Park in Santa Monica and is ready to take on the grind of doing a weekly television series. She's nine years younger than Stanwyck, and it becomes the role of a lifetime for her. She has done the producers a huge favor, of course. I cannot imagine *Falcon Crest* being successful without her.

Jane never comes across like a spoiled diva on the set. Believe me, if anybody has the right to be one, she does. She never assumes a sense of privilege because of who she is and what she's done. She uses the same size trailer we all use—a caravan of them, called "honey wagons," hooked together on a diesel truck, seven or more depending on the size of the motor of the truck that is pulling them.

Jane sets the tone for the rest for us. She never bullshits anyone. She has an incredible work ethic and, like clockwork, she's always on time, always prepared, happy to be there, ready to rehearse every single day. She also has an incredible affable quality about her. As we sit and wait around for the production crew to light or prep a scene, Jane always hangs close with us, her Nilla Wafers and Vantage cigarettes on a little table next to her. When we break for lunch, she never bails on us to go to a local restaurant or to her trailer dressing room. She eats right there on the set with the rest of us, at the same tables with the cast and crew and everybody else. All she eats are Nilla Wafers, and she smokes Vantage cigarettes all day. I swear she smokes more cigarettes than Vantage made. It is how she kept her svelte figure, I guess. I never see Jane eat food unless it is in a scene. Even then she takes only a small bite of salad.

During production, Jane never talks about anything but what we are shooting. Certain people learn very quickly not to bring up her second husband, former-actor-turned-president Ronald Reagan. If they do, she just gives them a withering look, like, Why don't you go crawl back where you came from? The subject is closed; she never mentions him.

Jane reminds me a lot of my father. She never speaks of her career, never rests on her laurels, and never takes personal, selfish credit for anything. She and my dad are both of the same mind-set. They were at the right place at the right time and took advantage of it.

From producers to television executives to visitors on the set, Jane, much like my father, defers every compliment given her. Always cordial and hospitable, she never gets too personal.

"Take a picture? Sure. Where do you want me?"

"You get the picture?"

"Can I sign that for you?"

Then move on.

Jane thinks of herself as one of the guys. A good poker player in her day, she loves playing with the crew every chance she gets. Bob Caramico, director of photography, and Michael Preece, our director, are two of her favorite poker pals.

That filming season, I hardly see Dad. It is horrible. I miss him so much. I cannot go to Dad and Esther's house with Victoria because they do not get along. On the other hand, if I have dinner with Dad and Esther without her, then I'm not being supportive of Victoria.

Finally, Dad agrees to meet me for lunch. Occasionally, we go to Carney's, the famous train-on-the-track restaurant on the Sunset Strip, and have hot dogs, or sometimes to Mirabelle. But our relationship is just not the same. We do not have that old comfort level. Victoria has become a wedge between us.

After a few months, we finally patch up our differences. Of course, I make the first move. I never wanted my marriage to Victoria to come between us. While having lunch with Dad, I remember saying, "Dad, I love Victoria and married her. In my heart, she is the woman for me."

Nibbling at his food, Dad pauses for a second and says, "Son, I understand your feelings and I hope you can respect mine."

"I do. I just wish you could accept Victoria the way I do."

Dad breaks into his familiar grin. "I cannot make that promise, but I will do this. I will always love you because you are my son."

Just as I did as a child, I simply nod. I know in my father's case that is the best I can expect.

The next six months, Dad and I spend quality time together, and I am able to mend my relationship with him. That's so important to me. We go to boxing matches together at the old Olympic Auditorium, something I stopped doing after marrying Victoria, and we sit with Dad's friend, fellow actor Robert Conrad, the star of my childhood

TV favorite, *The Wild Wild West*. It is like old times being with Dad. We laugh. We joke. We hug. We have the best times together.

One of the highlights that first season of *Falcon Crest* is working with Dad, who signs on to direct the episode "For the Love of Money," filmed in the winter of 1981 at CBS Studios, with some exteriors shot that summer in Napa. In demand these days, Dad directs fourteen hours for Lorimar that season, including such shows as *Flamingo Road* and *Falcon Crest*. Unlike the first time he directed me, I am more comfortable in my own skin this time around. As a director, my father knows what he wants and how to get it from us. On the set, I am just another actor and he lets me know when I do not get it right!

Before filming, Jane bends her hard-and-fast rule a little about talking about anything but the show in my father's presence. It is fun to see two industry giants like them chat and reminisce. The first day of rehearsal is like a family reunion as Jane tries to steal a little of Dad's thunder.

"You know, Fernando," Jane says in that whispery voice of hers, "I still have not forgiven you for walking out on me that night at NBC."

Without missing a beat, Dad breaks into his infectious grin and playfully responds, "Why, Jane, I have no idea what you mean. You must be talking about another actor."

They share a good laugh over it. Jane, of course, is talking about the night Dad ran out on her when I was born.

SEVEN

Twice the Heartbreak

ICTION HAS A WAY of mirroring reality. Such is the case in 1982 after CBS picks up *Falcon Crest* for a second season, and we hit our stride as a top 10–rated show. My character, Lance, becomes less of a one-dimensional figure, with more heart and human qualities, when he finds happiness after being stuck in a bad marriage. He was in a marriage of business and convenience rather than emotion and love. But then he falls in love with a new character, played by Maggie Cooper, after years of being on guard. In many ways, I fully identify with the direction my character is taking. My own marriage to Victoria, built on a faulty premise of its own, is on the verge of melting down due to a combination of things I never see coming.

Before the start of the second season, Dad calls me. He is busy prepping to do a new project to mark his television comeback. Producer Leonard Goldberg has signed him to play Robert Urich's pal Caesar Tortuga in *Gavilan*, a new action/adventure series set to debut on NBC that fall after the World Series. Caesar Tortuga is a charming, once-wealthy South American gourmet cook and bit of a con man who shares a house with Urich. Filming will be in exotic locales, including the Caribbean, and Dad plans to direct a few episodes as well as costar.

Dad is very excited about the opportunity. He loves the part. He likes Goldberg and Urich, whom he directed once before in an episode of *S.W.A.T.* He is hopeful his on-camera role translates into a boon for his career the same way *Fantasy Island* has for fellow Latin actor Ricardo Montalban. Thinking of it as a paid vacation, he says, "I'm doing this for fun and money."

For my father, working with Urich, who plays an ex-CIA agent who finds adventure and intrigue while working for an oceano-graphic institute, is like old times. They develop an immediate rap-port. Robert finds Dad a warm individual, one who makes everyone around him feel good. It is the happiest I remember my father being in a long time.

Filming is intense. Dad is on his feet all day long, working ten to fourteen hours a day for seven days, filming scenes for the pilot and four additional episodes. That summer, Dad phones me a couple of times while on location. He complains about back pain, which, he thinks, is the result of a swashbuckling sword-fighting sequence he filmed.

"I forget I am not a young kid," he says with a laugh. "I probably just pulled something."

Months before, I started seeing a terrific chiropractor in Beverly Hills. Victoria had introduced me to him so he could treat me for a neck injury related to my previous motorcycle accident and also from performing in karate tournaments since 1979. I recommend Dad see him when he returns to Los Angeles. By September, the pain is so se-vere in his lower back, Dad sets up an appointment. Dr. Fareed does a complete and thorough examination. Under the circumstances, my father is understandably worried.

"What's going on?" Dad asks.

Dr. Fareed is unable to determine the root cause. "We're left with no alternative but to send you to UCLA for some blood work."

Even though he has been playing macho guys in movies and in real life, Dad has a fear of going to the doctor. But if there is one doc-tor he trusts, it is Dr. Fareed. Dad goes to UCLA to have the blood test. In a few days, the results come back. What my father thinks is simply back pain is far worse: He has Stage 4 pancreatic cancer. Caught early, it is treatable with radiation. Unfortunately, his cancer is much too advanced. It is the harsh reality of how fragile life is— one day on top of the world, the next rock bottom.

One of the first calls Dad makes is to producer Leonard Goldberg to withdraw from *Gavilan*, ending plans for his much-anticipated television comeback. Patrick Macnee, best known for his role as the secret agent John Steed in the popular series *The Avengers*, takes Dad's place in the series, and the producers refilm all of his scenes with Macnee.

After his admission to UCLA Medical Center, Dad quickly goes downhill. It is heartbreaking to watch such a vigorous, physically active man, one so full of passion, simply waste away. My father was a two-pack-a-day smoker after marrying Mom until he suddenly quit cold turkey. He also gave up drinking. Never again does he give in to either temptation. Instead, he swims and plays tennis every day. He has been a picture of health.

Dad first changed his ways after Mom introduced him to Dr. William Hornaday, a leading minister of religious science and the clergyman who baptized me into the church. The last couple of years of their marriage, my parents became practitioners of religious science after attending a religious science school in New York with Dr. Ernest Homes, founder of the International Religious Science movement and author of the book *The Science of Mind*. Holmes's book is about combining the power of your mind with your belief in Jesus Christ to make a difference in your life and to help you visualize your successes. As practitioners, Mom and Dad gave pep talks and treated people based on the book's philosophy, guidelines, and doctrine.

Any free time I have, I visit Dad and help him any way I can. He has more bad days than good. It is tough to watch the man I worship— my father, my hero, my mentor, my everything—slip away a little each day.

Dad is always on my mind while I'm shooting interior scenes for *Falcon Crest* at Warner Bros. My *Falcon Crest* family rallies around me. Occasionally, Jane asks, "How are you holding up?"

Before rehearsals, Robert Foxworth puts his arm around me like a brother. "Hey, kid, we're pulling for him."

Ana Alicia, who plays my on-screen wife, Melissa, pulls me aside and tells me simply, "I love you. If you need anything, just call."

As most men do whenever there is an emotional crisis in their lives, I focus on my work. Acting becomes my release, my solace. It also offers some semblance of joy at a time when there is so little reason to be happy, knowing my father's time is fleeting and the inevitable is coming.

On the *Falcon Crest* set, in front of the cast and crew, I put on a good face as much as possible. I never let anyone know how painful this is for me. At times, I privately tear up just thinking of my father.

Before rehearsals, Jane, who will become like a surrogate parent after my father dies, comes up to me and asks, "Are you going to be seeing your father?"

I tell her, "I think he would want me to be *here*."

With a touch of emotion in her voice, Jane says, "I think you're right."

It is the way my father would have wanted it: for me to honor him through my work. Naturally, I do what I know he would expect.

Yet I visit my father as much as possible. One day, after doing something in Westwood, I drive to the hospital with Victoria. As she waits in the car, I run in to see him. I feel downcast afterward. Victoria is still in the car when I walk out of the hospital. As I hop in, I say to her, "I don't know, Victoria, this feels really weird to me. I don't know if Dad's going to ever make it out of the hospital. He really looks sick."

Victoria and Dad have that history, of course. Victoria, who always spoke negatively of him, suddenly says, "Well, if he dies, he'll finally be put out of his misery."

In a flash of anger, I take my hand from the steering wheel and slap her right across her face. "Don't you ever say that again!"

It is a coldhearted and shitty thing for Victoria to say, especially the way I am feeling at that moment. In no way does that justify my action, however. Every time I play that scene in my head, I realize now what she was saying that day she meant spiritually, and with no ill will toward my father and me. That my father is in pain, stuck in this world, and death would free him. But I didn't see it that way then; I didn't understand what she was saying. My father is dying. My heart is breaking. Then she goes and says that.

Until then, I had never touched a woman, or anyone, like that before. It is the first—and the last—time I do. Moments after, I know it is over between us. There is no going back to mend what is broken.

Horrified, Victoria sits there without uttering a word as I drive off. Back at the house, I start packing my suitcase. I announce to her, "I'm done. I'm out of here."

"Don't leave me, Lorenzo," Victoria says, crying. "I'm sorry. I didn't mean it the way you took it."

"I don't believe you," I counter. In my mind, our marriage is over. Consciously I know I have to end this relationship to salvage what relationship I have with Dad.

I move into the Holiday Inn on Sunset Boulevard and see Dad every day. During my visits, he could still talk. The last time I see him I tell him that Victoria and I are divorcing.

"I'm sorry to hear that," he says, weakly. "Soñ, as I have said before, you must be very, very careful where you place your heart. Make sure that your heart is taken care of."

"I was just following my instinct," I explain.

"You know how I feel about Victoria," he says.

"Yeah," I say, "but I wanted you to know she meant no harm. That she really loved me."

Even as death stares him in the face, there is no convincing my father. "Yeah, right!"

In late September 1982, Esther suddenly tells me to stop coming to the hospital. "Out of here, kiddo!" she says.

"Why?"

"Lorenzo," Esther calmly explains, "he just doesn't want you to see him, not in his condition."

Dad is such a proud person, I understand. Yet I am his son. I should have gone there anyway, but instead I honored Esther's (and his) wishes.

Esther, his devoted and loving spouse, is at my father's side every hour of every day. She even arranges to have a rollaway bed put in his room to stay with him in his final days. Then, on Friday, October 7, 1982, moments before his death, with the cancer having spread throughout his body, Father is ready to face his maker.

Dr. Hornaday, there with him at his bedside, asks him, "Fernando, are you happy?"

Breaking into that wide grin that once made fans swoon, Father weakly responds, "Yes, I'm happy," before breathing his last. The hospital pronounces him dead; he's sixty-seven years old.

The outpouring of well wishes and condolences from colleagues and friends is unbelievable. Dr. Hornaday delivers the eulogy at Dad's memorial service at the Church of Religious Science Chapel in Los Angeles. My *Falcon Crest* family is there for me throughout it all, including Jane, who attends the service. After the funeral, my father's ashes are fittingly scattered from Jonathan Goldsmith's boat over the Pacific Ocean, the same place where we shared so many memories together, swimming, surfing, and laughing our way to shore atop the white foamy waves. The fact my father and I became so close—and had no "should haves" between us—made his loss a little easier for me. I knew the closeness was there to the very end, and I could live with that. As a result, I carry his spirit with me always. Because of him, I have never lost sight of what it is to be a classy, no-nonsense guy with a sense of humor.

Unfortunately, despite my best efforts, my father died still believing Victoria was using me. She never did. She just had trouble sharing me with somebody else. I think that was a big part of it. At least I am comforted by the fact that Dad died knowing that he and I had reconnected and he didn't suffer the heartbreak of losing a son.

AFTER WORD OF MY BREAKUP with Victoria leaks to the press, *US* magazine dashes its plans to publish a happily-married-ever-after story about our marriage for its October 12 issue. As a result, I find myself faced for the first time with a much greater challenge: ensuring that the public does not start to believe I and the philanderer I play on *Falcon Crest* are one and the same.

Three months later, Victoria learns the startling news that she is pregnant and has been since three months before we separated. When she finally tells me, I am at a loss. "Oh, my God," I say to her. "Victoria, what do we do?"

"I want to have the baby," she says firmly.

I am completely honest with her: "I don't see us together."

Victoria pauses and says, "It's okay. I'll raise the baby. I don't want to burden you with a child. You know, you're barely an adult yourself. I'll take care of the child. Just send me what you can when you can."

Victoria is in such a fragile, emotional state over the heartbreak of our separation that after she tells me her plan, I become seriously concerned about her health and safety, and that of the child as well. I question her ability to provide a loving environment for the baby.

As it happens, she miscarries at seven months. The news deeply saddens me. I am sad for her, sad for the baby. Sad our marriage did not work out.

In the winter of 1983, after living apart all of this time, Victoria and I officially separate and file for divorce shortly thereafter. She is amicable and civil throughout the proceedings. At first, Victoria never seeks or wants anything from me. "I just want you to be happy," she says.

Finally, she asks for some support, so I give her $20,000. It is all I have at the time. She never asks for alimony, which is very generous of her. She reminds me a lot of my mom. Mom would never ask for a dime, even if she never had money in the bank.

After much reflection on it, I know I could have handled everything better with Victoria. I would do things differently today if given the chance; I would have acted more mature. I really did love her, but the strain of trying to please my father let my emotions get the best of me. I regret breaking her heart the way I did and leaving her son, Shile, fatherless a second time after our divorce. It is not what I imagined when I married her. The raw emotions kept me from seeing the truth.

Years later, after entering into another relationship, Victoria gives birth to a baby daughter. Mom, with whom Victoria has had a close relationship over the years, calls to tell me the news. I am so happy for her.

EIGHT

Rocking the Boat

MY FATHER'S DEATH is like a wake-up call for me, one with a simple message: "Whatever you're doing, make sure it's what you want to do, because you could go at any time."

After his passing and my separation from Victoria, I decide it's time for an attitude change. I need to enjoy work more, be thankful for my many blessings, and see the humor in what's going on rather than take myself so seriously. The secret is not to tiptoe through life. Instead, walk with some kind of purpose and attack it, because if you have the verve and if you have passion, life can—and will—be more enjoyable.

As sincere as my intentions are, staying true to that plan proves to be difficult.

One of my dearest friends and closest confidants throughout all of this is *Falcon Crest* costar Abby Dalton, who plays my screen mother on the show. In many ways, Abby is like a real mother to me. I have long talks with her about what's going on in my personal life, and she always offers great advice. Her husband, Jack Smith, is like a father figure to me, and the two of them are both so supportive. So is Kathleen Kinmont, their beautiful seventeen-year-old, five-foot-eleven-inch statuesque daughter and frequent visitor to the set. I had met Kathleen for the first time in 1982.

A friendship between us blossoms instantly. Kathleen slowly becomes a big part of my life, even through my first two marriages and divorces and later broken engagements. Throughout it all, we remain close friends and develop strong feelings for each other. Other than Ana Alicia, my *Falcon Crest* costar and on-screen wife, Kathleen is the only woman I consider a true friend. For me, she's on that same natural level as a close guy friend—someone I can talk to openly about anything, even all my rants and complaints. Never once does she judge me. She doesn't question me. She never says, "You're an idiot," even when I'm acting like one, or asks, "What are you doing?" even when I'm doing something dumb. She is a true friend.

But Kathleen is young, six years younger than I am, and that's what keeps me from seeing a future for us. She should get out and explore life more; she should experience other relationships. If after all that, she still has strong feelings for me, then maybe we can move forward together. But now does not feel like the right time. It's too soon.

In October 1982, not long after the death of my father, CBS sends me on a whirlwind publicity junket to New York to promote the first season of *Falcon Crest*. The network assigns a publicist from PMK, a big publicity firm with offices in Los Angeles and New York, to handle the tour. She is a dark-haired, vivacious, and attractive woman named Michele Smith. She keeps me on a tight schedule doing back-to-back interviews for numerous print publications and local and national television shows.

I am still on speaking terms with Victoria even though we have split up, so I've brought her with me to New York. Victoria immediately notices the interactions between Michele and me and says, "You two have some kind of chemistry."

I haven't noticed. "What are you talking about?" I ask. "She's a great gal, but I'm lucky you and I are still married."

Fast-forward to December 1983. I'm now legally separated from Victoria and am sent to New York again for another publicity tour with Michele. Not surprisingly, what Victoria said about chemistry ends up being true. My marriage to Victoria is over, with no chance of reconciliation, so the second I get to New York, Michele and I bond. We become inseparable. I blow off a couple of morning interviews, including an early-morning radio gig, because we're spending most of our time in my hotel room, between the sheets. I do get in trouble for missing those interviews, and I do care and feel bad. But more important to me is staying in the hotel room with Michele.

After that one week of publicity, I stay on for another week, shacking up with Michele in her apartment. I meet her friends. We hang out together, clubbing at night in places like Studio 54 and Heartbreak. We have a great time in everything we do. I am surprised and delighted by the similarity of our childhoods. Her parents also separated when she was a child. They shuffled her around from a boarding school to her mother's New York home and her dad's Palm Springs house. It is as if destiny has brought us together. Even though I've been wining and dining Michele for only a short period of time, I know deep in my gut that she is it for me.

Returning to Los Angeles, I move back into my A-frame and let Victoria live in the house we had been renting in the Mandeville Canyon area of Brentwood. The whole time Michele is back in New York, of course, so the two of us burn up the phone lines talking to each other every other day, running up bills like crazy. She wants to make a go of our relationship but her job, her career, is in New York.

"PMK has offices out here," I point out. "Why don't you see if they have openings here and come on out?"

Michele checks into transferring, but there's nothing available in California and they really need her in New York. For about four months, we continue the calls and when we can manage it, I fly to New York to visit or she comes here. I stay with her in her apartment for a weekend or so and then fly back in time to resume work on *Falcon Crest* on Mondays.

One afternoon weekday when Michele calls me, I can tell by the sound of her voice she has something on her mind.

"What is it?" I ask.

"I'm pregnant," she says.

Michele got pregnant after that first week we hooked up in New York. She is now four months along.

"That's it. That settles it," I tell her. "You're coming out here. You're moving in with me."

"What about my job?"

"We'll worry about that later. We'll make the most of this."

Michele quits her job and moves to California. I have no idea if I am going to marry her. Yet she is pregnant with my child. I feel in my heart this can work—but if it is to work, she needs to move in with me.

After she does so, we have fun and laugh. It's like old times. Things are going so well I finally pop the question: "Will you marry me?"

Michele immediately jumps into my arms and says, "Yes!"

At the time, marrying Michele seems so right. Because she is four months pregnant, we rush the wedding, and on May 22, 1983, three months after my divorce from Victoria is final, we are married on a yacht in Marina del Rey. We have known each other only five months.

The day of the wedding, however, I start having second thoughts. Early that morning I start downing screwdrivers and lose count. Everything is happening so fast. Too fast. My father had died in October of the previous year. The ink on my divorce to Victoria is hardly dry. Now I am tying up with Michele, who is pregnant. Suddenly I have doubts. Yes, Michele loves to party and hang out with friends. And yes, the two of us have a great physical relationship. But we have little else in common. Our physical attraction has led to the conception, and in keeping with that old-fashioned mind-set, I feel I must do the honorable thing: marry her. But deep down I wonder if maybe I'm just going along for the ride.

Michele and I marry, and we make a go of it. I buy us a much larger house: a three-bedroom California ranch on a half acre of property in luxurious Hollywood Hills, with a fabulous pool just steps down from the front of the house. I now have a beautiful home. I am married to a beautiful brown-eyed, brown-haired woman who seems to fill the hole in my heart. I am excited about becoming a father and having a family of my own, and professionally things have never been better.

But I soon discover the genuine happiness we project is just the opposite—nothing more than superficial.

When you are on a hit television series, many doors open for you that otherwise might not. Some trappings of fame become more easily available to you when you have the means and opportunity. I'm talking about drugs, specifically cocaine.

Beginning in 1983 in Napa during location filming for *Falcon Crest*—and before becoming involved with Michele—I had fallen into the deep hole of drugs and alcohol. Cocaine was the drug of choice back then. I got friendly with some of the crew guys on the set, and we start doing coke parties. After wrapping the show, we would go back to the hotel, lie down and catch some z's, get up about nine or ten o'clock at night, and then the guys and I would hit the bars in Napa looking for local talent, i.e., single women. Some of the crew guys had families back in Los Angeles, so they never did the coke thing much after returning home—only when they were on location.

Now Michele and I have developed a common interest in coke. During the days when I'd be shooting, I'd often invite the production crew up to party at our house, just ten minutes from CBS Studio Center, where *Falcon Crest* films. The crew comes up during our lunch breaks. We hang out by the pool and do some lines—or "rails"—of cocaine. We party only on the days when we wrap and do not have to go back to work after lunch or even the next day.

One day after partying hard around the pool with three close friends and members of the production crew who had come over to the house to do a few lines with us, I throw my golf clubs into my car and go hit balls at the nearby driving range in Studio City while coming down from my high.

Back home from the range, I jump into the pool, swim, and party some more. I figure since we have wrapped I have the rest of the day off. Suddenly the phone rings. Dripping wet, I run inside to answer. It is our first assistant director.

"What are you doing?" he asks. "We're looking for you."

I'm confused. "You're looking for me?" I ask. "Why? I'm wrapped."

"Lorenzo, the show hasn't wrapped," he says. "You still have to show up for work."

I'm like, "What?"

"It's for a scene with Jane," he says.

I always prepare for my scenes with Jane Wyman. I never take them for granted and never want to get caught not knowing my lines. Nothing but professional. Now I am really scared shitless. My heart is racing; I start sweating profusely.

I find the script. It is a three-page scene with *lots* of dialogue. I tear out the pages, jump into my car, and speed off. Driving to the studio,

I am gripping the steering wheel, white knuckled, scared out of my fuckin' mind, trying to memorize the lines for my scene with Jane.

Screeching into the parking lot, I run straight to my dressing room and change into my wardrobe while trying to calm down. I look the scene over some more and try to really focus and comprehend what I am reading without panicking. Suddenly there's a knock at the door. It is one of my crew buddies who was at the house partying earlier that day.

"Hey, buddy, are you fuckin' scared or what?" He's laughing his ass off.

"Get the fuck out of here!" I shout. "I do not want to see you right now."

"Don't worry, man," he says, still stoned out of his mind. "It's going to be fine."

I shoo him away with the script pages I'm clutching in my hand and start screaming at him, "Leave me alone! Get away from me! Get the hell out of my face!"

"You'll be all right, man," he says." Don't worry."

"Thanks, man," I say as I close the door on his face so he'll leave.

Pulling myself together, I practice my lines some more and finish changing before heading to the makeup trailer. I'm sweating excessively as I sit down in the makeup chair. Our makeup artist and my dear friend to this day, Monet Mansano, says in his flamboyant Israeli accent, "Lor-r-r-r-enzo, did you par-r-r-r-ty? You're sweating!"

"Yeah, I partied," I say, panicky. "You got to fuckin' fix me up. Where is the anti-shine shit? You gotta give me that anti-shine shit." (Anti-shine chokes off the sweat glands so actors do not develop moisture that will come through their makeup.) "Give me that anti-shine, Monet. I have to get through this."

"Okay, don't worry. It will be okay," he says as he blasts me with almost a whole can of the stuff. "You study your script. I don't talk." But Monet *loves* to talk.

So Monet talks and I am cool with it. I learn my lines and leave the trailer, covered with anti-shine shit so I am not sweating, and walk on the set to film my scene with Jane. It is a restaurant scene and she is already sitting at the table, waiting for my ass, which makes me even more self-conscious. The set is quiet as a morgue. Everybody knows how pissed Jane is. She has had to wait at least an hour for me, her twenty-five-year-old idiot costar, to show up.

"Hi, Jane," I say as I sit down, ready to do the scene.

"Do you know your lines?" she asks sternly.

I am dying inside. "Yes, I do."

"Would you like to rehearse them once?"

"Thank you," I respond with a smile. "Yes, that would be nice."

We start rehearsing the scene and I mess up my lines.

Right away Jane asks, "Did you study your script?"

"Jane, I have to be honest with you," I stammer. "I didn't know we had to shoot the scene today."

Jane is unflinching: "Are you ready to do the scene?"

"I think so."

"But you don't have your lines memorized."

The anti-shine shit is wearing off; I am sweating like a rain forest. I am dying, just dying. Finally, I say, "Jane, I'm so sorry."

Jane sees right through me. "You're high, aren't you?"

"Yeah, I am."

She looks at me sternly. "Wouldn't your father be disappointed in you?"

That digs deep. It hits a raw nerve. Of course he would. I feel so ashamed. How could I have let things come to this?

I immediately flash back to the first time I came home stoned to my father's house. I was seventeen years old and had just graduated from the academy. I hung out at the beach every day with my friends Jon and Cary Gries (their father was director Tom Gries, a very good friend of my father's and with whom he had worked on the movie *100 Rifles*). That day, I went over to their house in Beverly Hills after the beach, and we smoked some pot. I rode my bike home and when I got there, Dad immediately saw my eyes were bloodshot and asked, "Have you been smoking pot?"

"No," I lied.

"Don't you fucking lie to me!" he exploded.

Finally, I confessed. "Yes, I was."

"It's one thing to smoke pot, another to lie about it," Dad said, fuming. "Don't you lie to me or ever smoke pot again."

My father hated the whole drug scene. And he would have hated that I was high on anything at any time. But now if he had witnessed

Jane Wyman having to dress me down like that in front of the cast and crew, he would have been so humiliated and mortified. Jane was a special person to him and she is to me. She gives me heartfelt, valuable advice; she keeps me honest and focused.

She's still waiting for an answer, so I finally mutter, "Yes, Jane, you're right. He would be disappointed."

Without batting an eye, she says in that grandmotherly voice of hers, "This is what we're going to do. We're going to take a fifteen-minute break. You're going to memorize your lines. And you're never going to come to work high again. Are we in agreement?"

"Yes."

"Fine."

To the director, Jane barks, "We need fifteen minutes."

Gently rising from her chair, she gives me that classic withering stare. Then after lighting up a cigarette, she walks off, leaving me there to study my lines. I can tell you this: I never forgot what she did for me that day and I learned from her example. She could have had my ass fired but gave me a second chance. And I knew there would never be a third, a fourth, or a fifth chance. I never came to work fucked up again.

As any father or mother will tell you, becoming a parent changes your perspective on just about everything. It certainly changes mine. A.J. is born in Cedars-Sinai Medical Center in Los Angeles on December 9, 1983, and it becomes the happiest day in my life. After holding little A.J. in my arms for the first time, I have an epiphany: We have to stop with the drugs.

I know if A.J. is going to have a chance in life, I have to do right by him. But Michele, I believe, still wants to have a good time. I admit we are our happiest when we fill the house up with people to party, drink, and carry on, but after it ends and they all leave, we are just miserable together. That has to change for A.J.'s sake.

I try talking to Michele about it. "Look, we have to pull back," I say. "We can't be partying every single night. First of all, I have to get up at six in the morning, and secondly, A.J. is here. We can't be doing that stuff around him."

"You're right, you're right," she says.

But Michele has more problems kicking the party scene and all that goes with it than I do. It becomes a major issue in our marriage. Even though Michele is not working, I hire a nanny to help her around the house with A.J. I try to get her to go back to work, but she gives me the same pat answer: "There are no openings. I don't want to start from the beginning again."

Consequently, Michele becomes a homebody. I can't relax until the nanny gets there at nine or ten o'clock in the morning. Only then do I know for certain A.J. is in good hands. A couple of times I come home early and, to my utter shock, find A.J. crying and wriggling uncomfortably in his crib. I confront Michele. "This is not working. Either we're going to make a go of this marriage completely straight and sober or it's not going to work out."

It doesn't. In July 1984 I split from Michele. It's simply not working between us. Outside of the physical attraction, we—a couple in our midtwenties—do not have the depth or the tools to cope with our situation. Our relationship cannot continue down this same path. With A.J. in the mix, I was willing to try to change, but I don't believe Michele was.

The supermarket tabloids love it. Our separation becomes fodder for gossip and innuendo. The media cast me as the bad guy in all of this, apparently assuming there is no difference between me in real life and the philandering character I play on *Falcon Crest*. During our separation and divorce, I take the polite way out. I never speak ill of Michele to the press, nor do I try to defend my actions. I decide that someday I will have my say on the matter, but now is not the time. Ironically, just as my marriage to Michele is ending, Mom marries her sixth husband: Marc Rosen, a perfume executive eighteen years her junior. They are married by the captain of the cruise ship *Sea Goddess* during a voyage from Marbella, Spain, to Monaco.

That summer, while doing location filming on *Falcon Crest* in Napa, I have Michele and A.J. come to stay with me for a while in my fancy two-room suite. But Michele sleeps in one room while I sleep in the other. We have no physical contact. She has been invited for the sole purpose of bringing A.J. He and I play in the pool every day and have loads of fun. It is so cool having A.J. there. A week later, the two of them return to Los Angeles.

In March 1985, after twenty-one months of marriage, I file for divorce from Michele, citing "irreconcilable differences," and seek full custody of A.J. Because the court papers that are filed only hint at the real issues that ripped our marriage asunder, A.J. need never know the whole truth.

I tell Michele she can keep the Hollywood Hills house until we can sell it and I move back into the A-frame I still own. I hire my attorney and Michele hires hers. Then it all becomes a very combative and very expensive civil war between us. After receiving a check for $75,000 from the probate settlement of my father's estate, I remember taking it right over, endorsing it, and handing it to my attorney. Yet it's not near what the divorce ultimately costs me: $150,000 total. As the only one gainfully employed, I end up paying for Michele's attorney fees as well. It is just a nightmare.

I try appealing to Michele's common sense. "Let me take the boy," I plead. "I'll take care of him. You can see him whenever you want."

Later, *People* magazine publishes a story—not favorable to either of us—in which we sling mud at each other. I say she indulges in substance abuse; she claims I'm an absentee father causing the child I love emotional and psychological pain. It's just the beginning of the legal wrangling to come.

Later that month, I fly to New York on a publicity junket for *Falcon Crest*. Michele and I are not yet divorced; our case is still working its way through the courts. Michele comes to visit me at the Ritz-Carlton with A.J. She puts our son in a playpen and then one thing leads to another. We have not made love for about six months, but that first night when they are in town we end up hooking up in my posh hotel room.

After making love, Michele says softly, "Let's try to make this work."
The whole idea leaves me flummoxed. "I don't want to," I reply.
"You have to."
"Michele, we don't have enough between us to keep this marriage together."
Furious, Michele soon flies back to Los Angeles with A.J. while I stay in New York to tape a television special, *Night of 100 Stars II*, for

ABC. It is then that I meet the lovely and talented Jennifer O'Neill, who is costarring in the special with me. I find her just stunning. She is the girl in the *Summer of '42* and the fantasy of every young boy who ever saw that film—including me when I was fourteen. And now I am instantly smitten with her, and we have an affair. Jennifer is thirty-six and I am twenty-seven.

Back in Los Angeles after the taping of the special, I make the mistake of telling Michele how I met Jennifer on the same trip she came on with A.J.

"You did not!"

"Yeah, I did," I say. "As I told you before, I don't want to get back together."

"You son of a bitch." Blah-blah-blah-blah. "You piece of shit!" Da-da-da-da.

Michele and I never talk after that. My affair with Jennifer only fuels her rage. Things become very contentious between us. Michele's attorneys try dragging Jennifer into the center of our divorce. Jennifer is now starring in her own television series, *Cover Up*. Her costar is male-model-turned-actor Jon-Erik Hexum, who later will accidentally kill himself while joking around with a prop gun that has a live charge in it. I frequently visit Jennifer on the set of *Cover Up*, and our relationship blossoms.

For months, Jennifer and I remain an item in the press. I plan to take Jennifer with me on a five-week cruise that May on the *Pacific Princess*, the flagship for *The Love Boat* television series. I'll be filming a guest spot for my third series appearance, the first since my ear-piercing fiasco. Jennifer will be making a guest appearance in an episode on the next cruise after that. Our trip as a couple, however, never happens. The month before we're to depart, Michele calls me. Our divorce is nearly final, but she drops another bombshell: "I'm pregnant," says Michele. "Now will you marry me again?"

Apparently, her pregnancy is the result of us hooking up together that one time at the Ritz-Carlton in New York when she and A.J. came to visit.

"Michele, you cannot have this child," I say as firmly as I can.

She's firm as well. "I don't know what it is, Lorenzo, whether it's a boy or a girl. But I am not going to let our son, A.J., grow up without a sibling."

"Michele," I say even more emphatically, "we are not going to be married. Can you understand that finally? Doing this is not going to make me get back together with you. So doing this is wrong."

"Well, I'm having the baby," she says. And that is that.

I tell Jennifer, of course, but it all is too much for her to bear. After all, she has lived through five divorces of her own. "Honey, I can't do this," she says. "The whole time we've been together it's been this drama with you and your ex-wife. Now she is pregnant because you hooked up with her in New York the weekend you met me. I can't."

I can't think of anything to say that will make this bad situation better. So instead, I gently lean over and peck Jennifer on her cheek. Her blue-gray eyes growing moist with tears tell what could have been, what should have been. She pulls away and I whisper one last goodbye. I, too, will always wonder what could have been had our relationship continued.

Prior to that sad, final breakup, Jennifer and I had agreed to appear on ABC's two-hour *Battle of the Network Stars XVII* special. The producers recruited me to captain the CBS team that includes Jennifer and fellow CBS stars Lucie Arnaz, Mary Frann, Jenilee Harrison, Doug McKeon, Dack Rambo, and my *Falcon Crest* costar and buddy Billy Moses. The show must go on, and so Jennifer and I both honor our commitment.

The special is set to air in late May and is the first in this series to be filmed outside the United States, in the sand-and-surf resort of Ixtapa, Mexico. We compete against teams of well-known celebrities from other ABC and NBC network shows. Four new events—the beach relay, mixed-doubles tennis, volleyball, and fishing boat races—have been added to the usual running relays, tug-of-war, and swimming competitions.

Competing in the event is fun and challenging. Billy and I each win new Mitsubishi automobiles. Working with Jennifer so soon after our split is awkward, of course. I still have feelings for her; I still love her. In front of the cameras, we are completely professional, and we go our separate ways after shooting. But my life feels empty without her.

Later, I try to reconcile with Michele for the sake of our second child, but it never sticks. In late April, we separate a second time and

I subsequently refile for divorce. Once it is decreed, a mix of emotions runs through me. Most of all, I think about the two kids and what kind of future they will have without a father. For their sakes, I so wish things had turned out differently. But now that the final divorce judgment is in, I know it's as it should be. Unless the other person is willing to change, there is zero chance for success; any second chance is bound to fail. It is that simple.

I proceed without Jennifer to film *The Love Boat* episode on the cruise once intended for both of us, in and around the coastal cities of Spain. To my surprise, Billy Moses is on the cruise with me. He is filming a different episode for the same four-episode, two-hour extravaganza. I will appear in one episode as the grandson of a famous matador (played by Cesar Romero) who falls for Mary Crosby and wants to become a writer rather than a bullfighter. Billy's then girlfriend, Tracy Nelson, whom he marries two years later, joins him on the last part of the cruise.

Billy is like a brother to me on the trip. He consoles me, chews the fat with me, and makes me laugh at a time when laughter is absent from my life. We hang together, dine together, and have more fun than any two guys should be allowed. He brings out the playful, lighthearted side of my personality, a side some people never see.

One day when we are docked off the coast of Spain, *Entertainment Tonight* shows up with a crew to do a feature story. Suddenly I get this bright idea to dive off the Promenade, the highest deck on the ship, into the coastal waters below. I turn to Billy and ask, "Are the cameras around?"

"Yeah," he says and points, "right over there."

Billy looks into my eyes and breaks into a wide grin. "What are you going to do?" he asks.

"I'm diving off the deck."

"No, you're not."

"Yes, I am. Watch me."

I go over and climb up on the railing. Mary Hart of *ET*, who is there doing the story, smiles broadly and asks, "Lorenzo, what are you doing?"

"Are the cameras rolling?"

"Yes," she says, her smile even wider.

I commence to do a swan dive off the Promenade into the bay. Little do I realize that with the ship ported in shallow waters, jagged rocks lurk just below the surface. Fortunately, I miss them. Unfortunately, and to no one's surprise, I am now in major trouble with the crew. The captain reprimands me sternly: "You can't be diving off the ship like that!"

I apologize. "I'm sorry," I say.

After pulling myself back up on the deck, I ask Mary Hart, "Was it good for camera?"

Mary winces and says, "Well, we got the first part, but we missed the second part."

I am not about to disappoint Mary, so I decide to do it all over for *ET*. As I am getting ready, I turn to Billy and say, "You don't have the balls to go off this deck."

"Oh, yeah," he replies with a smirk, "I'm going!"

I dive first and then Billy jumps in after me, both of us off the Promenade deck. We make *ET* very happy. They get the shots they need. Billy and I have a good laugh over it. In fact, everyone laughs except the captain, who almost kicks us off the ship, and the producers of *The Love Boat*, who never invite us back again.

YEARS BEFORE, I had begun to pursue other aspects of the film business, including directing—just as my father did. Even before that, however, I had gotten into another area of the entertainment biz: music. Long before acting, I was singing—only not professionally. Then in 1982 I signed a record contract with Scotti Brothers Records to embark on a music career as a sideline to my acting. I recorded ten songs for my first album at a studio not far from my alma mater, Santa Monica City College. Unfortunately, Scotti Brothers never released the album. But then in April 1983 I cut my first single, "Fools Like Me," which I also sang in the New World Pictures movie *Body Rock*, a film in which I costarred. "Fools Like Me" was released by CBS Records, with my recording of "Smooth Talker" on its B-side. "Fools Like Me" became my first and only hit, making Billboard's Hot Top 100 chart in 1984, climbing to the eighty-fifth position.

Also in 1983, my manager, Herb Nanas, and Scotti Brothers Tony and Ben invited me to join them for a weekend of horse racing in Del Mar, a suburb of San Diego. Herb and the Scottis were, and still are, huge racing fans. Herb had arranged the trip under the pretense of my meeting with Mike Greenfield, an agent who wanted me as his client. Shortly after we took our seats at the track, Mike showed up with this gorgeous, voluptuous brunette on his arm. Heads turned as she sashayed down the steps to their seats. She is Patty Kotero, better known then as Apollonia, Prince's girlfriend and costar of his movie *Purple Rain*.

That first night, Mike set me up on a date with Patty. We became extremely close quickly and had an amazing weekend together. I remember this much: We barely saw any horse racing.

During the fifth season of *Falcon Crest*, 1985–86, the producers decide to shake things up a bit with my character. To add more intrigue to the story lines, they pair me with a new actress to play my girlfriend for ten consecutive weeks. She walks onto the set on her first day, the same gorgeous bombshell who turned heads (including mine) at the Del Mar racetrack two years earlier: Patty Kotero.

She looks as amazing as ever. As we film our scenes in our first episode together, we can feel the attraction we both still have for each other. But we never act on it. What is different this time is that both of us are married (since I am not yet legally divorced). Had we not been married, I am certain something more would have developed between us. Instead, we become and remain very good friends to this day.

On November 6, 1985, Michele gives birth to our second baby—a girl. We name her Shayne. When Michele goes into labor, I immediately put aside our differences. I am right there at her side to help her through the labor and the birth of our daughter. And I have been a part of Shayne's life ever since.

Finally, after a bitter and drawn-out battle, my divorce from Michele becomes final. The judge never grants me full custody of A.J. Instead, he awards us *shared* custody of both A.J. and Shayne. Before our daughter's birth, I had moved into a house on Venice Beach and then into one in Malibu. It's there where I spend almost every weekend and as much quality time as possible with A.J. Yet whatever time I have with him is never enough. I understand now how my father must have felt after his separation from me following the divorce from my mom.

Shayne adds a whole other dimension to my life. As with A.J., I do everything to make her a part of who I am and what I do. Over time, she finds having a famous father surreal. To this day, she relishes the time I took her and A.J. to Disneyland. At the top of my game then, I could not go anywhere without creating a frenzy. That day, a crush of fans surrounded us and we could hardly move or breathe as I posed for pictures and signed autographs. Later Shayne described it as "like you were Michael Jackson, Daddy."

I wish I could have done more. I wish I could have been an even bigger part of A.J.'s and Shayne's lives. Not being there for them is something I am not very proud of. Between constant career demands and turmoil with Michele after our divorce, I missed some pivotal times. Fortunately, I have now made my amends and have a great relationship with both of them. I am just so very happy to know they are part of my life.

Rebounding from my divorce, I date Kathleen a second time, but it can never evolve into something greater without affecting our friendship. It is mostly my fault. The heartache of two divorces weighs heavily on me, and I cannot commit to another relationship until my heart mends. Until such time, Kathleen remains my closest confidante. She's always ready and willing to listen, to provide encouragement, and to be there when I need her.

NINE

Finding My Way

N THE EARLY 1980S, I develop a love of race cars. During my off-hours every summer after filming exteriors in Napa Valley for *Falcon Crest*, I first nurture my affection for the sport by attending the races at Sears Point (now known as Sonoma Raceway). The sport feeds the daredevil inside of me, much like motorcycling, but even more. The high-speed derring-do by the drivers, the intense competition, the burning rubber, and the roar of the engines—I love it all so much I decide to race myself.

In 1985, I enter my first pro-celebrity competition, the Toyota Grand Prix, one of the biggest race car events in Southern California, held in Long Beach. That weekend I mix with all the famous race car drivers, including Mario Andretti, and more importantly, win my first race in the pro-celebrity division. After that, I am hooked. I start flying around the country to race in other pro-celebrity races, including the IMSA Camel Lights and USAC/Toyota Sportsman series, and make many new lifelong friends from the world of auto racing. The sport proves a great escape for me from the trouble and turmoil in my life, and I can never get enough of it.

In early November 1985, on a spectacular, cloudless, sunny weekend, I compete in a Formula Ford race at Riverside International Speedway. I am excited to drive in the competition before thousands of devoted race car fans.

As we wait for the flagman to officially start the race, my car is in position and ready to roll. As soon as he drops the flag, we are off and running. Every kind of Formula Ford you can imagine is burning rubber and tearing around the racetrack, trying to stake out their positions and move up in the pack. Every time we pass the ninth turn, I start gaining on the leader. As we get near the end, I successfully jockey my car into second position, right behind the lead car. My entire focus is on the leader. The crowd is really into it now, on their feet and cheering like crazy. It appears it'll be a close finish.

As I'm taking the last turn and going wide on the highest bank at one hundred miles per hour, I suddenly lose control and crash into a concrete retaining wall. I'm powerless to do anything, and my car spins around 180 degrees—without hitting a single other car—and smashes hard into the pit wall and then bounces thirty feet back onto the track.

The flagman immediately red flags the race to an end. Meanwhile, a hush falls over the once-cheering throng. At this point, all eyes are on my car. I'm trapped inside, unable to move. My car looks like a chunk of compacted scrap metal at a junkyard; the only thing left intact is the driver's cage—in which I sit. I try moving my arms and legs but feel paralyzed. Everything is numb.

An emergency crew speeds out onto the track. A worker hollers inside to me, "We're going to get you out."

Working feverishly, they pull away the wreckage and remove the fiberglass to get to me.

They take almost twenty minutes trying to pull me out of the car, but I am really out of it and pass out for a minute. A worker gets inside and revives me. When they try to pull me out, I suddenly feel shooting pain in my collarbone and right leg. They keep tugging on me, hard. The pain intensifies, becoming excruciating, and I cry out in pain, "Hold on!"

Finally, I see the problem: The steering arm has driven itself through my leg, right through my calf muscle.

"Stop pulling!" I shout to the worker in earshot of me.

It takes a major effort to pull the steering arm out of my leg. It turns out my right foot is also broken. As they put me on a stretcher, I pass out. I lapse in and out of consciousness and do not remember a single thing after the accident—the ambulance ride to the hospital, my time in the emergency room, or my stay in the hospital. They

keep me pretty doped up to treat my injuries and then discharge me
the next morning.

Without the use of my arms, I cannot ride my motorcycle home to
Venice where I live. I have the hospital call Kathleen, who then has a
boyfriend. I talk to her and tell her of my accident. She immediately
drives to the hospital from Los Angeles to get me. Afterward she
moves in with me to take care of me. She feeds me, bathes me, and
wipes my ass. She does everything for me.

That Monday, with Kathleen's help, I make it to the set of *Falcon
Crest* at CBS Studio Center without telling a soul about the accident
or my injuries. (Under the terms of my contract, I am not supposed
to be racing.) The wardrobe guy fits me with a jacket to compensate
for the fact I cannot lift my arms. It is crazy, but I go through rehearsals that day for that week's episode. It is one of my best acting jobs
ever. I carry on throughout as if nothing is different. For a while, it
all works pretty well. Finally, even my fitted jacket cannot conceal
the fact something is definitely wrong.

During rehearsals, Jane says to me, "Is everything all right?"

"Why?" I ask coyly.

"You don't seem yourself." Jane lowers her voice and adds, "You
aren't using again, are you?"

"No, no, Jane, it's not that," I tell her.

"Then what?"

I cannot lie to Jane, not after the last time I tried. I tell her the
truth. "I was in a serious race car accident over the weekend and
broke my shoulder and my collarbone and—"

"You did what?" she interrupts.

I think, "Oh, God, Lorenzo, you have done it now. Now she is
going to bring your father into this and go down that *Wouldn't your
father be disappointed in you?* trip." I think fast.

"Well, Jane, I have been racing cars now for a year. It's just a hobby
of mine."

"Some hobby. You could have killed yourself."

"I know, I know."

Jane pauses. Her maternal side seeps through. "Well, *we* better tell
them what has happened. You cannot work like this, and they have
a right to know."

Jane barks to the director, "We need to break for fifteen minutes."

The director shouts to the cast and crew, "Fifteen, everybody."

Walking off the set, Jane shoots me that classic withering stare before lighting up a cigarette.

I follow Jane's advice. We—I mean *I*—tell the powers that be the whole story. The producers are not very happy with me, while the network loves the story and jumps all over it to promote the show. They decide to work around my injuries. The director shoots my scenes in a way that nobody watching the episodes that follow has any idea I had just survived a horrific race car accident.

After the accident, I test my luck and race intermittently through the mid-1990s, including again the Long Beach Grand Prix. I hang up my racing gear for three years before returning to the sport in 1998 for a series of US F2000 National Championship competitions.

Back to the accident. A day after almost killing myself, I have an epiphany: My life is careening out of control like my race car on that track. I am flying around the country and driving race cars, not spending enough time with A.J. and Shayne. I'm trying to avoid the reality of my divorce and my responsibilities as a father. The wreck helps clarify my purpose on the planet and helps me recognize some very important things about myself I need to change. First and foremost, I need to be a better father to my son and daughter; I need to be much more involved in their lives than I have been. They deserve better from me. After the accident, I make a real and conscious effort to become the father they always hoped I would be.

After nursing me back to health, Kathleen moves back in with her boyfriend, and I go on to have other relationships. Her selflessness in my time of need, however, is something I can never forget. Her caring actions distinguish her from all the rest. It's a major reason why I later go back with Kathleen and let her know how I truly feel: "You're the one, you're my gal."

After the accident, my life is as much a work-in-progress, if not more so, as I admitted to you earlier. I continue to act as the person I think people want me to be instead of changing and growing into the person I want to be. I do not always use the best judgment or show the greatest self-control when letting circumstances and my heart's desire dictate my life, including with the women I date.

The following season, the *Falcon Crest* producers once again spice things up by casting an aerobics instructor as my girlfriend in an episode. She is actress Robin Greer, drop-dead gorgeous, with blond hair, green eyes, and a striking body to match.

We immediately start having an affair. Robin breaks up with her boyfriend. Back in Los Angeles after wrapping location filming in Napa that August, we take the next step in our relationship: I have her move in with me in my Malibu beach house. Five months later, I propose. Before I know it, our engagement and pending nuptials become the subject of intense gossip, until we confirm the rumors that May.

At this point in my life, I am very happy working as an actor. I do not have any major business aspirations or the time to pursue anything else but acting. I feel very satisfied with the direction of my career. Robin, however, has different ideas. It seems like I am not doing enough for her. We have several conversations about that.

"What are your long-term goals?" she asks.

"Well," I say honestly, "I'm living my dream. I'm on a hit show. I'm making very good money. What are you talking about?"

"It's not going to last forever, Lorenzo—the future, the money."

I take everything the wrong way. What Robin says offends me. Immediately I get defensive.

"What? Am I not good enough for you? Just because you were married to a multimillionaire, now I'm not good enough for you?"

Looking at the expensive engagement ring that I just gave her—it cost $20,000, a lot of money—I am thinking, "What else do I have to do for this girl?"

I realize now Robin was probably looking out for our best interests. Back then, however, I had a bit more Fernando in me than was good for me. Consequently, I end our relationship for the simple reason that she apparently thinks I am not good enough for her.

It is heartbreaking. Robin falls to pieces over the breakup. I feel terrible about it. At the very surface, I am not looking at her concerns going forward, only mine. It is unfortunate when things end the way they do, but in my current state of mind, I cannot see any other way.

After breaking up with Robin, I go back to a familiar place: I date Kathleen again. Anytime we are together, we have fun. It is as if you have a best friend in school, then after school ends, you go your separate ways for summer vacation. When you come back and see your best friend and the old gang again, you have that comfortable feeling. That is exactly the feeling I have anytime I get back together with Kathleen. Despite all of my failed marriages and dustups with other women, Kathleen and I remain close friends and develop strong feelings for each other.

This time, things get serious between us after Kathleen breaks up with her boyfriend and because I had broken off my engagement to Robin. For a good six months, we see each other and hang out. We go on long motorcycle rides with my friend Mike Liakos and his wife, Sandy. In the summer of 1986, the four of us embark on a motorcycle ride to the Kern River, where we camp out in sleeping bags and tents and swim in the river. We have a great time. I remember sitting on the bank of the river, looking over at Kathleen, and feeling just so content while thinking of my father. How he would really like Kathleen because she is so sweet and supportive. Kathleen and I stay together until that fall, when something happens that surprises even me.

In the fall of 1987, I feel an undeniable chemistry with this tall, beautiful blond actress the second she walks on the set of *Falcon Crest* to costar in an episode that season. Her name is Daphne Ashbrook. The chemistry between us is evident right away in our scenes together. It is not something you can invent or make up. It is tangible and real.

Acting on impulse, I immediately ask Daphne out. We have a torrid love affair that starts shortly after her appearance. We both dig each other and hang out a lot together. I love Daphne because of her independence and the fact she is a doer. I respect her for that, especially after being with Michele, who really did not do anything after my going with her and marrying her. Along with being a great actress, Daphne is very athletic, something I find very attractive. She can throw a football—a real tight spiral—as well I can. That clinches it for me.

Our relationship starts out well. We have lots of fun. After only a few months, the flames of our passion produce an unexpected surprise: Daphne becomes pregnant with my third child, a daughter she names Paton Lee. I am like, "Damn it!" The last thing I want is to start another relationship built on the wrong premise, without a strong foundation first. Yet I am so deeply committed to Daphne, I try to make the relationship work.

We end up living together in Daphne's house in the Hollywood Hills. For about six months, I am so busy between working and taking care of Daphne through her pregnancy that I never see A.J. or Shayne. Harnessing her skills as a former publicist, my embittered ex-wife Michele spins a story for *People* she hopes will get my attention: The headline in the *People* piece says she is taking me to court to force me to spend more time with our children and that she wants to make a "precedent" out of me.

Michele hires a high-powered attorney, an associate of Marvin Mitchelson, the famous divorce attorney for the stars. I receive horrible press and publicity over all of it. It sets the tone for a very contentious relationship with my ex-wife and has a serious effect on my relationship with Daphne.

I stay with Daphne until a few months after Paton is born in September 1988. By then I am miserable and unhappy. I start to believe that because of my fame, not only did my ex-wife Michele have an unexpected second pregnancy, but other women are also trying to trap me into relationships by getting me to father their children. Furthermore, Daphne's personality is so opposite of mine that I come to believe we are not such a good match after all. Finally, I tell her, "I can't go through with the marriage. I can't do it."

The old saying "Hell hath no fury like a woman scorned" is fitting for what happens next. Daphne takes the breakup so hard she sees to it that she makes my life a living hell. She gives birth to Paton and then keeps me from seeing her. My greatest heartache becomes never getting to know my daughter, something I could never talk about for a very long time. It was far too painful. There was nothing I could have done—outside of taking Daphne to court and making a big deal out of it. I wanted to see Paton and spend time with her, to get to know her and let her know who her true father was—and is. Daphne would not hear of it. She would not let Paton and me even talk to each other.

Maybe it was better this way. Paton would know who I was later, when she was older, when there was not anything between us and the relationship between a father and his daughter could blossom. It is something I prayed for.

I agree to provide child support. I send Daphne a check every month without fail. I decide that even if Daphne remarries or meets some guy who raises Paton as his daughter, I will at least be happy for Paton.

At times like these, I miss my father. I often wonder what he might say or do. I know if he were around to provide counsel, I might be mature enough to listen to him. Even though I'm taking full responsibility for my actions, I doubt he would be very proud of me right now. He always warned me to be careful where issues of the heart are concerned. It takes a series of bad judgments on my part to understand my failings. To conclude: I cannot keep marrying every single woman I love.

After my terrible breakup with Daphne, I call Kathleen's brother, Matt. "I've been thinking about your sister a lot," I say. "I've separated from my girlfriend. Is she in a relationship?"

"Well, no, brother," he says. "As a matter of fact, I think she's broken up with her boyfriend."

"Do you think she'd be interested in taking my call?" I have not spoken to Kathleen in about a year.

"Well, Vites"—we call each other "Vites" like the Vito brothers in the movie *The Godfather*—"I don't see why she wouldn't be interested. Of course she'll see you. She's never stopped loving you."

Just hearing that brings a smile to my face. "Matt, I finally realize that Kathleen is the one I am supposed to be with from the very beginning. She's always been there for me."

"I know, I know, brother," he says. "She's always loved you, Lorenzo."

"I think I'm going to ask her to marry me."

Now listen to what Matt says to me. I have known him as long as Kathleen; he is a year or two older than she is. "Why should she be the only one left out?" We both laugh.

"Okay, brother, I appreciate it. I'll give her a call."

"You do that."

Matt gives me Kathleen's phone number. On Halloween 1988, a month after Paton is born, I call her from my dressing room at CBS

Studio Center after filming scenes for an upcoming episode of *Falcon Crest*. I get her answering machine and am unsure if she is going to pick up. But she does.

"Hey, Keene," I start. Keene is her nickname.

"Happy Halloweenie!" she says, cheerfully.

We laugh, and after talking for forty minutes to an hour, decide to meet. At the time, I am driving a Jeep Wagoneer that needs new shocks. I pick her up at her town house on Sarah Street, and we drive to a hot dog stand right across the street from Bob's Big Boy in downtown Toluca Lake. The Wagoneer has a bench seat in front. Every time I turn the corner, the whole car lifts to one side and she slides back and forth next to me. We are just hysterical laughing about it all the way to the hot dog stand.

Although Kathleen and I are crazy about each other physically, I do not want to complicate our relationship right away. I keep it like a real friendship for a couple of months.

After breaking up with Daphne, I let the lease go on the Malibu place. In early December of that year, I move in with Kathleen after asking her, "Do you think I could room with you for a couple of months until I find a place?"

"Yeah, it won't be a problem," she says.

After not even two nights living together, we end up in the same bed. I remember waking up the next morning and looking over the sheets at this beautiful twenty-three-year-old girl, my best friend in the world. Suddenly it dawns on me: She is the person I am meant to be with.

At that very moment, Kathleen opens her eyes and looks at me. "What are you thinking about?"

"I'm thinking that we should be together."

"Well," she says with a smile, "you know you're going to have to marry me now."

I laugh heartily. "Yeah, I kinda figured that."

"You are going to have to marry me for what I've put up with," Kathleen adds seriously. "There's no way we're going to live together and I'm not married to you."

It made perfect sense. I broke her heart three times before—once with Michele when I went and married her, then with Robin after breaking up to date her (a shitty thing to do, I admit), and then with

Daphne when I took up with her and had a baby with her. Therefore, I realize that, you know, if Kathleen is going to take me seriously, I am going to have to do something drastic. Instead, she beats me to the punch and does something drastic of her own.

Before marrying her, however, I experience the first red flag in our relationship. After coming home from a day of filming *Falcon Crest*, I find Kathleen in the upstairs bedroom on the phone whispering as I enter.

"I have to go," she says hurriedly. "Bye." Then she hangs up as soon as I inquire softly, "Who's that?"

Kathleen never says a word.

"Is that Michael?" I ask.

Michael is Kathleen's now ex-boyfriend Matt told me about. He is a lowlife who lives high above Laurel Canyon. Following their breakup, I went with Kathleen to his place to get her cassette tapes and personal stuff Michael was hanging on to. She was too afraid to go there alone.

Kathleen finally says, "Yes."

"What are you talking to him for?"

"I don't know," she says with a shrug. "I'm talking to him because he called me."

"He called you or what?"

"Yeah, yeah, he called me."

I can tell Kathleen is being less than honest with me. Finally, I say, "What's going on, Kathleen?"

"Nothing."

"Why do you look so frickin' guilty? What is going on between you two?"

"Nothing is going on, Lorenzo."

I confront the situation head-on. "After all the things you told me about him. Now you're calling him? Get Michael back on the phone."

Kathleen calls him and hands me the phone. "Michael, this is Lorenzo. What is going on between you two?"

"You better ask Kathleen," he says, "because she just left my house."

I turn and face her. "Kathleen, he said you just left his house. What's up with that?"

Kathleen has this guilty look on her face.

"Did you go up there and fuck him?"

"No."

Then I ask Michael. He didn't have to confirm what I already knew. He goes, "Yeah, man. You don't know the whole story."

I explode. "Get in your car and come over here!"

I hang up and look at Kathleen, incredulous.

"You know what is going to happen, one of two things," I tell her. "You are going to look at him and me in the room together. You are going to decide whether you want to be with him and I'll take off. Or you are going to decide to be with me and he'll be out of the picture forever. You'll have to make that choice."

Kathleen just sits there.

Finally, Michael shows up. The three of us sit down in the living room. Michael sits in one chair, I sit in another, and Kathleen takes the couch.

"Okay, Kathleen, who's it going to be?" I begin. "Michael or me?"

"I don't know..." she whispers and starts crying. "I don't know what I'm going to do."

"No, it's simple. You are looking at two guys right here, right now—me or him."

Kathleen points her finger at me. "I choose," she says, sobbing, "you!"

I look Michael straight in the eye. "Michael, did you hear that?"

"Yeah, man, I heard it."

I let him have it. "Then get your shit and get the fuck out of here. Don't ever come back, and don't you ever talk to her again."

Michael quietly gets up, grabs his stuff, and walks out.

Kathleen never moves, never gets up, and is still crying as I lay it all out for her. "Kathleen, you will never talk to him, you will never see him, you will never have any more contact with him or I am history. Understood?"

"Yeah, honey," Kathleen says tearfully, "I love you. I am so sorry."

"Fine, I'll give you this one. Don't be mad at him."

Later, some of my friends would ask me, "Why the hell did you marry her?"

I could never explain it other than to say that I know Kathleen well enough—or I think I do—that if she tells me she will not do anything, she won't. I guess she just has to get him out of her system.

She had to see the two of us together to decide, or whatever. As far as I know, she never contacts him or sees him again. We move forward in our relationship.

Kathleen and I spend the Christmas and holiday break with her parents in their mountaintop condominium in Mammoth. I officially ask her father, Jack, for her hand in marriage. In January, after returning to work on *Falcon Crest*, I get this impulsive idea to run off and elope with Kathleen without telling anybody. On a Friday afternoon, I run across the street from CBS Studio Center to a jewelry store and buy a gold amethyst ring—something small I can give Kathleen until I can buy her a more fitting wedding band later. That night, I drive us to Vegas in my Jeep Wagoneer, bad shocks and all, to marry her and follow in the footsteps of my dad and mom, who became husband and wife in Vegas four years before my birth.

We are like two giddy schoolkids laughing the whole way. As we pull into town, the first place I take us to is the Clark County courthouse to get a marriage license. Then we head down the Strip to find a fitting place to exchange our vows. My eyes immediately lock on the flashing marquee in front of the famous Graceland Wedding Chapel (I am a huge Elvis fan):

MICHAEL JORDAN AND JOAN COLLINS
MARRIED HERE

"This is a great idea!" I say to myself, pulling into the parking lot. Kathleen and I run inside.

An hour later, January 21, 1989, we make it official. We are married. Like young-in-love teens, we are both very excited.

We skip a honeymoon for now, and I return to work. We joyfully share the news with Kathleen's parents. Jack is fine with it. But her mother, Abby, is slow to warm to the idea. She is very disappointed that we sneaked off and married on the sly instead of doing it in front of family and friends. A few months later, to make it even more official, Kathleen and I have a bigger wedding and repeat our vows in front of fifty invited guests at Lakeside Country Club, where Jack is a member. It is a nice ceremony. Abby now feels better about it all. After the ceremony and reception, a helicopter lands on the golf course to whisk us away to the Biltmore Hotel in Santa Barbara, where we honeymoon for the weekend.

As we whirl our way into the blue sky above to the cheers of family and friends below, Kathleen and I smile and wave before I plant a big one on her lips. I remember thinking: "This is the one. This union will last." She is "good-time Keene." She never judges me. She loves me unconditionally despite everything I have done. I feel so lucky. I know even my father would approve of this one.

TEN

A Renegade in My Midst

THAT YEAR, Kathleen and I buy a beautiful ranch-style house in the Rancho area of Burbank, not far from the famous Walt Disney Studios. Kathleen owns her own horse, and I think how neat the location will be for her. She can stable her horse there, go across the street, and ride the nearby trails every morning with her girlfriends.

For the first six months to a year, our marriage is bliss. We have fun, laugh, and love each other's company. My kids, A.J. and Shayne, who still live in Los Angeles, often come over and bunk together in another room in the house. It is such a happy time in my life. We ride and hike together and take the two kids bike riding at the nearby park, just like a real family. Because they have known Kathleen since they were young, they instantly feel comfortable around her.

Over time, Kathleen changes. Reality sets in. I have responsibilities beyond just the two of us. Every time I pick up the phone to call Michele to arrange for A.J. and Shayne to come stay with us, I feel her resentment. Yes, I had another life and kids before I met and married her. But I was never aware of her feelings about it before we married.

I feel guilty anytime I pick up the phone to call Michele. Kathleen seems angry or depressed whenever I make those calls. Even though she denies the resentment toward Michele and my past life, every time I hang up the phone after a conversation with Michele, I find myself dealing with a very moody person. It is not exactly how I thought our marriage would work out. She is not the same person, and the changes alarm me. Soon it wears on the relationship—on both of us.

About a year into our marriage, other issues arise, this time over my doing love scenes with actresses on *Falcon Crest*. Throughout the season, the producers cast beautiful actresses to play opposite my character, Lance, and he ultimately becomes attracted to them. That was never a problem before with Kathleen, but now suddenly it is. She asks me all about the scenes I do. "How did you do them?" "Are you ever turned on?" "Is the actress you sleep with turned on?"

Sometimes in the heat of doing love scenes and kissing an attractive woman, you become aroused. Sometimes nature takes its course. One day, I make the mistake of telling Kathleen about a love scene I had done with actress Kate Vernon in 1984, after she had joined the cast to play Lorraine Prescott, the nineteen-year-old stepdaughter of Richard Channing (David Selby). The daughter of the great actor John Vernon, Kate is very pretty. Our characters engage in a hot romance that season. For the scene we are filming, wardrobe dresses Kate in this see-through negligee, while I wear a pair of boxers. Her negligee is so transparent you can see *everything*.

We are under the sheets, rolling around, making out. One thing leads to another. Kate is really getting into it. She is feeling me; I am feeling her. After the scene ends, I look at Kate and laugh. "I'm sorry."

"Sorry for what, Lorenzo?" Kate says matter-of-factly. "If I wasn't feeling you feeling me, then I'd think something was wrong."

"You're very, very kind. I appreciate it. I'm a little embarrassed."

Flashing a wicked smile, Kate says, "Lorenzo, you've got *nothing* to be embarrassed about."

I've always been honest with Kathleen about everything. I think we have that kind of open and honest relationship where we can express our thoughts and feelings openly without issues. Yet after I tell her what happened with Kate and me, even though it was a long time ago, Kathleen becomes livid. She's not the same person I could once tell everything to.

From that day on, I never tell Kathleen anything anymore. It breaks my heart to act that way. It breaks my heart because I have waited a long time to find someone as special as she is. As a result, the lines are now drawn. My relationship with Kathleen is never the same.

Unable to share that part of my life with her anymore, I become very depressed. I fall into a deep funk. Kathleen is not the only moody person in the house anymore. Because she is wife number three, I am figuring, What the hell am I doing wrong? Why can't I get a break here? You think you marry your best friend. Then, suddenly, she is this person with all these hang-ups, someone I cannot share everything with anymore.

The fact I work with other beautiful actresses on *Falcon Crest* now becomes a major issue. Kathleen wants to rehearse the love scenes that I am going to be shooting, not only on *Falcon Crest* but also on independent movies I make in between, including a series of *Snake Eater* movies I film in Canada for Cinepix starting in 1989. I actually put Kathleen in the second one of the series, *Snake Eater II: The Drug Buster* (1989). While I'm rehearsing my scenes with Kathleen, she wants to know exactly what I am going to do with whatever actress I'm working with. If I don't kiss open-mouthed when we rehearse, I had better not kiss open-mouthed in the scene. Suddenly I feel trapped in a relationship with a person I seem to hardly know.

The final straw comes a month later. During the first year of our marriage, Kathleen had introduced me to a sweet girlfriend of hers, Peggy McIntaggart, a gorgeous blond Canadian-born model and *Playboy* Playmate of the Month. She and Kathleen made a movie together in 1988, *Phoenix the Warrior*, just prior to us getting back together. Now Peggy frequently hangs out with us and comes over to the house for dinner.

One day, Peggy drops by looking for Kathleen. I am busy working on a dirt bike in the garage—changing a spark plug, starting the bike up, riding it up and down the street, and adjusting the carburetor a little bit afterward—when she walks in.

We start talking about how great it is Kathleen and I found each other after all these years. I am positive and upbeat about it with Peggy. "Yes, it's just great."

I never get into any gossipy stuff with her. Of course, deep down I am thinking, "If you only knew the truth." We are good friends, but she is more Kathleen's friend than mine. Therefore, I am respectful.

Peggy ends up staying longer than I think. She is there maybe an hour or an hour and a half, the whole time talking while I am working on my bike.

Peggy leaves. Kathleen comes home. With a wrench in one hand and my back to her, I tell her, "Peggy came by."

"What did she want?"

"I don't know. She was looking for you. We just hung out and talked in the garage."

"What were you talking about?"

Kathleen moves off to the side of my bike and is in my peripheral vision as I answer. "You and me and how happy Peggy was that we found somebody. That we seem like the perfect couple."

"Well, how long was Peggy here?"

I look up from what I am doing. "An hour and a half."

Kathleen walks off, goes into the house, and calls Peggy. She asks Peggy what we talked about. Peggy tells her, "I told Lorenzo how lucky you are to have a guy that is as sweet and nice and as cool as Lorenzo is and who cares for you and provides such a nice life for you." In other words, what every woman wants.

"How long were you here?" Kathleen asks.

Peggy pauses. "I don't know...maybe *three* hours."

I never wear a watch when working around bikes and machinery, and I didn't have one on that day. Never for a second did I think Peggy was there that long.

Kathleen storms down the stairs into the garage and says, "Peggy says she was here for three hours. You say she was here for an hour and a half. What the hell, Lorenzo. What the fuck did you do?"

I am just stunned. "What? What did you think I did?"

"You know damn well what I think you did. And you better be honest with me."

When Kathleen asks, "What the fuck did you do?" I know exactly what she is implying. That Peggy and I made love. Her accusation crushes me. I have this feeling in my stomach I have only had a couple of times in my life. The first is when my dad died in the hospital. This is the second.

I look across the garage at the person I am completely in love with, the one I think I am going to spend the rest of my life with. And she just accused me of something I would never do. The bottom line is she does not trust me. You cannot really love a person unless you trust them. It all comes down to that. If she does not trust me, she does not love me. If she does not trust me and does not love me, then she cannot even like me. Therefore, our relationship is a charade.

Furious, I charge through the entry door from the garage into the kitchen, grab a chair, and throw it right against a wall, leaving a hole the size of a basketball. Since striking Victoria outside the hospital that day my father was inside dying, I have never hit another woman. I have kept that promise to myself.

Storming into the room after me, Kathleen eyes the damage and with a suspicious tone in her voice says, "Oh, is *this* who you are? Are you going to hit me, too?"

"No, Kathleen, I will never hit you."

Without saying another word, I walk upstairs to our bedroom, undress, and head straight into the shower to cool off. As beads of water from the showerhead spray evenly across my face, I sentence myself as punishment for being an idiot again. "Okay, Lorenzo, you have done it to yourself again," I say to myself. "You are going to stay married to this person for five years."

True to my word, I stay married to Kathleen for four more years. During that time, I continue to do *Falcon Crest*. In the process, I earn nominations for two Soap Opera Digest Awards and a Golden Globe. I become the only actor to appear in all 227 episodes thanks to my agent, who negotiated that for me in my contract. Then in 1990, CBS cancels us after our ninth season.

To further transition myself from prime-time soap opera hunk to movie action hero, as I had already begun doing with the *Snake Eater* movies, I star in a number of other action movies for the next two years, including *Final Impact*, *The Swordsman*, *Snake Eater III: His Law*, and *CIA Code Name: Alexa* (the first of two, which I also direct). Then Stephen Cannell calls. He wants me to star in *Renegade*, an action/adventure series he is developing exclusively for first-run syndication.

Stephen's latest brainchild casts me as Reno Raines, "an innocent man on the run." Raines is a former police officer framed for murder by a crooked cop (played by Stephen, no less!). He tries to prove his innocence while bounty hunting on the lam for Bobby Six Killer, a professional bounty hunter whose life he had saved.

I love *Renegade*'s premise (it was originally titled *Vincent Black*, after the motorcycle the title character owns: a black Vincent) and sign on to do the series. We film a presentation pilot that Ralph Hemecker directs. It includes some fight scenes with me and scenes of me riding a motorcycle through Old Town Mesa and Julian against the backdrop of Bon Jovi's energetic 1986 ballad "Wanted Dead or Alive." Stephen presents the video at the annual National Association of Television Program Executives convention that year. Based on that presentation pilot alone, he ends up getting clearances for the series to air in 90 percent of the markets in the U.S.

While shooting a Spanish telenovela, a six-hour miniseries, in Columbia, South America, Stephen phones me with the good news. "Lorenzo, *Renegade* has been picked up."

I know this is my big shot and everything I have been looking for in my career: my own show.

"Stephen, thanks. I don't know what else to say."

"Don't worry, kid. Enjoy the ride."

Immediately after hanging up, two thoughts come to mind: I am happy not only to play a cool character on television, but also that my seven-year-old son A.J. will get to see his dad play a hero and what fun it will be for him.

Before I begin shooting the series, Kathleen and I throw a huge invitation-only Mexican-theme pre-launch party, complete with hay bales and a mariachi band. Party honorees are Stephen and the show executives, and we also invite our many close friends. One person I invite is my stepmom, Esther, who has known Kathleen since Kathleen was twenty (the two of them will remain close friends until Esther's death).

During the party, Esther sits and chats with Stephen. At one point, she whispers to him, "Stephen, you have to write a part for Kathleen in the show or you're going to break those two up."

Filming *Renegade* entirely in San Diego and the surrounding suburbs means I will have to live there and come home for the weekends to Kathleen and our Burbank house. I will hardly see her. I know, as does Esther, that is not going to fly with Kathleen. If anything, the separation will only accelerate our breaking up. Dad used to tell me, "A man is only as good as his word." And although I never tell Kathleen of my self-imposed "sentence" to stay in the marriage five years, I know I must see it through to the end.

Consequently, Esther is responsible for Stephen writing in a series part for Kathleen as Cheyenne Phillips, Six Killer's sexy sister and computer nerd, who bails my character out of many precarious situations.

Kathleen and I go down to San Diego and have fun working on the show. I make a great, lifelong friend in my costar Branscombe Richmond, who plays Bobby. Branscombe is a terrific guy, family man, and actor. We do stunts and fight scenes together and have a ball. It is a dream job for a guy who's been riding motorcycles for fifteen years, a job that utilizes everything I love, even martial arts. I owe a great debt to Stephen Cannell for giving me my shot.

Premiering in syndication on September 19, 1992, *Renegade* becomes a major hit in the U.S. and abroad. At its peak, the series airs in nearly one hundred countries (including Latin-speaking countries, where I remain immensely popular to this day) and in a dozen languages, rivaling syndication powerhouse *Baywatch* as one of the most-watched syndicated programs around the world. The fact there are so few martial arts shows on television is a big reason. Other than the huge success of martial arts movies and television shows such as *The Green Hornet*, costarring Bruce Lee as martial arts master Kato, and *Kung Fu*, with David Carradine as the wandering kick-ass monk Kwai Chang Caine, the genre had little presence on television until the arrival of *Renegade* and Chuck Norris's *Walker, Texas Ranger* in the 1990s.

In addition to creating the concept, Stephen oversees the writing of *Renegade*. Credit deservedly goes to a great staff of writers for the show's success, including Rick Okie, who has a great feel for my character and pens many of the scripts. A master of the craft, Stephen reads every draft and occasionally tweaks the dialogue or story arc in line with his vision of the characters and series as a whole. Usually his changes are spot-on and seamless; he makes everything fit together perfectly.

My character, Reno Raines, is like someone straight from a romantic novel, Fabio on a motorbike. Long, sun-streaked hair, knitted brow, bronze-sculpted body, bulging biceps and tattoos, a shirtless swagger—the kind of man who makes women swoon. Not only women, but men as well become huge fans of the series, a carryover from my days on *Falcon Crest*, where I carved out an image as a "television bad boy." Motorcyclists also identify with the show because television has not seen many positive-image riders like my character.

One problem we have doing *Renegade* is finding stunt men with a martial arts background to do fight scenes with me. They are a rare commodity. Stephen hires a bunch of cowboy stunt men out of Los Angeles who have experience doing fights in westerns. They know how to take a punch or fall off a horse, but if I try to flip them or do a wrist-lock on them and throw them, they resist and can get hurt. Taking a kick is far different from taking a punch. There is more force behind it. You have to let more air out to sell it. It is really a dance between two skilled people: the actor on the offensive doing the kicking and the stunt man selling the kicks and punches to the audience. If they both cannot sell it, the action looks stupid and people watching it soon know it's not real.

As a result, I not only act in my *Renegade* scenes but also serve as stunt coordinator and martial arts instructor. Those lucky enough to visit the set must wonder what's going on as I put the others through some drills.

"Okay, roll!"

At once, you see these studly cowboys in western wear and jeans rolling on the grass.

"Now the other way," I shout.

Back they roll on the other side.

"Again!"

To the naked eye, it looks like child's play. Actually, the drill will loosen them up and make them more flexible when it's time to do their kicks and punches in their scenes with me.

I usually spend most of the lesson time teaching them how to take a fall. That is one maneuver, believe me, you do not want to know.

Overall, the stunts play out better than I imagine. One favorite is in a first-season episode featuring World Wrestling Federation superstar Jesse Ventura. He plays a bad guy. My scenes with Jesse are just hilarious. I devise all the stunts in our fight scene to make sure they look realistic, and Jesse is the perfect pupil. Jesse is a monster of a man who towers over me, and he certainly does so in the scene. In a series of fight sequences I coordinate, Reno's job is to wear Jesse's character down. I let Jesse have the upper hand at first. With his brute strength, he picks me up and throws me against a tree, then picks me up and throws me over a log, and then whales on me.

Rolling myself into a ball like an armadillo, I block his punches until Jesse punches himself out. From below, I start working on his knees. I kick him in one knee. That brings him down on one leg. Then I kick him in the other. That brings him down to my size. Then I really let him have it. We have fun shooting that together. Afterward, Jesse and I both laugh over the kicking-him-in-the-knees scene.

"I hope your show has insurance," Jesse says in that deep, husky voice, as he fakes hobbling off to laughs from the crew.

Except for dangerous scenes, I do every stunt on the show. It is far more important to me that the stunts look real, even though doing them results in tremendous wear and tear on my body.

The actual motorcycle I use in *Renegade* is a customized 1989 Harley-Davidson Softail (or "A" bike) with a V-twin 1340 ccm engine with painted fire flames on its black fuel tank. We have three bikes that we use altogether: the "A" bike for close-ups; the "B" bike for long-shot footage of me rolling down the highway; and the "C" bike, a dirt bike made to look like the *Renegade* bike that my friend/stunt biker Paul Lane uses for real difficult stunts, including jumps on the bike. Everything else I do, including riding down rocky riverbeds, through sand, over rocks and gravel. I hit the ground a lot and fall off the bike twice—once in motion, once when getting off.

As with any film or television series, sometimes things go the opposite of how you plan. We are shooting a scene down on Imperial Beach. Whenever filming on the beaches of San Diego, we always draw large crowds of onlookers. This time is no exception. Production assistants do their best to keep the fans behind crowd-control ropes during filming. In the scene, I am supposed to ride my Harley almost to the water's edge to engage in dialogue with a fellow actor. The bike is so heavy—it weighs more than 650 pounds—that riding it on the beach will result in the rear tire spinning and digging itself into a hole in the sand. To avoid that, prop men lay a hundred feet of plywood down just under the sand to make a hard surface for me on which to ride.

We do the scene. I ride the Harley out on the plywood surface. Coming to a stop, however, I pull too much on my front brake. The front wheel locks; the bike buckles under me and then falls on its side as I quickly hop off. The crowd immediately starts jeering. "The guy can't ride!" someone yells and they boo me mercilessly.

The production assistants try quieting the crowd as I prepare to do another take. A smart-ass hollers, "Do it again, Reno!"

I am so frickin' embarrassed, but I never show it. Keeping my cool, I act professional. This time I stop, get off the bike, walk over, and do my scene with the actor without a hitch. The crowd reacts with stunned silence. Immediately after finishing, I ride out to the parking lot where all the trucks are. Hopping off, I get the rear tire loose and do doughnuts for everybody, just to prove I can ride a motorcycle.

The crowd cheers, and even the rowdy bunch of characters who minutes before jeered and booed me now wolf whistle and holler, "Way to go, Reno!"

ELEVEN

Starting Over

LITTLE DO I KNOW that after playing an action hero on television, I will soon find myself playing one in real life. In the winter of 1992, Kathleen and I are riding in the backseat of a black stretch limousine with our publicist, Joan Carey, on Fifth Avenue in New York. We're on our way to a press event to promote *Renegade*. Suddenly, a sedan coming westbound runs the red light as it crosses Fifth Avenue and careens out of control in front of us. It smashes head-on through a park bench and straight into the wall of a towering building behind it. Within seconds, smoke envelops the car.

"Stop!" I yell to the driver.

"What are you doing?" Kathleen says.

"I have to take care of this." I admit I have no idea what I'm going to do, but I have to do something!

I jump out of the limo and run fifty yards to the corner where the car has smashed into the wall. White smoke is billowing from under the hood, most likely from a busted radiator. I run around to the driver's side. The driver, an elderly man, is unconscious and slumped over behind the wheel, his head in his hands. I immediately reach inside and put my hand on his shoulder. "Are you okay? Can you hear me?"

The man groans but never says a word.

"I'm going to open the car door," I shout.

It gives me a better look. The man is seriously injured. He has a large gash on his forehead that is bleeding profusely, probably from hitting his head on the steering wheel. Suddenly, he moans and says, "My foot, my foot!"

"I'm going to help you out," I say, trying to stay calm.

I pull the man out as thick smoke sweeps toward the windshield, lift him into my arms, and carry him over to a park bench. His foot is definitely broken; the bone is protruding through the flesh. By now, a crowd of curious onlookers is on the scene.

"Call 9-1-1!" I shout out to them.

"They're already on the way," a man hollers back.

I stay with the elderly man until paramedics arrive. Tearing off my shirt, I wrap it around his head to put pressure on to slow the bleeding. I cradle him against my shoulder to keep him elevated. Minutes later, the ambulance, its siren blasting, pulls up to the curb. I inform the paramedics of the situation and they load the man on a gurney and take him away to the nearest emergency room.

Many of the onlookers, realizing who I am, start cheering as I run across the street bare-chested and bloodied, back to the limo. Joan greets me excited and breathless. "I already called the *New York Post*," she says, almost gleefully.

"You didn't."

Joan is over-the-top in her excitement. "We have to take advantage of this," she says. "This doesn't happen every day. This great opportunity just fell in our lap."

I am like, "Oh, no!"

Within minutes, word of my daring rescue spreads to every major media outlet and all the way to City Hall and the office of then New York mayor David Dinkins. The following day, the mayor, in front of flashbulbs and whirring television news cameras, awards me a commendation for saving the man's life. Action hero indeed.

THE FIRST TWO YEARS of working with Kathleen on *Renegade* pass without incident. During filming of the fourth season in November 1993, however, an earlier issue rears its ugly head: Kathleen's problem with me doing love scenes with other actresses. Not only is she making me crazy asking about it at home at night, but she's also making me rehearse with her the scenes I am set to play with whatever actress.

Then Kathleen takes it even further. She starts coming to the makeup trailer, sitting down next to the actress in the scene with me, and giving her the evil eye without saying a word.

One day, in the middle of filming, one of the makeup ladies lets me in on what is going on. "Lorenzo, please have a talk with Kathleen," she says. "The makeup trailer is like a mausoleum or a morgue when she comes in. She is making everybody uncomfortable."

I knock on Kathleen's dressing room and enter. "We have a problem."

"What about?"

"This deal you have about these actresses...They are very uncomfortable about you coming into the makeup trailer."

Kathleen immediately gets defensive. "I don't know what you're talking about."

"Nobody can talk in the trailer with you there," I counter, "because the vibe is so negative."

Kathleen is steadfast that she's doing nothing wrong. "I don't know what you're talking about," she insists. "I'm not doing anything. I don't have to talk to anybody."

"No, you don't have to talk to anybody," I tell her, "but you can at least be nice and welcome them to the set or something."

"I don't have to do that." Kathleen storms out of the dressing room.

About a week later, I reach my limit and go to her dressing room to tell her I want a divorce. But I make the mistake of actually telling Kathleen that while we're still on the set. She begins screaming hysterically.

I tell her, "I can't do this anymore, Kathleen. You're making my life miserable and everybody else's. I can't do it."

Kathleen starts screaming obscenities at me. At that point, I leave and return to my trailer as another actress enters hers to try to calm her down.

Branscombe knocks on the door to my dressing room. "Brother, this is not good," he says as he steps inside.

"I know, I know. I don't know what to do about it."

"She's exhausted," Branscombe says, exhausted himself from the whole sorry episode.

"I know, I know," I tell him. "We just have to finish the rest of the shooting tonight and then we can go home."

"Brother," Branscombe says after a long pause, with a smirk on his face, "couldn't you have done this at home?"

We laugh, but Branscombe is right. I have no business bringing my personal business onto the set.

Driving back that night to the apartment we are sharing in San Diego, Kathleen is sobbing uncontrollably next to me. Suddenly, she blurts out, "I can't live without you." An emotional wreck, she keeps crying. "I just can't think of my life without you."

It breaks my heart to see Kathleen like this. But she is beyond my capacity to reach anymore. After exhausting every avenue, including the two of us seeing a marriage therapist—but just one time, because Kathleen refused to go back again—divorcing her is my only option.

"We can work together," I tell her. "I'm not going to take you off the show. But I will find another place to live."

On Veterans Day 1993, we officially separate. We issue one statement to the press on the matter: that our marriage had "run its course" and that we had "mutual respect" for each other. Meanwhile, I move out of our apartment into a new place in a complex called La Mirage, near what is now San Diego's Qualcomm Stadium, just down the street from her. She comes to work every day as always and goes to Los Angeles on weekends. And I do my own thing. By mid-January 1994, Kathleen files for divorce.

Six months later, she meets a new guy—an actor.

"Great, I'm happy for you," I tell her.

"Would you mind," she says, "if he read for a part in the show?"

I oblige. "Of course."

Kathleen brings the actor down from Los Angeles with her. He auditions and gets a supporting role in an episode. I do a couple of scenes with him. He is a cool guy and a good actor. I am very happy for Kathleen. In fact, I'm relieved she is able to move on so quickly after our separation and that things are working out between us without any other issues.

BY NOW, MY EX-WIFE MICHELE and I are civil toward each other. The contentiousness between us finally ebbs after I start talking to her about A.J.'s and Shayne's well-being and invite the two of them to start spending three weeks every summer with me while filming *Renegade*. I love having them and we have a blast together. Michele also has since remarried. Her new husband, Craig Pike, works in construction. Lately he is spending most of his time in Arizona, building housing developments. In 1993, after doing a lot of work in Lake Havasu, Craig uproots Michele, A.J., Shayne, and their daughter, Dakota, and moves them all there permanently. That makes spending time with A.J. and Shayne even more difficult.

"Sure, okay, I guess I'll see the kids on vacation in the summer," I tell Michele.

But something always gets in the way, and it is harder on A.J. and Shayne to be away from me for that length of time. Both are suffering from separation anxiety. They are fighting and acting up all the time. A.J. is having problems in school, causing trouble and getting into fights. Michele calls and informs me, "A.J. is being difficult."

"Well, send him out to me," I suggest.

"A.J.'s in school," she says, "so I can't really do that."

Without the kids around or anybody to share things with, my life becomes very difficult. For the first time in a very long time, I feel all alone. The days are long, the nights longer, and every day is like Yogi Berra once famously said, "Déjà vu all over again." It is a huge change for me, especially for a guy who has always been in a "relationship." At the moment, however, I know I have to see it through and move to wherever life takes me next.

FOR ALMOST A YEAR after separating from Kathleen, I never date or see anyone and lead a celibate life. I focus entirely on myself and my work and, after hiring a trainer, get in the best shape of my life. One day in October 1994, a stunning twentysomething blue-eyed buxom brunette in a red bikini catches my eye. She is among the bevy of bikini-clad extras on hand for filming the beach scenes in "Muscle Beach," the eighth episode of the third season. This time Reno and Cheyenne go undercover as bodybuilders to solve a murder at the Hilton Hotel, right on Mission Bay in San Diego. Too shy to go over and talk to this beauty, I recruit Branscombe during a break in filming to relight the set for the next scene to talk to her on my behalf. "Do me a favor, brother, you see that girl over there in the red bikini?"

Branscombe breaks with that familiar smirk of his. "You mean, Code Red?"

"What?"

"Code Red, brother. You know, Code R-e-d."

I get the inference and laugh. "Okay, Code R-e-d, or whatever, just go over and talk to her and find out what her story is."

Branscombe walks over and talks to Code Red. She is smiling, he is smiling, and I am thinking, "Shit, what have I done?" I've sent "Wolf"—even though Branscombe is happily married and safe to send as my official emissary—into the henhouse.

Branscombe runs back to me with a big smile on his face. "Her name is Shauna Sand," he reports. "She grew up in La Jolla. She just graduated from college."

"Really?"

"Yeah, she also speaks French."

Now I am intrigued. "She does?"

"Yeah, she went to college in France."

My gut tells me she is somebody I can really like. "Well, what do you think of her?"

The wide grin on Branscombe's face evaporates into a serious frown. "She's been hurt, brother. So be careful."

Stupid me thinks, "I can help this person!"

On a longer break, I walk up to the craft services table and start talking to her. "How long have you lived in San Diego?" I ask casually.

"All my life. I went to school here," she says, flashing her super-model smile while fussing with her long brown tresses. "My parents moved me and my sister to Aspen, Colorado, just so I could go to a ballet academy there."

Shauna, it turns out, has been ballet dancing since she was a little girl. Her parents relocated her family to Aspen when she was thirteen just so she could attend a very prestigious ballet academy on a full scholarship, with the hope of turning professional someday.

Physically, Shauna is very attractive, with golden-brown hair that goes all the way down her back. Branscombe, however, is right. In talking to this pouty-lipped bombshell, I can tell something inside her is hurting. I later find out the cause: She had a difficult marriage with her first husband, who came from a wealthy French family. She had met him when they both were students at the American University of Paris in France and married him at the age of twenty.

I'm smitten with Shauna from the moment we meet, and we start seeing each other and grow close quickly. We are never apart even for one night. Besides working as an extra on *Renegade*, Shauna works on *High Tide*, a series Stu Segall is producing, starring rocker-turned-actor Rick Springfield. She goes back and forth as an extra on both. When working on *Renegade*, she hangs out with me in my dressing room and we become an item.

Although she's happy in her relationship with her actor boyfriend, Kathleen seems unable to accept the idea of me seeing anybody. Shauna's presence—in Kathleen's words, I am "flaunting" this so-called platform-wearing young girl around with me—really offends her.

Every day I depend greatly on Branscombe for his honest assessment of the vibe on the set. In the face of Kathleen's latest uprising, he says, "Brother, everybody is happy for you. This is fine. Just be happy."

I feel okay about my relationship with Shauna. I mean, we never carry on or kiss in front of everybody. During breaks in filming, we retire to my dressing room to keep our relationship out of plain view. I admit a few times I did not hear the first team call—when the cast needs to be on the set to resume filming—while in my dressing room. Kathleen immediately confronts me in front of everybody after a production assistant runs to get me. "We've been waiting for you!"

I immediately apologize. "I'm sorry, I didn't hear the call."

In 1995, my son and daughter, A.J. and Shayne, meet Shauna for the first time during a trip to Lake Havasu. I arrange to fly them to San Diego later to stay with me while I'm filming *Renegade*. In order for them to come visit me, they will take a commercial flight from Phoenix, then a connecting flight, and miss a day of school. Later, after getting my pilot's license, I will fly there to pick them up myself, bring them back for the weekend, and then fly them home.

During A.J.'s Little League practice in Lake Havasu, Shauna shows up dressed like a porn star in a halter top and the sheerest gym shorts you can imagine. His teammates rag on A.J. about her in the dugout. Embarrassed, he tells me afterward, "I can't do this, Dad."

A.J. and Shauna never become close, and although Shayne has her reservations about her, she just wants to see me happy. Kids have a way of seeing through the veneer better than adults do. My attraction to Shauna bedazzles me and prevents me from seeing what they do. Her physical beauty is toxic and every guy's fantasy, something I cannot live without.

In 1995, at the start of filming our fourth season, my relationship with Shauna is strong and I even give her her first on-camera bit, as a rollerblading brunette. Because of her presence on the set, tensions between me and Kathleen reach an all-time high. I do not want to take work away from her, but at the same time, if I don't cut her from the show, the working environment for me—and the rest of the cast and crew—will get even worse.

On Friday, December 1, 1995, we are wrapping filming of an episode of *Renegade*. That morning, on my drive to work, I flip on the radio station KIOZ-FM to listen to Howard Stern's radio show. To my surprise, his guest is Kathleen. She is on "live" along with her radio partner, Kimberly Hooper. They are cohosts of the popular weekend radio show "The Bad Girls" on KLOS in Los Angeles. Nobody knew she was going to be on his show—not even me. During the course of the interview on Stern's national radio program, Kathleen makes disparaging remarks about me, my relationship with Shauna, and Shauna as well that go beyond the pale.

At one point, Howard, referring to Shauna, asks Kathleen, "Did you ever clam on her? Pop a loogie on her? Anything like that?"

Kathleen snipes, "She's easy to trip because she's short and wears these really funky shoes."

Listening to her, I am left speechless. I cannot understand what would motivate Kathleen to do something like that. Previously I never sensed any bad feelings or vibes from her. In my mind, the interview is the last straw. Under the circumstances, I don't see how we can continue to work together. At that moment, I decide Kathleen can no longer be on *Renegade*. I go straight to Stu's office to meet with him. "Stu, I can't work with Kathleen anymore."

"What do you want me to do, man?" he asks.

"We have to get her off the show."

Stu calls Stephen, who backs me up. "Not a problem, Lorenzo, we'll have her do maybe two or three more episodes and it will be over."

Monday, midway into filming the fourth season, Stu informs Kathleen she is gone from the show.

After that, it is a much happier environment for everybody. Kathleen and I never speak. For now, it is better that way. Finally, I have some peace in my life, though it never lasts.

TWELVE

Slaying Demons

SHAUNA AND I ANNOUNCE plans to marry in April of 1996 in a small private ceremony at the upstate New York home of my mom and stepdad, Marc. With our marriage license in my hand, I quip to *Entertainment Tonight* prior to our nuptials that it is "the best $30 I've ever spent" and announce to journalists on our wedding day, "This is the last wedding in my life."

Every bit is true. Every word of it—real and heartfelt, an exact expression of my exuberance and my love for the woman I am about to marry. In the past, any time I think I have found true love, it only comes back to bite me in the ass. This time, I feel different. I feel Shauna is different, unlike all the others. She completes me as no other woman has, and I feel so fortunate to have this beauteous twenty-four-year-old in my life.

The day of our wedding, Shauna looks spectacular. Dressed in a sexy off-the-shoulder champagne-colored wedding dress, she has a lustrous glow about her as she joins me in front of family and friends. They say a person's eyes are a window to their soul. In her case, the look in Shauna's baby blues is telling: They have a vacant stare without any sparkle. A look I have seen only a few times before. That reminds me of what my *Renegade* costar Branscombe Richmond said to me the day I met Shauna, "She's been hurt, brother." It takes my marriage to Shauna to realize just how much.

Early in our relationship and our marriage, Shauna's sheer beauty helps mask the problems that will later surface. I always accept her for who she is, even before marrying her, unaware what trouble lurks beneath the surface. I got my first glimpse before we were married, but at the time I simply assumed it was a case of her personal taste versus mine.

To preface this story: Three years earlier, I had purchased a beautiful 3,500-square-foot home all made of imported Brazilian teakwood on a three-acre estate in Poway, a suburb of San Diego. The home was built by architect Ken Deleece and his wife, who spared no expense. It is my dream house, a little slice of heaven on earth: three bedrooms with an oversized family room that opens to a large deck with a specially designed glass fireplace and a separate two-bedroom guesthouse. The place also has a barn with four stalls, a pool and spa, two waterfalls, a natural running spring, and a volleyball court.

After announcing our engagement, I drive Shauna out to see the place and cannot wait to show it to her. We pull up in the long driveway and I offer my hand to escort her. We are there only a few minutes. Shauna takes one look at the place and says flatly with an expressionless stare, "I don't want to live *here*."

Shauna's reaction shocks and surprises me. She is talking about the home of my dreams, my little slice of heaven on earth, the place where I want to live, love, and enjoy the rest of my life. Finally, I counter, "Shauna, this will be yours, too, when we are married."

Shauna's bottom lip quivers for a second. She is steadfast. "I can't live here," she says, and storms off.

I never consider the fact then that this is a woman born with an air of entitlement, someone who has been given everything her entire life—and whose problems are much deeper than that. So what do I do? What any man would: make her happy.

I put the Poway ranch up for sale and buy us a $1.8 million house in the Los Feliz district of Los Angeles instead. Built in 1922 and completely renovated in 1990, the Mediterranean-style 4,348-square-foot home is situated on one acre, has four bedrooms and a maid's quarters, plus a guesthouse, black-bottom pool, and spa. Fifteen minutes from downtown Los Angeles and thirty minutes from Malibu, the gated estate includes a weight room in the four-car garage. It offers spectacular views of the city. I figure Shauna will be much happier living there, so close to the city and all of the amenities it has to offer.

In the interim, I wrap filming of the fifth season of *Renegade*. After the first four seasons in syndication, USA Network exclusively airs the series beginning in the fall of 1996. As a replacement for Kathleen, Stephen adds a new character as a semiregular, Sandy Carruthers (played by actress Sandra Ferguson). In April of 1997, the show ends its run on USA after 110 episodes.

Saying goodbye to the character of Reno Raines and the rest of the cast and crew is especially bittersweet for me. Deep in my soul, I feel so blessed and so lucky. It has been a great ride. I imagine that even as much as my father hated me riding "murdercycles," he is beaming with pride.

"Well, kiddo," he would say with a wide grin, "not too shabby."

Now married to a woman who is never happy, I find myself in yet another relationship I know is not going to end well. I do everything to make Shauna happy. Nothing does. Finally, I decide that maybe having a child—giving Shauna some responsibility and someone she can love and nourish—will make her happy.

On November 22, 1997, Shauna gives birth to a healthy baby daughter, Alexandra. Alexandra is a sweet child, but a handful from the day she is born. As it turns out, Shauna never embraces the responsibility of motherhood as I had hoped. Instead, I become a father and mother all rolled into one. Every night, poor Alexandra will not sleep or cries herself to sleep in her crib. Shauna never lifts a finger. I end up letting baby Alexandra sleep with us until eventually she is comfortable sleeping in her crib by herself.

Fortunately, in 1998, I land another series, as ex-Navy SEAL and CIA agent Rio Arnett in a new action-adventure series, *Air America* (no relation to the 1990 film of the same name), costarring with Scott Plank. Scott is a great guy, a theater-trained actor, and a fun person to work with, even though he has some demons of his own. The show is shot on location in Ventura County with a non-union crew, and so I drive there every day during the week for filming. I also make the series a family affair by casting Shauna and my mom in supporting roles in some episodes of the series. We film twenty-two episodes that first season, and the show premieres in early October 1998 in syndication. But doing the series beats the hell out of me. At the end of the season, I undergo reconstructive surgery on both knees due to the physical toll of doing so many daring stunts and fight scenes, first on *Renegade* and now on *Air America.*

The whole time I am recuperating at home, concerned whether *Air America* will be renewed for a second season, Shauna takes every opportunity to complain about our life. Her latest beef: She no longer wants to live in Los Feliz because she cannot take the kids to nearby Griffith Park anymore because of the element that picnics there on weekends.

Like a good husband, I try to make her happy. In November 1998, I put our Los Feliz home on the market for $2.5 million and look for another place for us to live. I could spend the rest of my life in that house, but even if I could move it elsewhere, I know Shauna would never be happy. As a replacement, I find in a million-dollar development near the golf course in the Braemaer Country Club in the hills of Tarzana a brand-new luxury home in the affluent, gated community of Mulholland Park. I buy it. I put Shauna in charge of doing whatever she wants to decorate it. She is just thrilled. But she ends up spending a fortune as a result. She puts in padded walls, silk wall coverings in three rooms, a wrought-iron balustrade in the foyer—you name it, she does it. I figure it is all fine if decorating the house to her satisfaction means she will finally be happy and have nothing else to complain about. She is not.

When Alexandra is about a year and a half old, Shauna gets pregnant and our second daughter, Victoria, is born on April 24, 1999. Because I'm now providing for a family of four on top of paying $8,000 monthly alimony to Kathleen, our marriage becomes fraught with worry. Shauna, however, is too much into herself to care. Nothing changes after Victoria is born. Shauna is not a hands-on mother. Diaper changing is not her thing. Consequently, I hire a live-in nanny to come to the house and do everything after I go to work in the morning.

Near the end of the year, I make an astonishing announcement: I am finished with acting and only interested in being with family. Six years of struggling with dull pain and four knee operations, most of them over the last several months, prompt my decision. Having said this more out of frustration than anything, I regret putting it out there and soon change my mind.

With all of this going on, I sign on to do a starring role in *The Immortal*, a new syndicated, hour-long sci-fi series. I play sword-wielding demon-chaser Raphael Cain (a male version of Buffy Summers, the Vampire Slayer), who's on an eternal quest to conquer the forces of darkness bent on destroying humanity while searching for his daughter, kidnapped by demons more than four hundred years ago. The show is not unlike the popular *Highlander* films and television series in that my character has three objectives: seek vengeance against the demons that killed my wife in the seventeenth century and kidnapped our daughter; send the demons back to hell (they've been initiating Satan's thousand-year reign on earth); and find my daughter. What attracts me to the property right away is the emphasis on the future and what it holds, something that has always intrigued me.

We commence production of *The Immortal* in December 2000, shooting the first six episodes in Prague in the Czech Republic—my first series filmed overseas—because production costs are much cheaper there. The show is special effects–driven and very difficult to do, and the role is very taxing physically. Rigged in a wired harness for hours at a time in front of a green backdrop, I chase demons up walls and on ceilings to kill them and send them spinning into a whirlpool back to hell. Making matters more difficult is the language barrier working with a non-English-speaking crew. I end up talking to the stunt men through an interpreter to explain the stunts.

We film the next episodes of *The Immortal* in Vancouver. I learned to fly in 1997 and bought my first plane a year later. Now Shauna stays in Los Angeles while I fly myself in my Piper Mirage back and forth to Vancouver so I can be with her on the weekends until completion of the seventeenth episode. We then take a two-week break from filming while the crew gets set up in Prague. We'll return there to film the remaining episodes—it'll save money.

I fly Shauna, Alexandra, and Victoria to Prague to join me—a huge mistake, since Shauna is eight months pregnant with our third child. When I come back to the hotel room at ten o'clock every night, physically and mentally exhausted from filming, Shauna invariably complains there is "nothing" for her and the kids to do. This even though I have arranged activities for them through a trip coordinator, including sightseeing excursions to the zoo. Physically, I am showing signs of wear: peaked and haggard looking with bags under my eyes all the time. I take B12 shots twice a week to keep my energy up, but through it all, I am just miserable.

Four months later, on February 2, 2001, Shauna delivers our third daughter into the world. We name her Isabella Lorenza; she's six pounds, one ounce, a beautiful new playmate for her sisters, Alexandra, now age three, and Victoria, now two.

Wrapping the first season of *The Immortal*, I return home to enjoy some quality time with Shauna and the kids while waiting to hear if the show will return for a second season. A few months later, former *Air America* director Dimitri Logothetis calls me. He has a part for Shauna in an episode ("Johnny's Guitar") of *Dark Realm*, costarring my buddy Corey Feldman, a new syndicated supernatural/paranormal horror anthology series he is filming and producing for Warner Bros. on the Isle of Man. I am nothing but supportive of the idea. As long as I have known her, Shauna has wanted to pursue an acting career. I had even offered early on to put her through acting school. However, she's unwilling to put in the necessary work. "That's boring!" she says.

Nonetheless, I now put Dimitri and Shauna together to discuss the role. Shauna accepts. I am happy for her; it sounds like a terrific career opportunity. Shauna flies to London and takes a ferry to the Isle of Man. With the difference in time, she is twelve hours ahead. I wake up early the first morning she is there to call to see how she is doing and how things are going. The phone in her room just keeps ringing. She never picks up. I call back and ask for the operator. "Give me Corey Feldman's room."

The operator connects me. Corey does not answer either.

By then, the girls start stirring, including Isabella, who is only a year old. I put her in the playroom with Alexandra and Victoria after breakfast and try calling Shauna and Corey again. The result is the same.

I call Shauna a third time at ten o'clock that morning—ten at night there. She's had a busy day filming, so I figure this is the best time to reach her. I call three different times. Again, she never answers.

Finally, I try one last time. I call Shauna at two o'clock in the afternoon—two in the morning there. The phone in her room keeps ringing. I ask the operator to put me through to Corey's room. Corey groggily answers on the first ring. "Hello."

"Hey, buddy, it's Lorenzo," I say. "I'm sorry to call so late, but I'm looking for Shauna. I have been trying for the past four or five hours to reach her."

Corey pauses for a long time and then says, "I didn't want to say anything, but she's been spending time with [a certain actor]. She was with him last night."

"You did the right thing in telling me," I say, trying to stay calm. "Go back to sleep. I'll handle it."

I call the hotel back and tell the operator to connect me to the actor's room. With the tone of my voice, I play it cool and never let on how mad I am when he answers. "Hey, man," I ask casually, "could you put Shauna on the phone for a minute?"

"Sure!" he says.

As soon as Shauna gets on, the charade is over. "What the hell are you doing?" I ask. "It's two o'clock in the morning there."

"Nothing," she says.

"Don't give me that," I say, my anger building. "I've called your room and you're never there. It's late and you're in another man's room. I'm not stupid. Are you fucking him?"

Shauna evades the question. "We're just having drinks together."

"That's not what Corey says."

Shauna immediately grows silent. Her silence is telling.

I tell her, "You just answered my question."

Furious, I hang up.

After Shauna returns home, we pick up where our phone conversation left off. Shauna continues to insist she did not have an affair; I insist she is lying. We are like two kids fighting in a schoolyard.

"We just had drinks together!"

"You did not!"

We go round and round. Finally, for the sake of the kids, I put our differences aside and move on, knowing it is only a matter of time before the truth will come out.

Despite the success of *The Immortal* in overseas markets, it is not renewed. After six months, I become free to pursue other roles. In 2002, with opportunities not as plentiful at the time, I accept an offer to star in *Raptor Island*, a sci-fi movie to be shot in Sofia, Bulgaria. I must return to eastern Europe for six weeks. Initially, I tell Shauna I will send for her and the kids after the first week of shooting. I like getting to the location first to get settled, get my bearings, and understand the demands of the production before I send for my family. It gives me a chance to prepare for my role without any distractions. That is my intention with this Bulgaria-shot movie.

After the incident with Shauna on the Isle of Man, however, I change my mind and decide not to bring them this time. I tell Shauna, "I'm just going to go to Bulgaria alone."

Shauna totally flips out. We have a huge argument. I am ready to forgive and forget. Shauna is not.

Then one morning at about two, I suddenly awaken and cannot breathe. Shauna has her hands around my throat. She is choking me. She's a small woman—something like ninety pounds soaking wet—so I'm able to pull her off me and jump to my feet. Shauna leaps at me, wraps her legs around my waist like a crazed chimpanzee, and tries to choke me again. I pry her off and push her onto the bed.

"Don't do that!" I warn her. "You can get hurt if I get any more upset than I am now. I might not be able to control myself!"

Shauna taunts me: "You won't do anything to me. You're a fuckin' pussy. You're a douche bag pussy. You have never stood up for anything in your life. You've never stood up to anybody."

I warn her again, "Shauna, don't push the buttons." I really do not want to hit her. I have only ever hit one woman, Victoria, and will always feel terrible about that.

Keeping my emotions in check, I grab the blanket and head downstairs to sleep on the couch, as Shauna shouts obscenities at me. Shauna attacking me in my sleep certainly marks the end of our marriage for me. I start thinking then about divorcing her. It is a hard decision to make, especially with three beautiful little girls. I really do not want to leave them alone with her.

The next morning, my first thought is I do not want the children to see us fighting and arguing all the time. I think enduring that kind of abuse and suffering, its damaging effects will be worse on the girls than us separating. At least when we're divorced and I have my time with the girls, I can be the kind of dad who gives them my undivided attention, without my narcissistic wife around to get jealous anytime I'm with them.

With the backdrop of my failing marriage, I fly to Bulgaria to film the movie. During the break from Shauna, I reassess things and come back with a new perspective. I decide for the sake of our three daughters we should try again to make things work. Upon my return, however, I barely set foot in the house and Shauna starts complaining about everything. It is then I realize why. Her constant complaining has nothing to do with our marriage, or our three beautiful children, or the spectacular houses, or the luxury car she has in the driveway, or the latest baubles and fashions she is wearing. She simply complains about everything; she is just personally unhappy, period.

I had never really considered this before. It makes perfect sense to me now, however, after flashing back to an event six years earlier when producer Gary Pudney asked me to cohost with Princess Stephanie of Monaco in a prime-time special for ABC called *The Champions of Magic*. The program, featuring magicians from around the world, highlighted Monaco's annual Festival of Magic. Shauna and I flew to Monaco and the producers put us up in two adjoining suites in the luxurious Hotel de Paris, right across from the casino, with spectacular views of the Mediterranean coast. The first thing Shauna said to me after we got into our rooms is, "Lorenzo, there is dust on the baseboard. This room is absolutely filthy."

I had no idea what Shauna was talking about. I inspected the baseboards closely. They seemed fine. I countered, "Shauna, this is the Hotel de Paris. This room that you are standing in is $8,000 a night during Cannes."

"I don't care."

Being a gentleman, I called and asked the manager to move us. He put us in a different luxury suite. I then asked her, "Is this going to be okay?"

"I suppose so."

While I was busy taping the special, Shauna created problems, day and night; she was miserable the whole time she was in Monaco.

Back to the present. She keeps carrying on, and I finally tell her, "Shauna, we have to go to therapy. There's a problem. You're unhappy. I don't know if you suffer from depression or are bipolar or what. Maybe a doctor can provide a prescription that will help."

"I don't need pills," she snarls. "I'm not going to any therapy."

"You have to go therapy, or we're finished," I say.

In September 2002, Shauna reluctantly agrees to meet with my therapist, a wonderful lady, Lyla Abouhamad, who practices in Brentwood. She is the same therapist I took Kathleen to see. The same thing that happened to Kathleen happens to Shauna. First, we meet Lyla as a couple several times so she can see the interaction between us. Lyla then wants to see Shauna individually. After going once, Shauna comes home crying. "I can't, I can't do this," she says. "There is nothing wrong with me."

"Honey, there is," I say. "It's not just you. It's me, too, because we are in a marriage. If Lyla feels you need to do some work, do so. You find out things you didn't know that are creating these traps you set up for yourself. I met with her by myself and discovered why I was doing the same harmful behaviors over and over. You need to find out the same thing."

"No, I won't," she insists. "I won't do it."

On October 7, 2002, without any hope of our relationship surviving, we separate after six years of marriage. I move out of our six-thousand-square-foot mansion to a Residence Inn, five minutes away, just off Ventura Boulevard in Tarzana. A few days later I tell Shauna, "I want a divorce."

My first call after moving out of the mansion is to Lindsay Miller, a nanny who had worked for us before. I want to rehire her. None of the nannies I have hired, not even Lindsay, have ever satisfied Shauna. She finds fault with every one of them. She fires one nanny, a sweet girl who took a silk flower because she was too afraid to ask. She fires another for "not folding the towels right." She fires Lindsay for being "too young" (then twenty, Lindsay is slightly younger than Shauna).

I ask Lindsay, "Can you help me with the girls?"

"Absolutely."

Lindsay bathes the girls in the morning, assembles a diaper pack for the day, takes the girls to the park when I am working—anything I need. She is a huge help.

Back in September 2002, when Shauna reluctantly agreed to see a therapist with me, I costar with fellow celebrities Traci Bingham, Coolio, Kato Kaelin, Tiffany, and Barry Williams as "recruits" in a new military-style reality series for Fox called *Celebrity Boot Camp*. It's a spin-off of the popular 2001 series *Boot Camp*, and drill instructors from that series put us through a rigorous week of military training. In the end, the two that survive will face off in a series of tests. The last recruit, the one who collects the most "dog tags," wins $50,000. The series is punishing to do physically as the instructors put us through tests of endurance, stamina, and fortitude. I'm happy for the exposure, yet I net little from it and continue to work feverishly to find suitable acting roles to get back on a network television series. I need to provide for my girls.

Not long after separating from Shauna, I move from the Residence Inn into a rental house in Malibu. I enroll Alexandra, Victoria, and Isabella in Webster Elementary School close to where I live. Shauna, meanwhile, continues to live in our big house in Mulholland Park until it sells and she can find a place to rent. Being a single dad is tough. Much tougher than I imagined. Juggling my career with parenting three young, excitable girls is even more challenging. Nonetheless, I am happiest when they are with me. We feel like a real family.

On weekends, Lindsay continues to help me with the girls. But when she decides to go to makeup school, I hire a replacement, Amanda, who works in the retail shop at the Sports Club where I work out. I bought some swimming goggles from her, and after seeing what a sweet person she is, I ask her straight up, "Have you ever thought of being a nanny?"

"Not really," she replies, "but I know you have three girls."

"You're right, I do. They're six, four, and two. Would you consider coming out to Malibu? I'd give you your own bedroom while I have the kids."

"Yeah, I could work that out."

Amanda steps in and does a remarkable job. The girls love having her around. She becomes a big help and a great friend of ours during this difficult transition period for all of us.

Now, with a much better living arrangement for everybody, I begin taking the kids for longer periods of time. What starts as Thursday through Sunday becomes Wednesday through Sunday and then Monday through Sunday. Essentially I end up getting the girls for fifteen days—two solid weeks—a month. Only a few times does something come up where I don't get the kids, but Shauna is usually good about working that out with me. I have to give Shauna credit. Despite our differences, she never tries to use the kids as pawns like so many other divorced parents do. And neither do I.

Alexandra, Victoria, and Isabella know they are free to call and talk to Shauna and see her whenever they want. I never step in the way of that. Shauna is their mother, and they certainly have that right. Gradually, more times than not, they find they are the happiest just staying with me.

In early December, I formally file for divorce. I never wanted it to come to this. I fully hoped that with Shauna seeing the therapist and getting the help she needs, we could save our marriage and spare dragging our kids through a long, messy divorce, with every tawdry detail and untrue accusation about us becoming public. But that's not what happens.

My main priority becomes ensuring our three young daughters are raised in a loving and stable environment. Given Shauna's previous meltdown and violent outbursts, I petition the court for full custody of the children. As my attorney, Cary Goldstein, makes a case against her, Shauna is very subdued in the closed-chamber divorce proceedings in Los Angeles Court. As expected, through her attorney, she does everything to discredit me. She says that I cheated on her for a year; had "no feelings" for our second daughter, Victoria, even striking her weekly and making fun of her; closed Shauna's bank accounts; and ripped up her credit cards. All of it is complete nonsense. I never hit our children, ever, and always provided well financially for Shauna and the girls during our separation, and would continue to do so after our divorce.

For the first year, I organize my life around my daughters. In January of 2003, I accept an invitation from producer Mike Fleiss to be a judge on *Are You Hot? The Search for America's Sexiest People*, a new reality series he is producing for ABC. Inspired by Ralph Cirella of *The Howard Stern Show*, the program features female contestants—most of whom want to pose for *Playboy*—and a panel of judges to evaluate their physical qualities in hopes they'll be proclaimed "the sexiest." I am thrilled over the opportunity to be back on a network series.

On Thursday, February 13, 2003, the day of the show's premiere, Shauna calls me and asks, "Would you take the children tonight?"

I say, "Sure. Do you want me to keep them through the weekend?"

"If you wouldn't mind."

I am always happy to comply when Shauna needs me to take the girls.

Later that morning, Kathleen's mother, Abby Dalton, calls me. We talk on occasion. I am once again on speaking terms with Kathleen. Abby and her husband, Jack, live in a beautiful new house with a pool in Camarillo, a suburb of Los Angeles. They love seeing the girls, and on a previous visit, the three girls enjoyed the fun and sun of being in the pool.

"Well, Abby, my show, *Are You Hot?*, is debuting tonight," I say to her. "Can we just stay and watch the debut with you?"

"Of course," she says, "so long as you bring the girls."

Kathleen is there. Her brother (and my friend) Matt is there. We have a great time. We laugh and joke and it is just like old times. That night, at eight o'clock, we watch the premiere together. It is just a ridiculously funny, hour-long romp, and everybody enjoys it. Abby and Jack wish me well with the new show. We say our goodbyes. I load the kids in the car and drive back to Malibu, which is about thirty-five minutes from Camarillo.

Around ten o'clock that night, I tuck Alexandra, Victoria, and Isabella into bed and think of retiring for the night after a long, exciting day. Suddenly, I receive text messages on my cell phone from Shauna: *What the fuck was that! You didn't tell me you were on a TV show. I'm taking you back to court for more money, you son of a bitch.*

I have no idea what Shauna is talking about. We already arranged for temporary child support and are still going through divorce proceedings. During the course of our separation, she is already receiving monthly alimony and child support payments from me. I do not pay much attention to her first couple of text messages. Then she starts calling me. I pick up and ask, "What are you talking about?"

"You didn't tell me you did a show on television."

"Shauna, first of all," I tell her, "the series is probably only going to last a few weeks. You knew I was making a show and—"

She interrupts. "You didn't tell me you were making it for ABC."

"What are you talking about? It's been in newspapers and all over in the press. ABC has been running ads to promote the show."

It's as if Shauna is on something. She is not even listening. "I'm coming to get my kids. I'm telling my lawyer."

I insist, "No, you're not getting the kids. It's after ten o'clock and they're in bed. Just come and get them tomorrow morning."

Shauna is unwavering. "No, I'm coming and getting them tonight. I don't care what you say. You're an asshole and a son of a bitch and you're keeping things from me."

Shauna is implying that I am hiding money from her, which, of course, is flatly not true. In the discovery process they do when you go through a divorce, all of your financial records, your tax returns, your bank statements, everything is all opened up and examined. Shauna is paranoid—and always has been—that I am keeping money from her. In truth, my only earnings that year are what I make from being on *Are You Hot?*, so I have nothing to hide. Right now, the only deal I have is to do this series for ABC and nothing else.

I end the call with Shauna, but she keeps calling me. I tell her again, "You're not coming over here. The children are asleep. You are acting irrationally. There is no reason to wake the children up."

Alexandra is in my bed; Victoria and Isabella are in the spare room. Amanda is not with me that night because it is not my normally scheduled weekend to have the kids. Finally, I hang up again and, thankfully, she doesn't call back.

I am in bed and watching television. Alexandra, now around five years old, is sound asleep with her head on my pillow. Her side of the bed is the closest to the window in the bedroom with a view of the ocean. Around midnight, I hear a noise and get up. I look out the window and see headlights coming up the driveway. Because the house sits on a summit, you can see the driveway from down off the Pacific Coast Highway. I am thinking, "It can't be. It can't be that crazy person I was married to."

Sure enough, it is. The car careens up the driveway and pulls to a sudden stop in front of the house. Suddenly, the car door slams shut, followed by the inevitable knocking on the front door. Shauna looks as if she is out of her mind. Like somebody took a fire hose to her. Her makeup is running down her face. Her hair looks like she stuck her finger in a light socket. I have no idea what is going on with her, but I am sure that whatever was going on in Hollywood that night, she was in the center of it all. She is completely out of sorts, not herself, and yells at the top of her lungs, "Open this fucking door! I'm taking my kids!"

I stand there and do not open it. I holler back, "No, you're not coming in here and waking up the kids. They're asleep. Just get in your car. I don't know what is going on with you. You're acting irrationally. Get in your car and leave, and I'll bring the kids to you in the morning."

She goes, "Fuck you, I want my kids!"

Shauna walks around the house and bangs her tiny fists on the windows. Now she is standing on the front lawn in front of a huge plate-glass living room window through which you could see the entire coastline, from Palos Verdes to Malibu. She has a huge rock in her hand.

I shout out, "Shauna, put that rock down or I'm calling the cops!"

"Fuck you, I want my kids!" she yells. She starts tapping the window with the rock like some kind of crazy person. The rock weighs about ten pounds and she has to use both hands to hold it up. She keeps tapping the glass the whole time, shouting, "I'm getting in there, you motherfucker. You can't keep my kids from me." She is acting like she is on speed or something.

"Shauna, that's it, I'm calling the cops!" I holler.

I walk into my bedroom, pick up the phone, and call 911. I tell the 911 operator at the Malibu sheriff's office, "I'm at this address. My wife and I are separated. We have separation agreements. She has legal custody of the children tonight, but she asked me to watch them.

They're asleep. They're in my bed. I don't want to let this person in. She is threatening to break through the window."

The operator says, "Hang on, we're sending out a unit."

I go back into the living room and Shauna is not outside the window. I'm thinking, "Where the fuck is she?"

I look around to see if I can spot her outside the windows. Then all of a sudden, glass shatters. It sounds like it is coming from my bedroom. I rush down the corridor through the hallway to the back of the house, where my bedroom is. Shauna has thrown the rock through the bedroom window. It has just missed Alexandra. It landed just short of the bed where Alexandra is sleeping.

Alexandra, now wide awake, is standing in the middle of the bed, screaming. She's looking out at her mother, who just threw this rock through the window, and wondering, What's going on?

I immediately grab Alexandra. She clutches onto me like we are jumping from a sinking ship. That is how scared she is. She wraps her hands around my neck, squeezing me as hard as she can, yelling into my ear, "Daddy, don't let her take me!"

"Honey," I tell her, "don't worry, Daddy is here. Daddy is not going to let anything happen."

As a cold, damp breeze whips its way through the broken pane of my bedroom window, I tell Shauna, "I've called the cops. You better get the hell out of here before they show up, or you're getting arrested."

"Fuck you!" she screams, and then runs off like a crazy, possessed creature of the night.

As a black belt in karate, I have been in situations where adrenaline takes over and creates this heightened sense of action in the body. The heart is pumping; you're thinking triple time what to do next. I quickly weigh all my options. Do I leave the house? Get into the car? Get the hell out of there? Or stay? I must stay to protect my daughters, of course.

With Alexandra still clinging desperately to me, I immediately run into the other bedroom to check on Victoria and Isabella. They are both asleep. They never heard the rock crash through the window or Alexandra screaming and yelling. I walk out and close the door behind me, still carrying Alexandra, who is still sobbing, still trembling, and still very upset. I quietly reassure her. "It's okay, honey, Daddy's got you."

"Don't let her take me," she says between tears, "don't let her take me."

All of a sudden, I look into the kitchen and this crazy person is standing in the middle of the room. Shauna. Later, I discover that she crawled into the house through a window in the guest bathroom. She jumped up to reach the window and pulled herself through, no small feat for someone her size and strength. It is one of those windows that pulls toward you from the top of the ceiling, down about fourteen inches. Somehow she squeezed her skinny-ass body through there, like a shape-shifter turning herself into a snake and slithering through. Now wild and out of her mind, she starts screaming at me, "I want my kids!"

It feels like a frickin' horror movie. Alexandra starts freaking out. She tries to get away from me, crawl out of my arms, and run away. She has that fight-or-flee adrenaline going. I say, "Shauna, the police are coming. You better leave."

"I'm not leaving!"

Shauna starts to walk toward me. I put Alexandra in my other arm and then turn my body so it is between this crazy person and my daughter. She intends to wrestle Alexandra from me, which is never going to happen. As soon as she is about ten feet from me, I hear a knocking at the door. Through the plate glass windows on either side of the door, I can see flashlights going back and forth outside.

I walk to the door, with Alexandra in tow, and open it. Two sheriff's deputies enter the living room. One of them says, "What's going on?"

I tell them, "This is my residence. This is my wife. We are separated. I have custody of the children."

Shauna interrupts. "You don't have custody. It's my fucking night! I'm taking my kids back."

I turn to the deputy in front of me and continue. "Officer, we have three children. This is my five-year-old daughter, Alexandra, who as you can tell is very upset by this."

The deputy says, "That's fine, I understand. You hang on to her. Where are your other children?"

"My other children are asleep," I explain, "in the other room."

The deputy turns to Shauna and says, "You want the father to wake the children up so you can take them home. Is that the deal?"

"Yes. They're my fucking kids and it's my night."

"Okay," he says.

He instructs the other deputy to take Shauna out of the room to the guest bathroom, where she climbed into the house, so he can ask me some questions without her around. Shauna sneers at me as she walks off with him. Meanwhile, the officer working with me says, "According to your legal documents, the custodial arrangement you have during this time of your separation, whose night is it supposed be?"

"Well," I tell him, "it's supposed to be hers, but she threw a rock through my window. She's acting irrationally. I don't feel safe letting her take the children."

"I understand that. We have two options here. You can press charges against her for breaking and entering and for harassment for what's she done. But you're both going to have to go downtown to make statements, and the children are going to have to be put into protective custody while the two of you are downtown. The other option is you let her take the kids home."

I say, "Shit, that's it?"

"I'm sorry to tell you," the officer explains, "but those are your only options. File a complaint; charge her with breaking and entering. That means both of you are going to have to go downtown, and the kids will be in protective custody for the next few hours until this thing is hashed out downtown."

I know if I press charges, my girls are going to be put into a room with a stranger from child protective services for maybe four hours, maybe longer. In my heart, I know I cannot do that to them. With everything they have been through already with our separation and pending divorce, the jumble of moving to a new house, starting over in a new school, and making new friends all over again, it does not seem fair to lay this on them, too. So I decide on the second option: wake Victoria and Isabella, who don't yet know anything about what is going on, and let Shauna take the three girls with her.

First, before I do any of that, I talk to Alexandra to try to make her understand. "Honey, you have to go with your mother. It is out of my hands."

"No, Daddy, no!" she screams. "You promised."

"You're right, honey, Daddy did. This one time, I need you to do this for me."

"But, Daddy, noooooooooooooooooooo…" The haunting echo of her plea rings in my ears.

I pick up Alexandra to console her and she sobs in my arms. It is such a helpless feeling, knowing I cannot help her the way I want, the way she wants.

It is one of the toughest nights of my life. Seeing Alexandra sobbing and shaking uncontrollably as I help her and Victoria and Alexandra into Shauna's car, and then watching them drive off down the winding driveway into the distance.

The deputy afterward tells me, "In the future, please be mindful that sometimes, as the old saying goes, 'No good deed goes unpunished.'"

The events of that night haunt me. Did she have no regard for her children? Was she insane? I mean, who in their right mind comes in the middle of the night to take their kids back because she thinks I am keeping money from her? What do her kids have to do with that?

From then on, Alexandra develops problems being scared at night, sleeping alone, having nightmares. Many nights, she comes into my room frightened and asks to sleep with me. That continues until she is almost twelve years old. I am sure all of it is because of the traumatic events that night with her mother.

Countering the heart-wrenching, emotional drama of the night before, the next day I receive some very good news. In the overnight A.C. Nielsen ratings, announced the following morning, *Are You Hot?* wins its time slot handily, attracting more than 10 million viewers. Furthermore, the show boosts ABC's total viewers by 4.7 million and adult viewers, ages eighteen to forty-nine, by 181 percent over the average of its regular programming in that time period this season. The series performs solidly thereafter and gives me lots of visibility on a major network again. But even though I'm trying to keep with the fun, outrageous spirit of the show, viewers crucify me for my scathing critiques of the contestants. That includes my use of a red laser pointer to highlight their "physical flaws" and the frequent risqué comments I make to these very attractive women, comments such as "I've got a burrito cooking down here."

On the upside, with *Are You Hot?* gaining traction every week, things look very promising for my career. That is, until the American military invades Iraq in March 2003 to remove dictator Saddam Hussein and his henchmen from power. Soon more than 200,000 U.S. troops are deployed in Iraq, and network coverage of the war is 24/7. ABC decides to cancel *Are You Hot?*, feeling it is too "hot" and "provocative" to broadcast against the backdrop of young men and women dying every day serving their country. They do not want to put out something light and frothy in such serious times. Of course, today the networks have no moral compass and the show would have stayed on. Shocking but true. I think *Are You Hot?* was simply ahead of its time, and years later Mike Fleiss agrees when the two of us are discussing his request that I star in another reality series, *Leave It to Lamas*. After ABC's cancellation, I beg off on doing any future reality series to focus on doing mainstream film and television roles instead.

Before getting into those, in September 2003 I parlay my notoriety into becoming the first celebrity drop-in on *Divorce Court*, 20th Century Fox's long-running syndicated television series. On the show I offer advice as an actor, a father of six, and a man married four times to Lawrence and Shenkika, a divorcing couple struggling to help their children through the split. On the surface, my appearance stuns the show's millions of viewers. In many respects, however, it makes sense to have me there. I understand the difficulty but worthiness of mending broken fences and rebuilding relationships with your kids. As I tell the couple, "It is important that you never give up on your children and understand your relationship with each is certainly worth fighting for." It is advice I would give anyone if asked, and I believe it still rings true today.

In the fall of 2003, Victoria and Isabella change schools. I enroll them in a Jewish preschool when my first choice, a Christian school, is full and has a long waiting list. Their grandmother, Shauna's mother, Lesha, is Jewish, and it becomes a great experience for them. They learn about different cultures, how to make Jewish crafts and foods. I never force the two of them or their sister, Alexandra, into any religion or into believing anything they do not want to believe.

They make their own choice, much as I did as a child. I let them know there is a universal power—a god—who makes the world revolve and who gives us choices in life. He is there to help us with the decisions we make. If we make a bad one, nobody holds it against you; learn from it and move on.

Every night before they go to bed, Alexandra, Victoria, and Isabella pray just as I did as a child. Seeing their sweet, innocent faces offering up their thoughts reminds me of heart-of-gold Emmy praying faithfully with me at my bedside nightly. It underscores the key role faith has played in my own life, how it has guided me through the choppiest of waters and the stormiest of seas, reminded me that every intention has consequences. And it has made me mindful that I am never alone.

THIRTEEN

Living in Anticipation

LEAVE BEHIND all the death-defying feats, explosions, and special effects as an action star in television and film and return to the basics. Without all the toys to fall back on, I put my acting skills to the test. In February 2004, the producers of the daytime soap *The Bold and the Beautiful* cast me as Hector Ramirez, a deeply flawed character who, on the surface, is nice and mild-mannered, but who has a darker temperament just beneath.

Hector is tailor-made for me. He is a guy with a contentious back story—a star high school athlete who went to public school and whose life is now rife with dysfunction. The opportunity is perfect for me at this stage of my career to get back to the real craft of acting. I have a wonderful fan base that loves to see me do action, but doing this series is a nice change.

Risking life and limb in an action series is not a big challenge for me. But now the thought of me, a forty-six-year-old man, stripping down to my skivvies and seducing a female costar on camera makes me a nervous wreck. Unlike my days in peak physical condition on *Falcon Crest*, the love scenes make me more uncomfortable and are more difficult for me to do. I know that sounds strange coming from a guy who seemingly built his entire career as a Hollywood heartthrob. But I never gave myself that title; it is something the media tagged me with. It is funny that some still think of me in those terms. There are a lot worse things I could be called, so I guess "heartthrob" is not so bad.

I do *The Bold and the Beautiful* for three seasons until my final appearance in my 240th episode as Hector in December 2006. I enjoy every second of working on the series with such a fine cast of actors and, unlike during my childhood, embrace the city of New York. At the end, I am ready for new adventures when that chapter closes. During this period, I also film two or three television pilots and another independent movie, none of which gain any traction.

One morning in 2006, my son, A.J., calls. He is now living in Los Angeles pursuing—to my shock and surprise—a career as an actor. I am in New York taping episodes of *The Bold and the Beautiful*. It is the best our relationship has ever been since divorcing his mother and my ex-wife Michele. I have admitted to both him and his sister, Shayne, that I was never around enough when they were young, when they needed me most as their father. So now A.J. and I have mended our fences and spend as much time together as our schedules allow. It is always enjoyable being around him and seeing life through his eyes.

There is a long pause after I answer the phone. I wait a second, and then I hear A.J.'s voice. "Dad?"

"Yes, Son, what is it?"

He pauses again. "Dad, I need to tell you something."

By the tone of his voice, I can tell it is something very serious.

"I went clubbing in Hollywood and, well, got drunk."

What any of that has to do with me escapes me for a second. "Are you okay?"

A long pause. "Well, not exactly." A.J. takes a deep breath. "I got together with Shauna."

It does not surprise me. Since our divorce, Shauna has a reputation for prowling the clubs at night. My first thought is that A.J. happened to run into her.

"When did you see her?" I ask.

"Two weeks ago."

A.J. pauses again. Upset, his voice cracks as he adds, "More than that happened."

Now I start to realize what this is all about. I blurt out, "Did you hook up with her?"

A.J. is silent.

I ask, "You had sex with her, didn't you?"

"Yeah, I did, Dad," he confesses. "I'm sorry it happened."

Just hearing it breaks my heart. I cannot talk anymore to him about it. "I have to hang up, Son."

I cannot believe my ears. It devastates me. For days, I cannot speak about it. I hate Shauna for creating this divide between A.J. and me. Finally, I call her.

"What is this about you and A.J.?"

Shauna is evasive about the whole thing. "Nothing happened."

"That's not what A.J. said. How dare you!"

Shauna tells her side of the story. She denies everything, claiming nothing happened between them. They ran into each other at the clubs. They both got drunk. Afterward she took him back to her Malibu condominium because, in her words, "He was upset."

"Say what you want, Shauna," I tell her, "but A.J. has no reason to lie to me. You do."

I hang up.

Getting to the bottom of it, I find out more than I wish. Their coupling is a classic case of misery loves company. Two people under the influence, who feel sorry for themselves, talk about what "a rotten guy" I supposedly am. Getting together afterward, they do the one thing they know will hurt me more than anything else: have sex together. I can never look at Shauna with anything but contempt after that.

I have survived many things in my life. I survived the fear of losing Dad and living my life without a father. I survived the fear of never finding true love. I survived the fear of losing it all financially and subsequently filing for bankruptcy. I am not sure how I will survive this and ever have a relationship with A.J. and Shauna again.

Forging ahead, I know I can count on one solid, sure thing: my relationship with my three daughters Alexandra, Victoria, and Isabella. They remind me of my sole purpose every single day at this stage of my life: to provide for them, to care for them, and to spend time together so they will never doubt how much they mean to me. All my motivation stems from them and my passion to do well for them. Whether it is starring in independent movies, flying to Chicago to do an autograph show, or taking a chance to do a stage play, I just do it. For them.

In February 2007, after exiting *The Bold and the Beautiful*, I return to Los Angeles to live, work, and reconnect with my twenty-three-year-old daughter, Shayne, while still having nothing to do with A.J. My aching heart is slow to mend over the incident involving him and Shauna, between starring in countless independent movies. Anytime I try to work out problems in my life, I get on my Harley and ride. Although they may not go away, an hour of riding on the open road pushes them to the back of my mind until I can work through them and face them again. To heal from the deep hurt within over A.J. and Shauna, riding my bike helps cure my heartache and lift up my soul more often than not.

As an actor and a performer, unless you have passion behind what you are doing, there is no point to doing it. The most amazing opportunities sometimes come from things you deep down think you will never, ever do. Like live theater. I have always been attracted to the idea of working on the theatrical stage, and that August I take the plunge by starring as the king of Siam in a reprisal of *The King and I* at the Ogunquit Playhouse in Ogunquit, Maine. It is a real adrenaline rush for me playing a character in front of a live audience for the first time, hearing the spontaneous reaction from a full house every night: the resounding cheers and applause, the roars of laughter. I find the whole experience nothing short of spectacular, including the impressive work that goes on behind the scenes to bring it all together, to make every actor shine, to make the production flourish. I enjoy the experience of working in the theater so much that I do even more in the future.

To my surprise, Mom is there for my musical stage debut. Now eighty years of age, she drives seven-plus hours to Ogunquit, Maine, from New York City, to be there for me. Seeing her there sitting in the front row, beaming with pride, reminds me just how important she is to me. How she has always been there for me, even though when I was much younger I never quite saw it that way. She was the proud parent standing there for my graduation from Farragut Academy. She was there after my divorce from Victoria. She has helped me through every personal disappointment, always sprinkling a little bit of her good-witch magic over it. Not to trivialize it, but I realize it is her way of handling the many tragedies in her life, the reason she has survived these many years.

I am beyond the resentment I used to have for my mother, feeling I wasn't loved. I understand now that my feelings way back when were simply a reflection of how I expected her to love, without regard to what she was dealing with. Seeing Mom there front and center that evening helps me realize that no one can measure up to our expectations, and it is not something you can force someone to do. My mom has loved me as much as she could, in ways that are unique and according to her personal life experiences. She is an amazing woman. A survivor. She goes through life looking at the glass half full, not half empty, and the older I get, the more I strive to be like her.

In fact, I am the first to admit that through all of the events in my adult life, both positive and negative, my New York family has stood firmly by my side. It might seem odd that I refer to them that way, but nearly all the events that have shaped my adult life have taken place in California. My career choices, with the exception of my stage and singing. My marriages and divorces, racing and motorcycles, the births and raising of my kids. All of them took place in California.

My family back East has been, in a way, a form of shelter and support for me in times of tribulation and reflection—almost an oasis, a place to escape the craziness of my life out West. My mom, Arlene, and her husband, Marc, have always been supportive toward me and have never criticized me or uttered a harmful word to me when events have gone south in my life. My mom has always tried to guide me without being harsh or insensitive, even when I was making some of my craziest decisions.

My New York family has been my rock. My little sister, Carole, and her now husband, Phillipe, have been there for me when I had no one to turn to for help. Carole, who hid chocolate under her pillow and whose dolls I used to undress and fantasize about, has been my sounding board and most loving and trusted confidante. I love her with all my heart and am so happy she has found such a generous and jovial person to share her life with.

My younger brother, Stephen, a gifted artist and scholar, has bridged the gap between our generations with his love of music and the arts. We connect on a spiritual level as well and, along with my sister, share a unique and common thread of understanding when it comes to our mother and how differently we were raised by her. I am grateful to have the balance that my New York family gives me, and I shudder at the thought of how my life might have turned out without them.

That same year, in 2007, I challenge myself and take a page out of Madonna's image book to reinvent my own image and keep people interested. I will sing. The fact is, I have been singing for years, as I noted earlier, but have never really worked on doing more with it. Sometimes I feel like I was born twenty years too late. Despite growing up with the likes of Pink Floyd and Led Zeppelin, I have always felt closer to the more melodic music my parents played and enjoyed, the American songbook. Working with a voice coach and seeking advice from industry pros, including family friends Vic Damone and Michael Feinstein, I start testing the musical waters. As a tribute to my parents, I begin doing a cabaret act in nightclubs, at casinos, and on cruise ships, singing the standards first popularized in the 1940s, and, between songs, regaling audiences with stories of my legendary parents.

Every time I take the stage, I feel their presence, especially Dad. I imagine him with a wide grin on his face, sitting in the front row. Unlike when he silently watched my first starring movie role early in my career, he is cheerfully applauding, nudging the person next to him, and saying, "That's my son!"

In 2008, after swearing off reality shows, I accept a tempting offer to return to television as a contestant for the second season of CMT's *Gone Country*. At the same time, I watch with pride as my charming, bubbly blond daughter Shayne walks off as the winner of ABC's *The Bachelor.*

Determined to make her own name for herself in Hollywood, Shayne teams up with Mike Fleiss, who formerly produced *Are You Hot?* for ABC, to develop a reality television show of her own. She calls and tells me Mike thinks he can sell a show about her and her life and A.J., with whom I have not had a relationship for three years now, since the incident with Shauna. I tell her, "That's great, honey, I'm happy for you."

Mike calls me soon after this and says the E! Entertainment network is interested in doing the show with Shayne.

"What would you like me to do, Mike?" I ask.

"We can't get the show on the air without you."

I tell Mike, "I'm trying to get some decent acting roles. This reality scenario isn't usually a good idea."

"We'll keep your appearances to a minimum," Mike promises. "Just do a couple shows here and there."

The show, now titled *Leave It to Lamas,* gets greenlit. I know once production starts it means I am going to once again see my twenty-seven-year-old son, A.J. The show presents a real opportunity for me to get closer to both A.J. and Shayne. To be honest, our relationship could be better.

In filming the series, Mike builds up the drama of me and my kids meeting again in a nightclub where I am performing a medley of songs as a tribute to my parents. Shayne is there, and her half sister, Dakota, whom I always treat as my own daughter, is also there. Shayne's friend Christine is there, and so is A.J. When it comes to the part of the show where I introduce them, I introduce A.J. last. It is an emotional moment for both of us, a very real, unstaged moment. After the show, with the cameras still rolling, A.J. walks up to me and hugs me because he has never seen me perform my live stage act before. With tears in his eyes, he says, "I'm so proud of you. I never knew you had this in you."

After we embrace, I tell him tearfully, "Thank you, Son."

We walk off. They film that moment to the very end. What Mike chooses to air, however, is nothing like what happened. Instead, he purposely cuts the part out where I introduce A.J. Therefore, the television audience thinks after introducing everybody else, I purposely slight him. And that the tears A.J. sheds are because I never acknowledge him, not because he is proud of me. Seeing the final cut, I call Mike, furious. "You're going to kill the show! The minute you make me out to look like a bad guy is the minute the audience will turn off the show."

Sure enough, after its October 11, 2009, premiere, the ratings for *Leave It to Lamas* go south, and E! cancels us at the end of November after eight episodes. The show relies too much on this heavy, contrived drama between A.J. and me, which is sad to watch. The viewing public does not want to see a father and his son working out issues on television. Our program is not Dr. Drew. It is supposed to be an upbeat, happy reality series about a very charismatic young woman going out with her girlfriends and having a good time.

Hanging a whole show on a negative event—the so-called drama between my son and me, a drama that did not exist—ruins what could have been a terrific opportunity for Shayne to create a "brand" for herself, just like Jessica Simpson and Kim Kardashian. She has more personality, charisma, and natural talent, and it is a great misstep on Mike's part. He blows any chances for her. The only good to come out of doing the show is I have a new relationship with A.J., which I would never have had had I not done the series. For that, I am eternally grateful. But I swear never to work in reality television again. It is a promise I try to keep.

On October 13, 2009, two days after *Leave It to Lamas* premieres, I am set to meet with a former producer of *Baywatch* at Sony Studios about a new series. He and I have been talking about doing something together since I came back from doing *The Immortal*. He is developing a new first-run, thirteen-episode series he wants to film in Puerto Rico. It's based on the legend of Blackbeard the pirate, and he owns all the rights. That afternoon, I sit down with him and three or four other Sony Studios executives to talk about the series. Unfortunately, it never comes to fruition.

After our meeting ends, I walk out of the producer's office to my car and the paparazzi who are standing there. They have their cameras out and start yelling, "Hey, Lorenzo, over here!"

I'm thinking, "Why are they here, on the lot? And how did they get on the lot?" It could be they happen to be there to cover something else. I know it is not about the Blackbeard show, since news of it is totally under wraps. I have always been friendly with the paparazzi. I feel it does not benefit me as an actor not to be friendly with them. They have always been fair to me. They have never shaken cameras in my kids' faces. They have always kept a respectable distance from me and my kids around Beverly Hills.

Just as I get closer to them, one of them shouts out, "Lorenzo, what do you think of Shauna's porn tape?"

I go, "What? What porn tape?"

Another says, "You don't know?"

"No."

"She's just released a porn tape on Vivid."

I honestly think the guy is joking. "Get out of here!" I shout. "I have no idea what you are talking about."

"You don't?" he asks again.

"No, I don't."

"Well," the reporter says, "what do you think about it?"

"If it is true, I think it is the most disgusting thing I have ever heard. We have three little girls. Why would somebody do that?"

The paparazzi keep peppering me with questions, but I hold back any further comment. "Thanks, fellas, I'm late for another meeting as it is."

I get in my car. I go back home and immediately call Shauna. "You'll never believe what a paparazzi guy just told me today. He said you did a porn tape?"

A short pause and then, "Oh, yeah, I shot a video with my boyfriend, and we did it together," she says, like nothing is wrong. "I think it's just wonderful."

"Are you fucking out of your mind? You did a porn tape? We have three children, three little girls, Shauna. What are you going to do when they grow up and somebody comes up to them and says, 'Your mom did a porn tape'?"

"Well," Shauna pouts, "if you'd pay me any money I wouldn't have to do porn."

Her statement really rubs me the wrong way. "I pay you the court-stipulated settlement amount every month. Don't you think of anybody else besides yourself, ever?"

"Well, I had to do what I had to do," she says. "By the way, they paid me a quarter of a million dollars."

I pause and say, "Well, aren't you proud of yourself. Aren't you just the smartest, most elegant, and classy person I have ever met. You got $250,000 for fucking some guy on a video. Congratulations."

"Well," she says, "you just don't understand."

"No, I understand perfectly. I understand that you are the most important person to yourself. That nobody else in your life matters. Your kids don't matter. Your mother doesn't matter. Nobody matters but you, to do whatever the fuck you want, whenever you want."

Shauna reverts to the same old refrain. "Well, I wouldn't have done it if it wasn't for you walking out on me."

We have this whole argument on the phone about whether I walked out on her. That we went to therapy. That she left therapy. That she wouldn't go back. And that is why I left her because I could not live with such an insecure, neurotic human being.

That same day, Vivid Entertainment officially releases the sex tape, filmed earlier in the year. The footage of Shauna and her French boyfriend (he is just the latest she picked up one night at a Hollywood nightclub) is, from what other people who have seen it tell me, very explicit and disgusting. To this day, I've never watched it, nor do I ever plan to see it. Vivid Entertainment bills the tape as "Hollywood's princess of pumps, queen of the eight-inch heel, the belle of brand-name garb," and naturally links her to me, riding on the coattails of my celebrity. The ad copy says: "Lorenzo Lamas never really could control her, and now the secret is out! Look who's the renegade now, Lorenzo!"

With the $250,000 she receives, Shauna proves once again that everything is all about her. She burns through money almost as fast as she gets it, even buying herself the most expensive vehicle on the planet, a Bentley. Never once does she think of setting money aside for her three daughters, doing something that might just benefit them in the future. Of course, the news makes me furious, yet confirms everything I know about Shauna and why we are divorced in the first place. At least I know that decision was the right one.

Back in 2000, before Shauna and I were divorced, I had made a conscious effort while starring in *The Immortal* to put money away, not for myself, but for my children. I put $90,000 into a trust for them. I did it because I wanted to make sure that if anything happened, my girls would have something. I owe it all to my business manager, Liz Kenney, for helping me make it happen. I remember her saying to me one day, "You know, Lorenzo, this is something you ought to think about, no matter what happens. I'm not saying it will, but if you and your wife, Shauna Sand, ever get divorced, the courts can't touch this money." Liz set everything up through Loeb & Loeb, a respected and very large law firm with offices in Los Angeles. That trust fund has since survived my divorce with Shauna and two bankruptcies; the money has never been touched. It's there for my girls when they go to college and start their lives, something I never had.

After the porn tape and all that, things just cannot get any worse. But my life is about to change again—this time for the better.

I AM A VERY PHYSICAL GUY and a big believer in staying healthy. My healthy habits include regular exercise, of course. I routinely swim, work out, and train at the Sports Club not far from where I live. It offers everything I need to stay fit and in shape, and it is such a great place for me to hang out and clear my mind as well as let my body rest.

In late October, after doing a two-hour workout, I decide to enjoy a drink at the café at the Sports Club. I sit down at a table there, and this young, attractive woman seated at another table keeps looking over at me. I try not to show that I know she is. She is engaged in conversation with a friend of hers, Mara, who is also an executive at the club, the person in charge of memberships. The dark-haired beauty who cannot take her eyes off me says to Mara, "My God, that guy looks like Lorenzo Lamas."

"You dummy," Mara says. "We're in Hollywood. That *is* Lorenzo Lamas."

"Nooooo!"

"Yes," Mara says confidently. "You want to go over and meet him?"

Suddenly, her friend is too embarrassed to look at me. "What is he doing now?" she asks.

"Come on, he's not going to bite you."

Mara gets up from her seat and brings her friend over to introduce her to me.

"Lorenzo, I want you to meet a new friend of mine. This is Shawna. She's moved up here with me from San Diego."

I get up and smile. "Oh, hi, how are you doing?"

Shawna, who I later learn is rooming with Mara in a house on Highland Avenue with four other roommates, has the biggest, widest, most natural smile on her face—just this huge grin. I shake her hand.

It turns out Shawna has had her eyes on me longer than just that day. A few days earlier, she is at the club and Saul, a friend I train with, sees her and asks her to have coffee some day. Saul is married and friends with Mara. Shawna sees the ring on his finger and says, "You're married. I'm not having coffee with you."

"No, no," Saul says, "just as friends."

"I can do that."

They sit and talk a while. Suddenly Saul says to her, "You know—" he points over at me sitting in the café—"he is in great shape, you're single. Why don't the two of you get together?" He says it just to be funny. I mean, I am fifty years old, for heaven's sake. Shawna giggles at the thought. I had been dating Nancy, a woman I met at a Planet Beach beauty contest in Las Vegas. She lived in Los Angeles. We dated a couple of times and were kind of in a relationship.

Now that Shawna and I have met and are sitting together in the café, I peer into her eyes and tell her truthfully, "I'm seeing somebody."

"Uh-oh," she says, surprised. "Okay, we can just be friends."

"I'd like that."

After we say our goodbyes, I leave the gym that afternoon a very confused person. Here is this young, beautiful woman, who honestly wants to get to know me, but I cannot because I am seeing somebody, although not seriously. I keep thinking about Shawna all day. Something about her is different than the others. I call Nancy to tell her. "We're going to have to move on," I say. "I don't see this relationship progressing."

"Why not?" Nancy asks.

"Well, I really haven't had that physical connection, which is really important to me," I confess. "And I imagine it is to you, too."

"Yeah."

"I don't feel it. Do you?"

"Honestly," she says, "I just think you are a great guy."

I tell her, "You know what, Nance, I think you are a great girl, too. Let's just move on and be pals."

I cannot wait to see Shawna and tell her I am available. I go to the gym the same time every day until I see her again, but I try to play it a little cool and not be a complete dork. I manage to wait until she comes down from the gym to the café, where she always eats after she works out. She sits down and waves at me, and I wave at her. Mara is with her. Writing down my home phone number on a piece of paper, I walk over to their table and put it down next to Shawna.

"How is it going?" I ask.

"Good, Lorenzo," she says with a smile, "how are you?"

Immediately sensing something, Mara stands up. "I think I'll leave you two alone." She exits.

Shawna is all smiles sitting next to me. "Do you like to go to the movies?" I ask.

"Yeah."

"Maybe we can catch a movie sometime."

Suddenly, her smile fades. "Wait a minute. You told me you were dating somebody."

"I was. It just so happens I broke up with that person."

That big smile of hers returns. "You did?"

"I did. You want to go out?"

"Yeah!"

Our first date is to a Mexican restaurant. With my black Escalade in the shop, I pick her up in my dad's Rolls-Royce. Waiting to pick her up, I keep thinking that as soon as she sees me she'll think, "Here's this old guy with this old car." None of that happens. She is all smiles and happy to see me. Any thoughts I have about *What could she possibly see in me? Why does she want to be with me?* fade the second she slides into the car next to me. Being in the company of this young woman who's so full of life, so full of plans—she came out here from Panama Beach, Florida, by way of San Diego to go to acting school and make a career for herself—just thrills me. I cannot get enough of her.

We date for a couple of months and quickly grow into best friends—something that was missing in my other relationships. Michele, Daphne, and Shauna were never best friends, just partners I had to take care of and do everything for just to make them happy. Shawna is not like them. She does not want to marry or have kids. She just wants to be with me and have fun. It is the perfect scenario for me at this point in my life.

But I grow tired rather quickly of going back to her house every time to pick her up; her place is filled with great young folks, but they are a little crazy for my taste. So one night when we are parked out in front of my Beverly Hills apartment after a date, I suggest, "Why don't we move in together?"

"Where?"

"Here," I say and point to the downstairs apartment I share with my three daughters when they are with me.

Shawna immediately looks concerned. "How is that going to work out with your girls?"

Sensitive about how this will look to my daughters, the last thing I want them to see is the two of us in bed together. "You know what," I offer, "I'll sleep in Alexandra's room with her and you take my bed. It will work out."

Honestly, it is a concern for me. As much as I love Shawna, my first concern is how—or if—the girls will accept her. No other woman has lived with them since their mother. Until I propose, I keep the same hard-and-fast rule with Shawna.

All three of my daughters have personal issues. With all the back and forth with their mother and the comings and goings on they have witnessed with her and all of her boyfriends—not to mention her explosive anger and acts of violence that result in a restraining order against her—they feel dumped on. Alexandra, the oldest, remembers more than her younger siblings. She has a much harder time accepting the idea of me sharing our life with another woman. The two of us have developed such a close bond since my separation and divorce from her mother. Her sisters, Victoria and Isabella, are more accepting. They are very happy to see me in a relationship. As Victoria, very wise beyond her years, says to me, "Daddy, you need someone to share your life and to do adult things together."

Early on, Shawna feels horrible about creating this kind of strain between Alexandra and me. At times, she is so upset she wants to move back to the house on Highland Avenue. I tell her, "Just be patient. Be yourself. Once they know you as I do, they will love you."

For three months, we try this arrangement. Anytime I have the girls over, I sleep in the room with Alexandra, and Shawna sleeps in my bedroom. In that time, Alexandra warms up to Shawna and sees she is a sweet person.

Then on Valentine's Day, I propose to Shawna at the Portofino Resort in Redondo Beach. I do it that morning after we wake up and order breakfast in our room. I have the ring tucked inside the pocket of my bathrobe. Shawna and I always played this game where one of us says, "I want to marry you," and the other says, "No, I want to marry you."

That morning, I start. "Good morning, honey, I want to marry you."

Shawna plays along and says, "No, I want to marry you."

Then I say, "No, I really want to marry you."

She says, "Well, I really want to marry you."

Finally, I pull the box with the ring out of my pocket. "Well, if you really want to marry me, then you better start wearing this."

I hand her the box with the ring. Shawna takes one look at the box, still closed, and screams, "Noooooooooo!!" Her "no" does not mean "no" in the literal sense, of course, but simply her disbelief about what is happening.

I laugh. "What do you mean, 'no,' if you really wanted to marry me?"

Now Shawna starts laughing. It takes her twenty minutes before she opens the box and puts the ring on her finger. When she finally does, she cannot stop smiling.

But days before I asked Shawna for her hand in marriage, I took the three girls aside and asked them how they'd feel about me marrying Shawna. Usually it is customary for the man to ask the father of the intended bride for his daughter's hand in marriage. My case is a little different, so I ask my daughters, "Is it okay that Daddy and Shawna are together?"

Isabella speaks up first. "Yes, Daddy."

Victoria follows. "Of course, Daddy."

Alexandra pauses. Our eyes connect and she feels the love I have for her. She nods affirmatively, smiles, and says, "Yes, Daddy, I just want you to be happy." We do a group hug and it is official.

That May, three months later, Shawna and I are married in a casual, romantic beachside wedding at the Casa Dorado Resort in Cabo San Lucas, Mexico, overlooking the Pacific Ocean. Immediate family are there, including my then-pregnant daughter Shayne and her husband, Nik Richie. Other friends also attend, including Ron Moss and Winsor Harmon from *The Bold and the Beautiful*. As the crystal-clear blue waves lap up on the shore, I immediately think of my father's sage advice regarding making "wise choices" where matters of the heart are concerned. This time I am certain I have.

Before the ceremony, Shayne teases me in front of everyone, "You better marry this girl or you are going to die old and alone."

"Don't worry," I tell her, "I have this one covered."

Shawna is simply radiant wearing a traditional white bridal gown and barefoot, while I am dressed casually in white trousers, a long-sleeve black shirt, and flip-flops. Under a large beige canopy, we lovingly exchange vows, with the ocean as our backdrop. Neither of us can wipe the smiles off our faces afterward. It is a fairy-tale wedding and honeymoon; we even take spins on a Jet Ski around this coastal Mexican paradise to celebrate our new life together.

My life with Shawna has been just great ever since. We have a solid relationship. Shawna has her own relationship with each of the girls. They love having her around. She's someone younger and relatively closer to their age than me, someone they can relate to and talk "girl stuff" to. It is nice to feel like a "normal" family again. It reminds me of what it was like as a kid, yearning to have a normal life like my friends did. Sitting around the dining table, doing the things that a normal family does every day. It is as if my life has come full circle.

Marrying Shawna gives me a whole new perspective on everything. I quit looking in the rearview mirror; I know the best days in my life and career are ahead of me. One of my favorite movie comedies of all time is *City Slickers*, in which comedian Billy Crystal goes with his two best friends to a dude ranch in search of the "one thing" that will make him happy. Many times, I kept searching for my "one thing," then several things, thinking I needed them to fulfill me. Instead, I found the one thing that makes me the happiest now is what is in front of me.

Now I wake up every day with an unwavering belief that my time is coming. I am like the guy who goes to the bar and the bartender takes everybody's drink order but his. If I stand there long enough, the guy thinks, eventually he will notice me and ask me what I want. That is how I see my career. Some things take a long time; be patient. But if I stay the course, opportunity will come knocking, even when I least expect it. Read for a part in a film or television series, and *Boom*! I will end up getting it.

I am always joking about it with my son, A.J., who's still seeking that big break in his acting career. "One phone call," I tell him. "That is all it takes."

That's how this business is: one call. Suddenly your life changes like that! You sign on to do a film or television series that has a life and you never look back.

FOURTEEN

That One Thing!

AFTER KICKING AROUND doing my cabaret singing act, theatrical productions, a myriad of films (including direct-to-video films for writer-director Chuck Walker, who is like family to me), and television shows (including voicing the character Meap on the Disney Channel's hit animated series *Phineas and Ferb*), I decide to try my hand at comedy.

It starts when W. D. Hogan, a very talented writer-director, asks me to star in a comedy short titled *Let Lorenzo*. The three-minute film, which premieres in May 2011 on FunnyorDie.com, is a play on my legend as "a television and film star of television and film." In it I use all of my knowledge to show people the way to happier and healthier lives. Shot as a series of vignettes, it is a hilarious venture for me, one that pushes all the right buttons and allows me to finally make use of all my talents. Furthermore, I get the chance to do stuff I have always done seriously, including martial arts and riding a badass Harley, but this time for laughs.

As the title implies, characters in each vignette let Lorenzo help them in their time of need. I change a flat tire for famed Apollo 11 astronaut Buzz Aldrin and his wife, Lois; I instruct a floundering couple (played by David Michie and Jacqueline Pinol) in the art of salsa dancing; I show a husband (actor Jay Lewis) how to please his wife (played by Shawna) in the kitchen; I help a married couple (Jeff Finn and Ann Marie Lindbloom) develop a better way to breastfeed their baby; and much more.

I find doing something so off-the-wall and laugh-out-loud funny a refreshing change, and I can't wait to do more. I take another comedy role, this time a guest shot on an *Adult Swim* series for Cartoon Network, *NTSF:SD:SUV* (*National Terrorism Strike Force: San Diego: Sport Utility Vehicle*), a parody of police procedural dramas and action films, created by comedian Paul Scheer.

Shawna encourages me to keep at it. "You have to do something with comedy now. You have to take advantage of this opportunity that is standing in front of you." I do not have a manager; my wife is managing me. "You're very funny, you should do this," she says.

Shawna signs me up for a comedy class at Joe Falzarano's LA Stand Ups school, billed as "The Only Stand-up Comedy Class You'll Ever Need." A veteran comedy writer-producer, Joe helped launch the stand-up comedy careers of Jon Stewart, Louis CK, Dave Attell, Greg Giraldo, and Dave Chappelle, besides running other stand-up comedy clubs, including New York City's Original Improv and Caroline's on Broadway. He also produced 120 episodes of the CableACE award–winning stand-up comedy series *Caroline's Comedy Hour* for A&E.

Joe is a master at what he does. He ascribes to the belief that everyone can be funny, and his classes teach you the art of stand-up from the ground up, including all the techniques, secrets, and shortcuts professional comedians and comedy writers use to write really funny material. He really helped me understand how to embrace my personality, develop my comedy persona, hone my jokes and material, and connect with the audience. It is a whole new ballgame for me, but I am open to trying.

By the end of the course, I have about ten minutes of stand-up comedy I can do. On November 30, 2012, I do my first stand-up comedy gig in front of a paid audience at the Comedy Store. I make fun of my legend as "a television star and former heartthrob" and the many roles I have played, from "a shirtless, long-haired, Harley-riding bounty hunter...an outlaw hunting outlaws...a renegade" to my more subtle character Hector Martinez, "the Latino firefighter" in *The Bold and the Beautiful*. From there, I move into comedy about contemporary issues, like how stupid it is to "drive a car that gets a bazillion miles per gallon but will kill you in a wreck with a Miata!...I drive a truck, man. I'd rather pay through the ass at the pump, but live to complain about it!"

That first stand-up engagement goes well. I do about ten more, including hosting a one-night "Comedy Showcase" at the Comedy Store in late January 2013. Now, if somebody asks me, I can do a six-minute stand-up act. It is a great experience that soon opens other doors for me.

Suddenly, that one thing I keep hoping for that will catapult me into the next chapter in my career happens. I am performing outside of Boston, reprising my role in *The King and I*, when John Stevens, the producer of *Are You Smarter Than a Fifth Grader?*, *The World's Worst Tenant*, and *The Joe Schmo Show*, calls me. John is laying the groundwork for a third installment of *The Joe Schmo Show: The Full Bounty* for SPIKE and wants me to be part of the cast.

"How would you feel about playing a comedy?" he asks. "You'd be yourself but be making fun of yourself in the show, a reality show. But all the people in the show are like comedy improvisational actors except the one contestant who thinks that it's real."

"I'd love to," I tell John. "I never heard of anything like that before."

I agree to meet with John and his production partner Paul when I get back to Los Angeles. I drive to their offices for my first face-to-face with them and executive producer/head writer J. Holland Moore. No sooner do I sit down than John asks me again, "How do you feel about poking fun at yourself?"

"Every action star from the '80s and '90s who pokes fun at himself has found a bigger audience for himself that way," I point out to them. "So I think it is a great way to reintroduce myself, since I have not been on a regular series in some time."

During the meeting, John touches on the process with me. It will involve two weeks of rehearsals with all the actors. The show, in a sense, is like doing comedy improv all day with cameras on us 24/7, capturing everything we do and say. I will play a comic version of myself: a hyper, narcissistic, self-centered television star who is trying to reignite his career. I am totally sold on doing it. I think John senses it, too, but there is a catch (isn't there always?).

John pulls out this tiny little thing in his hand. "Lorenzo, you don't have to do this, but it's something we've been thinking about."

I cannot take my eyes off whatever it is he is holding.

"It would really be great if you would wear this on the show as your own personal bottoms."

John unfurls the "thing" fully in his hand. It is a blue Speedo of sorts. "We're going to call it the Lorenzo Lamas European Casual Pouch," he says.

John pauses as I keep staring at this thing he is hoping I'll wear.

"The idea is that you've changed but you are not working as much as an actor and you've come up with this product to sell," he continues. "It sells great in places like Saint-Tropez, where men wear bathing suits like this, and on the beaches of Rio de Janeiro and even here in America, and you're going to try to get Chase [the unaware contestant] to put it on."

I have a big decision to make right then and there. They want me to do comedy, act like an idiot, and wear skimpy underwear on national television. I think, if I don't do this, the series might not have the impact we're all hoping for. Why just be another character on the show? The renegade in me gets the best of me. I'm game.

"Sure, I'll do it," I say.

John, Paul, and J. Holland are delighted.

We have a good laugh over it. I just hope I made the right decision and don't make a complete fool of myself on national television.

We film the series at an exclusive estate and former horse ranch property outside of Los Angeles in an area called Hidden Valley. It's a beautiful, serene setting, and the sprawling property is big enough to house a production trailer for the producers, along with its spectacular Spanish-style mansion where the cast will live during the weeks of production.

Prior to the start of production, the producers select Chase Rogan, a good-natured twenty-eight-year-old native of Pennsylvania and sports fanatic, as the "Schmo." Chase is under the impression he is competing on a real reality show for the chance to win $100,000 and a one-year contract to become a professional bounty hunter. There is one catch he doesn't know about, however: It's all fake. All of us actors and everything else on the show is scripted to test Chase and push him and his emotions to the limit. In case things go bad during the first few days of filming and Chase doesn't continue, the producers have a second "Schmo" contestant, also from Pennsylvania, holed up at a nearby hotel to take Chase's place. As it turns out, they never need him.

During rehearsals, I meet the rest of the cast of actors: our hosts, Ralph Garman as world-renowned bounty hunter Jake Montrose and Amanda Landry as Wanda Montrose, the Ditzy Wife; Rob Belushi, son of Jim Belushi, as Chase's buddy, Allen; Jo Newman as Karlee, a deaf ventriloquist; and Fred Cross as Stan, her interpreter; Segun Oduolowu as Lavernius, the Black Guy; Nikki McKenzie as Allison, the Overachiever; Lombardo Boyar as Chico, the Ex-con; Meghan Falcone as Skylar, the Widow; Michael Weaver as Randy, the Asshole; and Chelsey Crisp as Chloe, the Model. It is a wild cast and they get even wilder when we start making the show.

Because of the improvisational nature of the show and the fact we're working in character for ten to twelve hours straight, filming is intense. There is no room for slipups. It is like being part of a high-wire act but without a safety net. The fact Chase is unaware that the whole show is a sham makes it that much more pressure-packed. We all feel it, including the production crew, who are in the production trailer watching the minute-by-minute developments as they happen. Cameras are on us and Chase, inside and outside the mansion, 24/7. There are even cameras in Chase's room. The producers can see what he is writing in his personal journal and know what he is thinking, if maybe he is getting suspicious and starting to figure things out.

The producers waste no time bringing out the "European Casual Pouch." In fact, I parade around in it in the first episode. I remember thinking while wearing it, "If this doesn't work, I will never work again, not even in movies that go straight to video!"

Fortunately, it does the trick. The prop furthers the notion in Chase's mind that I am this shameless, ego-driven actor and self-promoter. Of course, I am just following the script, even saying the line that got a lot of airplay on Spike, YouTube, and elsewhere: "I've got the sack of a twenty-five-year-old!"

The rest of filming goes surprisingly well. There are a few close calls, however. The biggest is when Jo Newman, as the deaf character Karlee, reacts to Chase making a comment when his back is to her.

Jo, who is a certified yoga instructor in real life, is doing yoga poses against the wall on the patio when Chase says to her, "That looks hard."

Without hesitation, Jo responds, "It is."

The look on his face says Chase is thinking, "Can she hear me?"

In the production trailer, the producers are going ape-shit. They start to panic. Their biggest fear is that at any moment they will have to go on the set and defuse a situation or attempt to distract Chase from what he thinks has happened. They don't have to this time. Something distracts Chase and he moves on.

Throughout filming the series, Chase makes a great impression on all of us. He is the real deal. Many times he could have lied and cheated. Instead, he is forthright, legitimately competitive, and honest, and he proves over and over again what a great guy he is. You cannot help but like him.

Shawna ends up appearing in the ninth episode ("The Rise of the Lamas"). In this one, the competitions include tasing your partner. The winner receives $1,000.

John approaches me with the idea first. "Would Shawna consider coming on the show and let you use a stun gun on her?"

"Let me call her and ask."

I call Shawna. "Babe, how'd you like to be on television?"

"Really? Yeah!"

"All you have to do is let me use a stun gun on you."

There's momentary silence. "What? Lorenzo! Use what on me?"

I tell Shawna, "It's very safe. We've all done it to each other. It's just a little shock, a couple hundred volts."

"A couple hundred volts! Are you smoking crack?"

"Babe, honestly, it's a drama show. You're going to look hot, and everybody is going to see that we are a couple. It will be great."

At the beginning of our marriage, gossip bubbled up about Shawna being a gold digger, that she married me just to get attention, blah-blah-blah-blah. So I see this as an opportunity for America to see her as she really is: a really cool lady.

Shawna is a good sport about it. She comes and does the show. Of course, she still does not like the idea of me using the stun gun on her. I zap myself for good measure to prove to her that it does not hurt. Still, Shawna does everything she can to elude me. Finally, she lets me tase her. We do not win the competition, but we certainly laugh about it afterward.

On January 8, 2013, the evening of the premiere, I am out celebrating with Shawna and we are in the parking lot of the local 7-Eleven when suddenly she screams, "Lorenzo, my God, you're trending on Twitter!"

Shawna shows me her smartphone. All these hashtags are popping up at once on the screen: #LorenzoLamas…#EuropeanCasualPouch… #JoeSchmo. I can tell from tweets by folks watching the broadcast that response to the show is very favorable. One Twitter follower sweetly tweets, "Lorenzo Lamas makes the show watchable."

Needless to say, the premiere is a very exciting night for me, and I am very happy how well things turn out. *The Joe Schmo Show: The Full Bounty* is a huge hit. The advance trailer racks up nearly 2 million views on YouTube, while a ten-minute sneak peek on Spike's website gets more than 54,000 hits. Of course, the biggest surprise for me is the response to the so-called "European Casual Pouch." A clip of that on Spike.com and YouTube receives more than 30,000 hits combined. I am both humbled and amazed.

During its ten-week run, *The Joe Schmo Show* becomes one of Spike's highest-rated original series, with an average of 714,000 viewers each week. Parodying myself on the show proves to be a wise career decision. I receive some of the best reviews of my career. *TV Guide* calls my performance "surprisingly hilarious," while a critic for AVClub.com proclaims me a "comedy genius."

My appearance on the show does everything I had hoped for my career. I land an agent who is very active in comedy and a commercial agent as well. My commercial agent gets me an audition for a national Sears commercial ("A Monkey's Uncle"), which becomes another. I audition with fifty other actors as a guy just standing by a barbecue, flipping burgers. The producers in the casting immediately recognize me and a lightbulb goes off in their heads.

"Aren't you Lorenzo Lamas?" one of them asks.

"Yes. I am."

"Wow, would you mind if we played on that a little bit?"

"Absolutely not."

So what initially is a walk-on becomes a personal commercial for me, poking fun at my multiple marriages and my legend as a so-called "Hollywood heartthrob." It's another comedy bit for me as "Lorenzo Lamas," this time with a monkey on my shoulder.

Doing *The Joe Schmo Show* is the first step Shawna and I take to solidify our relationship in the public eye. For the most part, it works to show the public we are a regular couple and are together for the right reasons.

Not long after *The Joe Schmo Show* begins airing, I hear from an old friend, Ron Starrantino. I had met Ron twelve years earlier while hosting promos for a show on SPEED TV. A retired stockbroker formerly with Jordan Belfort, the real Wolf of Wall Street (later depicted in the 2013 feature film starring Leonardo DiCaprio), Ron was CEO of Von Dutch Motorcycle, the guy who put that brand on the map. He now manages Daniel "Dee" Snider, best known as the front man and lead singer for the heavy metal band Twisted Sister. Ron calls me and invites Shawna and me to The Revolver/Guitar World Rock & Roll Roast of Dee Snider on January 24, 2013, at City National Grove in Anaheim, California. It is a red carpet event, complete with maître d'. At the event, Ron asks, "Lorenzo, what's going on with you now since *The Joe Schmo Show*?"

I am bluntly honest in my response. "Good question. It has been good exposure, but has not lighted the world on fire like I had hoped."

Ron pauses a second. "Have you ever thought about doing *Wife Swap*?"

Now Ron really has my attention. I tell him, "As a matter of fact, Shawna and I had taped an interview for that show but the producers never called us back."

"Well, Dee just got finished doing that," Ron says, "and I know the producers and the people who make the decisions. Let me put in a call."

Ron calls the producers. The next thing I know Shawna and I are filming an episode of ABC's *Celebrity Wife Swap*, with comedian Andy Dick and his former companion Lina Sved as the celebrity couple with whom we will trade lives for one week.

Shawna and I want to do the show because it is so intrusive. The cameras and crew are in your face for four days, filming *everything*.

We feel this will be the perfect vehicle to show folks out there that we are a down-to-earth, real couple—a traditional family dealing with the normal day-to-day issues of raising three spoiled daughters: Alexandra, sixteen; Victoria, fourteen; and Isabella, twelve. With such a large national audience, *Celebrity Wife Swap* is the perfect platform for us to send that message.

To be taken out of your comfort zone, to suddenly have your life turned upside down by swapping spouses, is extremely challenging. But Shawna and I see it all as an adventure that will enable us to learn something new about ourselves.

It is amazing to see the differences between the two families. We live a very traditional lifestyle in our home in Beverly Hills, where I am a hands-on dad who always tries to know what is going on with our daughters' lives. Plus, we make it a point to have family time at the end of the day. I still tuck my girls in at night and pray together with them. It is all about building a relationship with them based on trust, something very important to me, as it took a long time for me to achieve that in my relationship with my parents.

Shawna is a great stepmom to them. The girls all have their chores, which we list on a whiteboard, to make things run smoothly around the house. Shawna cooks meals at the beginning of the week and portions them out into Tupperware containers for every day of the week. My girls, unfortunately, are completely addicted to their mobile devices, something I have yet to remedy, but am still working on.

Conversely, Andy lives a very nontraditional lifestyle in Calabasas, California, where he sleeps in a silver travel trailer, like something out of the Desi Arnaz–Lucille Ball comedy film *The Long, Long Trailer* (1953). The trailer sits outside of Lina's home, which their daughters, Rachel, Emily, and Meg (Andy's only biological daughter; he adopted the other two), call "a crazy house." Andy, like me, does not have the best track record. He has been on TMZ, the celebrity gossip website, many times; of course, so have I. That is where our similarities end. Andy, unlike me, is very needy and can get on people's nerves rather easily. He lives by his own set of rules, and that includes having a girlfriend who pops in and out whenever she wants. Andy likes to sleep late in the morning and then come in the house for his breakfast green shake. Besides doing all of the cooking and cleaning, Lina is expected to drive Andy to his various meetings and appointments. He clearly likes others doing things for him.

Lina, who feels so responsible for her family, really freaks out when she packs up to leave for the swap. She has no idea who her celebrity spouse is until she sets foot in our Beverly Hills abode and comes across a dresser with photos of me, one of them from *Renegade*. Lina's worried look quickly turns to smiles, and she immediately feels at ease after she meets Alexandra, Victoria, Isabella, and me.

The weeklong swap becomes a real eye-opener. Lina gets to experience my life and see how at times I like to live on the edge. That includes me taking her for an unexpected ride on my Harley, which she seems to really enjoy, and then on a helicopter ride with me at the controls. That one scares her shitless. It's all part of who I am; I love thrills and adventure.

At home, Lina gets an up-close view of what my life is like raising three daughters. She immediately offers some very sound solutions that Shawna and I later make a conscious effort to incorporate in our family routine. One of them is to actually cook meals with the girls and have all of us sit down for dinner as a family. Living the way I do, as an actor always on the go, and the way Shawna does, as a very busy working professional, we find it difficult to carve out as much quality time as we would like. Thanks to Lina, however, we find it's not as difficult as it seems.

Shawna, on the other hand, walks into a much stranger situation: a silver travel trailer that could be a dressing room but turns out to be Andy's living quarters, and then the main house, where she finds Andy, his daughters, and later Andy's girlfriend, who shows up unannounced. The one thing she fears most when she finds out her celebrity spouse is Andy is that she'll "have to raise another child."

SHAWNA'S WEEK WITH ANDY is more unnerving than Lina's is with me, to say the least. Yet she handles it gracefully, with all the aplomb I expected she would. Andy is used to getting everything he wants, when he wants it. That includes his green shake made perfectly every morning. Shawna introduces Andy to new ideas when it comes to food, not all of them well received. He is a creature of habit, slow to change. But Shawna keeps trying, and his daughters are especially receptive to her ideas.

The first time Shawna drives Andy to an appointment, he keeps telling her how to drive and where to drive. Shawna helps Andy realize he cannot have his way all the time. She shows how important family is, why spending time together and taking time to do things with his daughters is so crucial for his family. It is a real breakthrough for Andy, and Shawna is the reason.

One thing Andy discovers from sharing time with Shawna is the fact that she does not walk the red carpet with me at events. Shawna has never wanted people to see her as simply this attractive girl hanging on my arm like some kind of celebrity jewelry. So every time we go to an event, we walk in separately. I understand her reasons. I have a lot of baggage, more than most, and she does not want people to attach her to all that. She wants her own personality, separate from mine. I understand that 100 percent. I would never want her to feel buried by my stuff, by my personality. There are times, however, deep down, when I would like her to stand with me on the red carpet, the two of us as a couple. I am proud of her, after all. But her wish to protect her own personality is more important.

At the end of the show, we two couples finally meet each other in what is like a reunion. Stuff comes out about what we have learned from our experiences. It gets very emotional when we talk about ourselves on camera, especially when Andy brings up Shawna's reluctance to be photographed with me on the red carpet. He says, "She should be proud of what you have as a couple and take pictures with her man."

Andy gets a little emotional. Lina starts crying. Shawna gets emotional, and so do I. It is a very delicate subject with me, despite how much I understand and respect Shawna's feelings. I break down and cry, something I did not expect. Of course, much good comes out of having such a frank and open discussion about the subject. From then on, Shawna does walk the red carpet with me, and we make family time around the dinner table with the girls a greater priority. The swap has made us a stronger couple, a stronger family.

THE MORNING OF JUNE 6, 2013, I wake up to heartbreaking news: Esther Williams has died. It is shocking because even at the age of ninety-one, she has been in remarkably good health. Once the news breaks, Twitter is ablaze with tributes and condolences in remembrance of her. I tweet and release a statement to the press saying how she was "the best swim teacher and soul mom" to a kid struggling to find himself, his identity, and his place in the world. Esther is a big reason I am who I am today. She was very spiritually centered, perhaps more than my father was, and she and I had that in common. I truly treasured her and miss her greatly.

Former actor Edward Bell, Esther's husband (her fourth) for the past eighteen years, arranges a private, invitation-only memorial service in her honor at the home of actress Connie Stevens, a longtime friend of Esther's. Ed hires a producer to create a twenty-minute tribute movie. Shown in the backyard on a large movie screen, it features a montage of clips of her glittering water ballet numbers from her MGM musicals, including swimming scenes with Dad and Tom and Jerry from *Dangerous When Wet*. The movie is a fitting tribute. Ed also arranges a synchronized swimming team to perform an entire musical number in her honor. Kathleen is there, and so are her parents, Abby and Jack. Kathleen loves Shawna. It is also nice to see Esther's kids, whom I have not been in contact with for many years. Overall, it is a warm, positive memorial, the perfect way to say goodbye, giving Esther all the respect she so richly deserved.

On Sunday, July 14, 2013, the episode of *Celebrity Wife Swap* premieres on ABC in prime time. Ours becomes the second-highest rated episode of the summer, with more than three-and-a-half-million viewers. Only an episode featuring Joan Rivers and her daughter, Melissa, does better. We are thrilled by the positive response. If we never do another reality television show again, our mission has been accomplished. The world now knows what I have always known: what a wonderful stepmother and spouse Shawna is and how blessed I am to have her in my life, and what a great relationship I have with my daughters, Alexandra, Victoria, and Isabella. I am one proud husband and father, and the luckiest guy on the planet.

Since *Celebrity Wife Swap*, I am busier than ever. I continue to audition for many new starring roles. I am back making movies, including four full-length features—two action films, *Being American* and *Atomic Eden*, and two comedies, *American Beach House*, costarring Mischa Barton (of television's *The O.C.* fame), and *Bro, What Happened?*—all opening in theaters this year. Meanwhile, I am doing more television series work, including two additional appearances as Dr. Hollywood (a role I first played in 2010) on Nickelodeon's comedy-musical series *Big Time Rush*, as well as *Ghost Girls* and *Bike Cops Van Nuys*, a comedy series made exclusively for the web. It's a "mockumentary" police comedy in which I play a disgraced cop, Peter "Ponch" Rodriguez. I am also working on many new projects, including getting back on a regular prime-time series on a major network. Plus, I am leaving enough time in my schedule to do more stand-up comedy, stage productions, and whatever else comes my way.

It is a very exciting time. Every day in my life keeps getting better and better. God's perfect plan is starting to come together for me, and I could not be happier or more thrilled. I have come a long way in my journey from that wet-behind-the-ears kid, hardly out of diapers, whom my legendary father drove in his fancy chariot to studio meetings. From growing out of that awkward stage as a chubby kid with little self-esteem to finding much-needed structure and discipline and avoiding becoming a juvenile delinquent. To emerging from the shadows of my father's larger-than-life fame and becoming my own man and enjoying my own successes and failures, and finally to keep on truckin' until I get things right with me and my life. It has been an incredible ride, one I hope continues well into the future.

As a race car driver, I used to feel I may not be the best driver or have the best equipment, but if I am there at the end of the race, I have a chance to finish first. That sums up my life at this moment. I am healthy and in great physical shape. I still work out three times a week for two hours. I eat only food with a high percentage of protein and avoid those with high amounts of fat.

I am far less cocky and stupid these days and am so ready for whatever happens next. No matter what, I cannot wait to see what lies ahead. Every time I think about the future, I get chill bumps in anticipation. One thing is sure: I will be here. Ready, willing, and able. And, as always, still a renegade at heart.

EPILOGUE

Family Footsteps

BORROWING DAD'S ROLLS-ROYCE for the day, I am on my way to pick up the girls from school while Shawna is at work. My late stepmom, Esther, and her husband, Ed, have kept the Rolls in mint condition all these years. The car is in amazing shape. Backing down the driveway, past the wrought-iron gates of Dad's old sweeping ranch-style house and onto Beverly Hills's Readcrest Drive, I cruise up Pacific Coast Highway to the school. The car purrs to perfection, as if it just rolled off the showroom floor. It is a wonderful Southern California afternoon, with cirrus clouds sweeping the blue sky ahead.

At school, my eldest daughter, Alexandra, comes running out to meet me. She suddenly stops and stares at the long, sleek car that awaits. I think she wants to make sure it is me.

"Dad-where'd-you-get that?" she asks. "Whose-is-it-Dad? Do-you-have-a-new-car?" Her words are all running together.

"It's Papa Fernando's," I laugh.

Gingerly, Alexandra climbs up into the car's front seat. "Wow! It's big," she says, with the wonderment of the child she is. "What's that smell?"

"It's Connolly leather," I explain.

"It's a fancy car," she notes.

"Yes, it is, Alexandra," I assure her.

Before I know it, Isabella and Victoria are running excitedly toward us. Isabella is naturally curious about the car, as is her youngest sister.

"Can we come, Dad?" Isabella asks as if she needs permission.

"Of course...this is your history."

Immediately, I think of my handsome and elegant father sitting behind the wheel and my history a very long time ago, and how the wisdom and experience he shared I am now passing on to a new generation.

"Papa Fernando loved his history," I remind them.

Victoria can barely conceal her excitement. With a squint-eyed smile, she says, "I love history!"

"Well, consider this your first of many history lessons."

I turn on the ignition, and we start to cruise up the coast. I take them to the many places I hold dear. Memories shared a lifetime ago with my legendary father. Even to the now-famous lamppost named after me, "Lo-ren-zo Place." Bubbling with enthusiasm, my daughters ask more questions than I have answers.

"How did Papa Fernando know there was a street named after you?"

I answer, "Papa Fernando was a very wise man."

"Did the kids at school really pick on you because of your name?"

"Yes, honey, they did," I explain, "but times were different back then. Papa Fernando knew that and made sure I did, too."

I pull over and park. We get out and walk down to the beach. The girls run to catch up as their flip-flops sink into the sand. "This is the spot," I tell them and point.

"What spot do you mean, Dad?" Alexandra asks, cupping her hand to shade her eyes from the sun's brilliant rays.

"This is where Papa Fernando always brought me, to this very spot."

"Cool!" Isabella shouts.

"Another history lesson?" Victoria asks with a smile.

"Yes, another history lesson, honey."

I point straight out into the blue Pacific as the waves roar and crest toward us. "Papa Fernando was a champion swimmer."

"Were you ever frightened swimming in the ocean with him?"

"A little at first," I admit without hesitation, "but Papa Fernando always made me feel safe."

Just as I finish my sentence, the mighty waves crash onto the sandy shore. Suddenly they lather our feet in white foam, just as Mother Ocean did many times before when Dad and I went surfing and swimming together on this very beach. It is like history repeating itself. The unexpected rush of the waves sends the girls running and screaming with delight.

I laugh. "Girls, you are missing the best part!"

As the sun's rays reflect off the blue watery coast, I pause for a second. I understand now exactly why Dad brought me here. How he felt every time he took me for a ride in his precious Rolls-Royce. It was more than just another day at the beach to him. It was more than just another ride we made countless other times in his spiffy chariot. The grandest of days in our life are those we spend together…as a family. Laughing, loving, and sharing precious memories (and yes, history!). Enjoying the most special bond of all, between a father and his children. That comes around only once in our lifetime, and only if we are lucky. There is nothing more to it than that. Dad knew what he was doing from the start, and I am the better for it.

Every time I stand at the water's edge, I instantly become a child again and think of Dad. It is only natural. After all, it is my history!

"Here, Dad, come here!" Alexandra shouts excitedly.

I realize how lucky I am. I could not be happier. This is what my life has become: I am a father and mentor to my three daughters, just like my father was to me. It is why I am here.

"I'm coming, Alexandra!" I shout back.

To carry on the family lineage and prepare this generation of Lamases perhaps better than my parents did me.

"Victoria thinks she saw a dolphin, Dad!" Isabella cries out.

To build a solid relationship—something I did not always have growing up with my parents. To spend time and cherish the moments—something I wish I had done more with my other children. It is what drives me.

"That's great, honey!"

My father, I am sure, is proud. He is smiling down on me from the high hill above the Pacific. It is how he would have wanted it. I will be happy to see it through to the very end, wherever the journey takes me.

"Hurry, Dad, you're missing it!" Alexandra screams.

It is true, as a wise man once said, "Life is littered with good intentions. What you make of them is what counts." I have learned from my disappointments and my mistakes. I am in a good place right now.

"Dad's here!" I call out. I stop after running clear across the sand to them.

By now, the girls are jumping up and down and breathlessly pointing. "There, Dad, there!"

A man of stature, tall, refined, yet inconspicuous with gray-streaked hair, is out surfing. He catches a tall wave and rides it for however long he can. Excitedly, Alexandra, Isabella, and Victoria wave as he comes closer to shore. He waves back as another arching wave crashes behind him. The brute force of it pushes him on his board fast and furiously toward the beach. He doesn't fall off.

Pausing, Alexandra looks up at me. With a broad smile on her face, she says innocently, "Just like Papa Fernando, right?"

I laugh. "Right, honey. You're right."

Now more than a half century later, my three daughters are the ones nodding as I carry on the family tradition started by my father: "Remember, you have a history!"

As long as the sand and surf are here, I always will. This is where my journey started; this is where it will end someday. Until then I am going to enjoy every second. I'll be there for Shawna and my girls as long as there is one last breath left in me. For a renegade like me who has searched a lifetime for the peace and happiness that has eluded him, it is such a liberating feeling, to know at this stage of living that every intention of mine was not in vain, even the most foolish. They are all part of a bigger plan. From Dad, to Mom, to Esther, to Emmy, to Lola, and every other guiding hand before, after them, and in between, from every failure to every success, all have played a role in shaping me as a man, as a husband, and as a father.

The best role is the one I am living now. For the first time in a very long time, you are looking at one very, very happy and fulfilled man.

ABOUT THE AUTHORS

LORENZO LAMAS, the son of actors Fernando Lamas and Arlene Dahl, is best known for his roles as Reno Raines, the framed ex-cop turned professional bounty hunter, in creator/producer Stephen Cannell's first-run syndicated and USA Network action series hit *Renegade* (1992–1997), and as the handsome playboy Lance Cumson on CBS's long-running prime-time soap *Falcon Crest* (1981–1990).

JEFF LENBURG is a prolific, award-winning author and Hollywood movie star biographer. He has written more than thirty books, including eighteen acclaimed celebrity memoirs and biographies and two national bestsellers. His books have been nominated for the American Library Association's Best Non-Fiction Award and the Evangelical Christian Publishers Association's Gold Medallion Award for Best Autobiography/Biography.